W9-DEA-342

DISCARDED

THE NATURE OF
INTELLECTUAL STYLES

The Educational Psychology Series

Robert K. Sternberg and Wendy M. Williams, Series Editors

.

THE NATURE OF
INTELLECTUAL STYLES

Li-fang Zhang
The University of Hong Kong

Robert J. Sternberg
Tufts University

LAWRENCE ERLBAUM ASSOCIATES, PUBLISHERS
2006   Mahwah, New Jersey   London

Copyright © 2006 by Lawrence Erlbaum Associates, Inc.
All rights reserved. No part of this book may be reproduced in
any form, by photostat, microform, retrieval system, or any other
means, without the prior written permission of the publisher.

Lawrence Erlbaum Associates, Inc., Publishers
10 Industrial Avenue
Mahwah, New Jersey 07430
www.erlbaum.com

Cover design by Tomai Maridou

Library of Congress Cataloging-in-Publication Data

Li-fang Zhang
   The nature of intellectual styles / Li-fang Zhang, Robert J. Sternberg
      p.   cm. — (The educational psychology series)
   Includes bibliographical references and index.
   ISBN 0-8058-5287-5 (alk. paper)
   ISBN 0-8058-5288-3 (pbk. : alk. paper)
   1. Cognitive styles.   2. Learning, Psychology of.   I. Sternberg, Robert J.
II. Title.   III. Series.

BF311.Z46   2006
153—dc22   2005055498
                                                        CIP

Books published by Lawrence Erlbaum Associates are printed on acid-free paper,
and their bindings are chosen for strength and durability.

Printed in the United States of America
10 9 8 7 6 5 4 3 2 1

To Ashley and to Seth and Sara

Contents

Preface

When one of the coauthors of this book studied introductory psychology, he received a grade of "C" in the course. The grade was discouraging to him and to his professor as well. The professor commented to him one day that "There is a famous Sternberg in psychology [Saul Sternberg], and it looks like there won't be another one." As a result, the coauthor decided to major in something else. He did worse in the something else and returned to psychology, now viewing the "C" as not so bad after all. In his upper level courses, however, he received much higher grades.

Over the years, we have found stories such as this one to be more common than we ever had expected. People take a course in which they are motivated to succeed, but somehow, they perform poorly. In later courses, they perform well. There is also a flip side to the story, as any professor could tell. There are students who do perfectly well in their early courses and then do poorly later on.

Such changes in performance may reflect many different origins, but one is almost certainly individual differences in *intellectual styles*—preferred ways of learning, thinking, and even teaching. Styles help one understand and organize the world. When one learns in a way that mismatches the way an instructor teaches, the result may be poor performance in a course, even if one has the ability to succeed. Styles affect many other things as well—performance on the job, performance in relationships, and performance in household chores. They are ubiquitous. This book is our attempt to understand styles in a unified way, and to bring order to what has been a fairly scattered research literature.

The book is intended for anyone—especially educators and psychologists—who is interested in understanding styles and their effects on daily life. The book attempts thoroughly to review the past literature on styles, including but by no means limited to our own work, and to answer basic questions about this work. A claim that often has been made is that styles are "value-free"—that one style is, on average, no better than any other. This is one of various claims that we examine in the book.

ACKNOWLEDGMENTS

We are grateful to our collaborators over the years in styles research for making this book possible. For Li-fang Zhang, these collaborators include Allan Bernardo, Albert B. Hood, Jiafen Huang, Gerard A. Postiglione, John Sachs, and Lili Zhang. For Robert J. Sternberg, they include Elena L. Grigorenko, Marie Martin, and Richard K. Wagner. We are also grateful to Cheri Stahl, Vincent Lee, Samsom Liu, Robyn Rissman, and Fanny Wong for their assistance in preparation of the book. Our sincere thanks go to Guohai Chen, Weiqiao Fan, Greg Fairbrother, Yunfeng He, Catherine Liu, Stanley Shum, and Shengquan Ye for their competent assistance in finding research materials used in this book. Our deep appreciation goes to Meng Deng, Hong Fu, Lingbiao Gao, John Hattie, Rongjin Huang, Sammy Hui, Raymond Lam, Edmund Thompson, Barrie Tse, David Watkins, Qiufang Wen, Minxuan Zhang, and Xinhua Zhu, as well as to the thousands and thousands of research participants, who were indispensable to the completion of our empirical studies centered on thinking styles. Our very special thanks go to Naomi Silverman for contracting the book. We sincerely thank our production editor Sondra Guideman for her unflagging support in the process of turning the manuscript into a published book. Financial support for this work over the years came in part from the Committee on Research and Conference Grants, the Wu Jieh-Yee Education Research Fund, and the Sik Sik Yuen Education Research Fund, as administered by The University of Hong Kong and from Government grants under the Javits Act Program (Grant Nos. R206R00001 and R206A70001) as administered by the Institute of Education Sciences (formerly the Office of Educational Research and Improvement), U.S. Department of Education.

—Li-fang Zhang
—Robert J. Sternberg

Chapter 1

Introduction

Some people prefer to think carefully and reflectively before they act. Others prefer to act quickly and on impulse. We sometimes refer to the latter kinds of people as ones who "shoot from the hip," or "shoot first, and ask questions later." These two types of people can be referred to as differing in their preferred intellectual styles, that is, in how they choose to use their intellects in solving problems and making decisions. Intellectual styles occur at the interface between personality and cognition.

Research results accumulated over the past half century indicate that intellectual styles play an important role in many aspects of our lives. Some of these aspects are learning performance, job performance, interpersonal interaction, communication, sense of morality, social behaviors, and psychological well-being. The differences made by intellectual styles have been documented in thousands of research articles and books. Under such a circumstance, one might naturally ask: "Why, if there is so much already written on intellectual styles, do we need another book on the nature of styles?" In the present chapter, we answer this question. Then, we define the concept of *intellectual styles*. Next, we put forward the major arguments of this book. The final part of this chapter lays out the structure of the book.

WHY SHOULD WE EXAMINE THE NATURE OF INTELLECTUAL STYLES?

Unresolved Issues

Until recently, the field of intellectual styles was characterized by the belief that different styles are supposed to be neither better nor worse than each other, but simply different from each other. In a similar vein, the field of styles has also generated two other controversial issues: styles as traits versus states, and diverse styles as different constructs versus similar constructs merely with different labels. One of the reasons styles research declined in the late 1970s and early 1980s is that many viewed the research as not living up to its promise. For the last two decades, however, scholars have expressed a renewed interest in styles. This recent renewal of interest in styles work has resulted in both better integrated models of styles and research studies that are more carefully designed and more theoretically based. However, these works still have not been understood within a unified scientific framework. Moreover, some of the major controversial issues in the study of styles (such as the three just mentioned) have yet to be systematically addressed.

Understanding these controversial issues within a unified scientific framework is important because their lack of resolution not only has inhibited the advancement of the field, but also has made practitioners, including educational and occupational psychologists as well as classroom teachers, hesitant to use the concept of styles in their work. For example, if styles represent fixed traits, any attempt to teach or develop particular styles would probably be in vain. If they are fluid, then attempts at teaching and development would make good sense. Thus, addressing these issues has the potential for both advancing the field of styles and providing clear guidelines for practitioners regarding how styles can be understood and used.

After a long period of research and theorization on styles, is there enough empirical evidence for us take an empirically defensible stand on each of the three aforementioned controversial issues over intellectual styles? Is there any way we can organize existing data on styles under a common scientific framework?

Goal of Book

This book presents a panoramic and updated picture of the field of intellectual styles. In particular, it addresses the aforementioned three major controversial issues in the field through both presenting our own empirical findings and portraying, analyzing, and integrating major theoretical and research works in the existing styles literature. After completing the book, readers will have a good understanding of the field of styles: its origins, historical development, theories, research, and applications, as well as the interrelationships among major theoretical constructs proposed by different theorists throughout the past few decades. In particular, this book will provide preliminary keys to unlocking the riddles relating to the nature of intellectual styles.

INTELLECTUAL STYLES

Definition

In this book, *intellectual style* is used as a general term that encompasses the meanings of all "style" constructs postulated in the literature, such as cognitive style, conceptual tempo, decision-making and problem-solving style, learning style, mind style, perceptual style, and thinking style. An intellectual style refers to one's preferred way of processing information and dealing with tasks. To varying degrees, an intellectual style is cognitive, affective, physiological, psychological, and sociological. It is cognitive because whatever styles one uses to process information, one must be engaged in some kind of cognitive process. It is affective because one's way of processing information and of dealing with a task (i.e., employing an intellectual style) is partially determined by how one feels about the task. If one is genuinely interested in the task at hand (assuming that the task does require one to be creative and to have a deep understanding), one may, for example, use a style that is creativity-generating. On the contrary, if one feels indifferent about the task at hand, one may simply use a style that is more conservative. It is physiological because the use of a style is partially influenced by the way our senses (e.g., vision, hearing, and touch) take in the information provided to us. It is psychological because the use of a particular style is partially contingent upon how one's personality interacts with one's environment. Finally, it is sociological because the use of a style is affected by the preferences for various ways of thinking of the society in which one lives.

Concepts Underlying Intellectual Styles

A careful examination of the nature of the various intellectual styles indicates that any style may have one or more of the following concepts as part of its underpinnings. These are one's preference for high degrees of structure versus low degrees of structure, for cognitive simplicity versus cognitive complexity, for conformity versus nonconformity, for authority versus autonomy, and for group versus individual work. Although these dimensions of preference are stated in bipolar terms, the pair of descriptors for each dimension can be viewed as two ends of a continuum.

MAJOR ARGUMENTS

In this book, we make three major arguments, each addressing one of the three controversial issues regarding styles.

Style Value

Are some intellectual styles better or worse than are others? In the long history of styles research, scholars seem to have deliberately avoided the comparison of styles regarding their relative superiority or inferiority. However, in the case of many style constructs, some styles do seem to be more adaptive than others. For example, field independence—a propensity for being able to orient oneself in space without regard to one's particular surroundings—is generally more adaptive than field dependence—the propensity to orient oneself in accord with the surroundings in which one finds oneself. In case of poor visibility, a pilot who is field independent, for example, is at a big advantage over one who is field dependent. Similarly, a diver under water who is field independent is less likely to drown than one who is field dependent. Reflectivity, a tendency to ponder what to do before doing it, is generally more adaptive than blind impulsiveness. In general, some styles are more adaptive than others. That is, such styles are value-laden. At the same time, other styles seem truly to be neither better nor worse. For example, being internal or external—more introverted or extraverted in one's work orientation—can be seen as equally advantageous, although their usefulness can depend on the situation in which one finds oneself. The internal person may be at an advantage when working alone, the external person, when working in a group. That is, such styles are value-differentiated.

Through empirical evidence and theoretical conceptualization, we argue throughout this book that styles are largely value-laden and that they are at times value-differentiated. We classify all intellectual styles into three types. Type I styles are perceived as being more positive because they generally have more adaptive value. Type II styles are considered more negative because they generally carry less adaptive value. Therefore, Type I and Type II styles are considered value-laden. Type III styles are value-differentiated (i.e., they can be either positive or negative) because they may possess the characteristics of either Type I styles or Type II styles, depending on the requirements of a task or of a situation (see chapters 3 through 8 for details).

One may ask: "Whose values are you talking about?" In the context of this book, we are talking about the values of those in democratic societies, or, at least, societies that value innovation.

Style Malleability

When Yan Zi came to the state of Chu as an envoy from the state of Qi, he was received by the King of Chu at a banquet. While they were drinking, two soldiers brought a tied-up criminal to the King in the hall. "Who's the man you've tied up?", asked the King of Chu. "He's a thief from the state of Qi," replied the soldier. The king turned to Yan Zi and said, "Why, he's your countryman. Men in the state of Qi must all be fond of stealing!" Seeing that the King of Chu was being sarcastic, Yan Zi stood to his feet and said, "I heard that when oranges are planted south of the river, they bear sweet oranges. When they are planted north of the river, they turn into trifoliate orange trees. Although their leaves are similar, their fruit is quite different. Why is that so? Because water and soil on either side of the river is different. People in the state of Qi never steal. But when they come to the state of Chu, they learn to steal. May I ask, is this not the water and soil of the state of Chu that have turned people into thieves?" (Translation by Zhao & Tang, in Si-Tu, 1990, p. 174).

The above is a story from *Anecdotes of Yan Zi*, recorded and compiled by writers of the Warring States Period (475–221 B.C.) in ancient China. The story illustrates the powerful impact of environment on human behaviors. Are intellectual styles malleable? Throughout this book, we present research evidence indicating that styles are malleable. They represent states, although they can be relatively stable over a period of time.

Style Overlap

In the literature, many style labels have been used. When reviewing the then-existing work on styles, Hayes and Allinson (1994) noted there were 22 different dimensions of cognitive style alone. Five years later, Armstrong (1999) identified 54 style dimensions, which he classified under the more encompassing term *cognitive style*. Some of these examples are field-dependent/independent (Witkin, 1954), scanning–focusing (Schlesinger, 1954), constricted–flexible control (Klein, 1954), intuitive–thinking (Myers, 1962), reflective–impulsive (Kagan, 1965a), splitters–lumpers (Cohen, 1967), serialist–holist (Pask & Scott, 1972), and activist–reflector (Kolb, 1976). Similarly, many style labels have been placed under the umbrella term *learning style*. Some of these examples include instructional preference (Friedman & Stritter, 1976), learning interest (Riechmann & Grasha, 1974), learning preference (Rezler & Rezmovic, 1974), study process (Biggs, 1979), and approach to study (Entwistle & Ramsden, 1983). Each style label has at least one corresponding assessment tool.

Are there any relationships among these style labels, such as cognitive styles and learning styles? If one prefers to use a deep approach to study in a learning context, would one also tend to use an innovative decision-making style at work? Such questions have been puzzling not only to scholars in the field, but also to laypeople who are interested in the notion of styles.

There are two levels at which we can address such questions. One is at the conceptual level, and the other, the empirical level.

Conceptually, the relationships among different style labels can be decided phered by examining three types of scholarly efforts: defining styles, integrating existing style labels, and proposing more comprehensive style terms. Without going into the specific definition for each of the individual style labels, we did a quick survey of how cognitive style and learning style have been defined. Not surprisingly, we found that, in terms of definitions, cognitive styles and learning styles share much in common. Consider some of the definitions for each in turn:

The definitions of cognitive styles are based on the notion that people are inclined to characteristic ways of processing information in various contexts. For example, Anastasi (1988) defined cognitive styles as broad, systematic features affecting an individual's responses to a variety of circumstances. Messick (1984) believed that cognitive styles are characteristic modes of perception, memory, thought, and judgment that reflect an individual's information-processing regularities.

By the same token, the definitions of learning styles are also dominated by the idea that people have predilections for attending information in certain ways, but not in others. The major noticeable difference between the ways cognitive styles are defined and the ways learning styles are defined is that the former concern multiple contexts whereas the latter pertain to learning situations only. For instance, Gregorc (1979) defined learning styles as the distinctive behaviors that indicate how a person learns from and adapts to his or her environment. Kalsbeek (1989) noted that learning styles can be viewed as one's preferred approach to information processing, idea formation, and decision making.

It is worth noting, however, that some scholars do not seem to consider it necessary to distinguish the two frequently used style terms: cognitive style and learning style. As pointed out by Campbell (1991), *cognitive style* and *learning style* have often been used synonymously. For example, Tennant (1997) stated: " 'Cognitive style,' 'learning style,' and 'conceptual style' are related terms which refer to an individual's characteristic and consistent approach to organizing and processing information" (p. 80). Indeed, some scholars do use the two terms interchangeably. For instance, Curry (1983) viewed her model as one of learning styles despite the fact that several style dimensions included in her model are cognition-centered. On the other hand, Miller (1987) referred to his model as one of cognitive style even though several style dimensions in his model concern learning activities. As a final example, although Kolb's (1976) work is normally discussed within the framework of learning styles, Hayes and Allinson (1994) classified Kolb's style dimensions as cognitive styles.

Efforts to clarify the relationships go beyond defining cognitive and learning styles. A number of scholars have attempted, and succeeded in varying degrees, in bringing order to the existing style labels. Sternberg (1997, see also Grigorenko & Sternberg, 1995) conceptualized the existing style labels into three approaches to the study of styles: cognition-centered, personality-centered, and activity-centered (see chapter 6 for details). Believing that many of the style labels are merely different conceptions of superordinate dimensions, several authors also have conceptually integrated these style labels (e.g., Curry, 1983; Miller, 1987; Riding & Cheema, 1991).

Sternberg (1988, 1997) proposed the notion of thinking styles. For two reasons, thinking styles are perceived to be more general than are cognitive or learning styles. First, they can be applied to both academic and non-academic settings. Second, thinking styles cover styles from all three traditions of the study of styles (see chapter 7 for details). Meanwhile, Sternberg (2001a) noted that although the three kinds of styles are often viewed as overlapping, they have been conceptualized in different ways. He offered his views of how cognitive, learning, and thinking styles might be used in processing the same information. Cognitive styles might be used to characterize ways of cognizing the information. Learning styles might be used to characterize how one prefers to learn about the information. Thinking styles might be used to characterize how one prefers to think about the information as one is learning it or after one already knows it.

So much for the endeavors in clarifying the relationships among styles. By now, one could easily come to the conclusion that, regardless of the kind of efforts that have been made and no matter how differently the existing styles have been defined, there is one essential common thread that links all different styles. That is, styles are not abilities; they are people's preferred ways of using the abilities that they have. Thus, inevitably, different styles overlap with one another, at least in theory. Yet, different style dimensions have different foci (e.g., personality-oriented, cognition-oriented, activity-oriented), which necessarily leads to our conclusion that each style also has its own unique features.

Empirically, the various styles overlap, despite the fact that each of the style labels (and its corresponding measures) was constructed independently. However, the shared variance between any of the two style dimensions under investigation ranges from 20% to 60%, on average. That is to say, a substantial part of the variance in the data is left to be explained by the unique characteristics of each of the two individual style dimensions concerned and by other possible factors (see chapters 3 through 8).

ABOUT THIS BOOK

This introductory chapter is intended to set the stage for an examination of the nature of intellectual styles. It provides an introduction to the key concepts and the major arguments of the book. The remainder of this book is composed of four parts. The first part (chapter 2) provides a general picture of the field of intellectual styles—its past and its present; it ends with reiterating the call for further understanding the nature of intellectual styles. Part II (chapters 3, 4, and 5) addresses the three aforementioned controversial issues regarding intellectual styles by reviewing and critically analyzing existing empirical studies based on previous individual style models. Chapter 3 concerns research on students. Chapter 4 pertains to research on teachers. Chapter 5 focuses on research in workplaces. Part III (chapters 6 and 7) explores the nature of styles through appraising style works that have aimed at conceptually integrating previous theoretical models and their empirical research. Chapter 6 discusses research based on four existing integrative models of intellectual styles in the field. Chapter 7 delineates research based on the latest individual theoretical model of styles: the theory of mental self-government. Part IV (chapters 8 and 9) further examines the nature of intellectual styles by re-conceptualizing works documented in the literature and making concluding remarks about the research and application of styles. Based on 10 individual classical style models and their research as well as on research evidence presented in the earlier chapters, chapter 8 proposes a new integrative model of intellectual styles that systematically addresses the three controversial issues over styles. Chapter 9 provides some concluding thoughts along with practical ways of using our knowledge about intellectual styles in a variety of contexts.

Part I

THE FIELD OF INTELLECTUAL
STYLES

Chapter 2

Surveying the Field
of Intellectual Styles

This chapter is organized into four parts and provides an overview of the field of intellectual styles. The first part is a brief account of the foundations of and trends in the styles literature. The second part specifies the difficulties in investigating intellectual styles. The third part describes some of the major efforts that have been made to rejuvenate the field of intellectual styles. The conclusion of the chapter pinpoints the need for further exploration of the nature of styles vis-à-vis the three controversial issues regarding intellectual styles.

FOUNDATIONS AND TRENDS

Foundations of the Field of Styles

The field of styles has diverse philosophical and theoretical foundations (e.g., Grigorenko & Sternberg, 1995; Kagan & Kogan, 1970; Messick, 1994; Morgan, 1997; Rayner & Riding, 1997; Riding & Rayner, 1998; Vernon, 1973). The origin of the concept of styles in cognitive psychology has been traced to different sources—to classical Greek literature (see Vernon, 1973), others (e.g., Martinsen, 1994; Riding, 1997), to conceptions of individual differences by Galton (1883), James (1890), and Bartlett (1932), and to Jung's (1923) theory of personality types (see Sternberg & Grigorenko, 1997). Similarly, works on styles have been ascribed to diverse research traditions, most notably, cognitive-developmental psychology, differential psychology, Gestalt psychology, psychoanalytic ego psychology, and the experimental psychology of cognition (see Messick, 1994; Morgan, 1997). Meanwhile, in his book *Cognitive Styles and Classroom Learning,* Morgan (1997) argued for the essential role of experience in the process of human learning (see also Denton, 1974).

Trends in the Styles Literature

Allport (1937) introduced the notion of styles to psychology when he referred to "styles of life" as a means of identifying distinctive personality types or types of behavior. Since then, styles have been the focus of research by many scholars, though levels of interest have waxed and waned in the past 60 years. In the long history of styles work, the notion of cognitive style appeared the earliest. The driving force behind the appearance of this notion was the need for a bridge between cognition and personality. Aiming to integrate personality theories into the study of cognitive preferences, *The Authoritarian Personality* by Adorno, Frenkel-Brunswick, Levinson, and Sanford (1950) exemplifies this endeavor. The effect of this work can be seen in the hundreds of cognitive-style studies that followed. In fact, this momentum was maintained for more than two decades. Sternberg (1997) referred to this flourishing of styles work as of the "cognitive-styles movement" (p. 135). Through this movement, many alternative dimensions of styles have been explored, among which Witkin's (1959) concept of perceptual style and Kagan's (1965a) notion of conceptual tempo have been the most influential.

By the late 1960s and early 1970s, the cognitive-styles movement reached its climax. The number of studies of styles diminished, in part because of the overwhelming earlier output of the field and in part because of its lack of internal dialogue (Jones, 1997a). When Biggs (2001) recalled his experience with this historical period, he stated: "Some years ago I was reviewing the styles literature to draw educational implications. I arrived at 18 different styles, then came across Kogan's (1971) review, which added another 8 to my list. I did not finish my review, convinced there had to be better ways of looking at educationally relevant individual differences" (Sternberg & Zhang, 2001, p. 76).

Partially in response to the proliferation of style labels accompanied by the number of style measures, and partially because of scholars' interest in applying the notion of styles to various specific disciplines, including education, researchers began to focus in the 1970s on the notion of learning styles. Two very different approaches were taken: the North American approach and the Australian/European approach (see Hickcox, 1995). The former approach, as represented by the works of Friedman and Stritter (1976) and Kolb (1976), originated from cognitive psychology, whereas the latter, exemplified by the works of Biggs (1979) and Marton (1976), was developed from observations of learning behaviors.

However, the learning-styles movement lasted for less than a decade before the field of styles began to die out in the late 1970s, for reasons we shall detail in the next section. But in the mid 1980s, there was a renewed interest in the notion of styles, for abilities and personality structure simply could not explain the whole story about individual differences in human performance. Efforts to rejuvenate the field are manifest in several types of works, which will be illustrated in the remainder of this book.

In the rest of this chapter, we focus our discussion on three topics. The first concerns the difficulties (challenges) created by the diverse historical roots of the field of styles. The second delineates the continuing effort to clarify the relationships of styles to abilities and personalities. The third points out the need for further advancement in the field.

PARADISE LOST—CHALLENGES IN INVESTIGATING INTELLECTUAL STYLES

In 1989, Tiedemann declared, "My personal opinion of the state of research into cognitive styles has to be: there is no point in chasing a chimera!" (p. 273). Tiedemann was not alone in expressing disillusionment with the field of styles (e.g., Freedman & Stumpf, 1980). What was happening? What had led some scholars to conclude that the field of styles deserved no further investigation? Many writers (e.g., Armstrong, 1999; Miller, 1987; Riding & Cheema, 1991) have traced the development of the styles literature and acknowledged that the field of styles was disorganized. Messick (1994) attributed the chaotic situation to the diverse roots of the field. These diverse foundations of the field allowed scholars to pursue their own interest in styles from different perspectives and to use different measures in investigating the nature of styles.

Inconsistency and confusion in terminology as well as goals of researchers arose, which presented challenges to the advancement of the field. Many (e.g., Messick, 1994; Miller, 1987; Riding & Cheema, 1991) have attempted to identify the challenges that faced the field at the time. We discuss three major challenges that are inextricably related: the lack of distinction of styles from abilities and personality traits; the lack of consistent definitions and reliable and valid measures for styles; and the lack of a global perspective. We consider each in turn.

Challenge One: Styles as Indistinguishable From Abilities and Personalities

As noted by Sternberg (2001b), one of the primary factors that contributed to decline in styles research activities in the 1970s was that some early theories presented styles that could not be proven to be "pure" style constructs.

These styles were not clearly distinguishable from abilities, on the one hand, or from personality traits, on the other. Consequently, the study of styles was easily immersed into the investigation of abilities or of personality traits, so the need for a distinct area of research on styles seemed to no longer exist. To some, styles research was ability or personality research.

For example, in the case of Witkin's construct of field dependence/independence (FDI), some scholars (e.g., Jones, 1997b; Richardson & Turner, 2000; Shipman, 1990) contended that the FDI construct primarily represents individual variations in perceptual/spatial/visual preference patterns. There is repeated empirical evidence showing that people's performance on the (Group) Embedded Figures Test (Witkin, Oltman, Raskin, & Karp, 1971) is only related to intellectual tasks that require disembedding, especially visual disembedding (e.g., Dubois & Cohen, 1970; Jones, 1997b; Satterly, 1976; Spotts & Mackler, 1967; Stuart, 1967; Weisz, O'Neill, & O'Neill, 1975). Such ambiguity of the nature of styles created an atmosphere that severely restricted researchers' ability and desire to study and apply the notion of styles.

Challenge Two: Conceptual and Measurement Problems

A second challenge recognized by many scholars (e.g., Armstrong, 1999; Campbell, 1991; Messick, 1994; Miller, 1987; Riding, 1997; Shipman, 1989; Vernon, 1963) was a result of the problems associated with conceptions and measurement of styles. Within the first few decades of research on styles, especially during the "golden age" of the styles movement between the late 1950s and the early 1970s, a diverse and massive collection of theories and models of styles resulted in various labels with the root word *style* (see Messick, 1984; Riding & Cheema, 1991), including *cognitive style, defensive style, expressive style, responsive style,* and *learning style,* among others. Yet, many of these styles had largely evolved from theories generalized on single experiments with little subsequent empirical support. Furthermore, different theorists emphasized different dimensions of styles in their conceptualizations and different criterion features in their assessments of styles. The quality of early research was also variable. When new styles were proposed, adequate means were seldom built into the research to provide both convergent and discriminant validation. The instruments assessing the style constructs were often introspective self-report measures. The result was one of problematically reliable and valid measures for the already somewhat faulty conceptions of diverse styles.

In the history of the styles literature, this diversity in theorization and research contributed to the sometimes chaotic state of the work on styles. This lack of convergence and, ultimately, aimlessness eventually led to a reduction in the quantity (and, arguably, quality) of styles research between the early 1970s and the mid-1980s (e.g., Jones, 1997a; Riding & Cheema, 1991). As Riding and Cheema (1991) explained, ". . . many researchers working within the learning/cognitive style research fail[ed] to mention the existence of other types of styles" (p. 193). Riding and Cheema (1991) compared the manner in which scholars were investigating styles to "the blind man and the elephant" (p. 193).

Challenge Three: The Need for a Global Perspective

The fundamental challenge to the field is the lack of a global perspective. This global perspective can be understood at two different levels. At one level, styles research and theorization were isolated from mainstream psychological literature. Even though styles were closely related to cognitive and personality traits, the appropriate literatures were not adequately addressed. At a second level, within the styles field, one could easily observe that "different groups of researchers seem determined to pursue their own pet distinctions in cheerful disregard of one another" (Lewis, 1976, p. 304). There was a lack of common language and common conceptual framework for styles researchers to communicate either among themselves or with psychologists at large. The inability to build this commonality, according to Sternberg (2001b), led to an untimely demise of styles research.

Obviously, for any academic field to prosper, a common theoretical framework and a common language are helpful. As Sternberg (2001b) observed, in the literature on intelligence, *g* theorists deal with a common conceptual framework using a common language. The theory may be incomplete, but it provides a common ground to unite a large number of researchers. The same can be said of the five-factor theory of personality. Although it is often seen as nothing more than a common language, it provides a common conceptual framework as well as language for personality theorists within the trait tradition. In the styles literature, however, there was neither a common conceptual framework nor a common language.

PARADISE REGAINED—EFFORTS TO REJUVENATE THE FIELD OF INTELLECTUAL STYLES

The last couple of decades, however, have witnessed a resurgence of interest in the study of styles in both academic and nonacademic settings. This interest is manifested through three types of work, each aimed at addressing its corresponding challenge, presented in the previous part of this chapter. The first is the continuing effort to examine the style construct against the ability and personality constructs, at both conceptual and empirical levels. The second effort is represented by empirical investigations geared toward clarifying the relationships among the different style labels. The third type is conceptual integration of previous work on styles as well as construction of new theories of styles. The latter two types are addressed in the remaining chapters of this book. In the present chapter, we devote our discussion to the first type of endeavor. Our rationale for examining the relationships of styles to abilities and personalities first rests on our belief that only when the identity (distinctions) of styles (from ability and personality) is established (are clarified) can one successfully pursue the nature of styles in other contexts.

Styles, Ability/General Intelligence, and Personality

As discussed earlier, interest in the study of intellectual styles came about partially as a response to the realization that neither ability nor personality alone, nor the two of them put together, can paint the whole picture of individual differences in human performance and behavior. So how do styles differ from abilities and personality traits? Are there data supporting the notion that styles make unique contribution to human performance and behavior over and above abilities and personality?

Style and Ability/General Intelligence. As Miller (1987) has rightfully noted, the relationship between styles and abilities has been a thorny problem in the literature. Indeed, this relationship has been repeatedly dealt with in the literature, at both the conceptual and empirical levels. At the conceptual level, there are differences but also some similarities between abilities and styles (e.g., Entwistle, McCune, & Walker, 2001; Furnham, 1995; Messick, 1984, 1994, 1996; Miller, 1987; Riding, 1997; Sternberg, 1997; Tiedemann, 1989; Witkin, Moore, Goodenough, & Cox, 1977). One of the earliest discussions on the basic distinctions between abilities and styles can be found in Witkin and his colleagues' work (Witkin et al., 1977). Witkin's group differentiated the two constructs by emphasizing the unipolar nature of abilities in contrast to the bipolar nature of styles.

Messick (1984, 1994, 1996) did a more comprehensive job of elucidating the differences between the two. According to Messick, both abilities and styles affect performance. However, there are two essential differences between the two constructs. First, abilities are competence variables, whereas styles are performance variables. As such, abilities pertain to *how much*, and styles are relevant to *how*. Having more of an ability is better than having less, but having the propensity for one style does not imply being better or worse than having the propensity for a different style, at least in theory. That is, abilities are unipolar and value directional, whereas styles are typically bipolar and value-differentiated. (It should be noted that in this book, we argue that styles are both value directional/value-laden and value-differentiated.) Second, abilities are domain specific, whereas styles are domain free: "An ability is usually limited to a particular domain of content or function, such as verbal or memory ability, whereas a cognitive style cuts across domains of ability, personality, and interpersonal behavior" (Messick, 1996, p. 359).

Other scholars have illustrated the distinctions between the two constructs in a rather similar fashion. For example, in discussing the nature of cognitive style, Riding (1997) stated: "The basic distinction between them is that performance on all tasks will improve as ability increases, whereas the effect of style on performance for an individual will either be positive or negative depending on the nature of the task. . . . In other words, in terms of style a person is both good and poor at tasks depending on the nature of the task, while for intelligence, they are either good or poor" (pp. 30–31).

Sternberg (1997) pointed out that "Styles do not represent a set of abilities, but rather a set of preferences" (p. 134). Styles are neither abilities nor personalities. They are at the interface between abilities and personalities.

At the empirical level, complex relationships have been found between abilities and styles. Some studies did not reveal a significant relationship (or found only a weak relationship) between abilities/intelligence and styles (e.g., Carne & Kirton, 1982; Keller & Holland, 1978b; Riding & Pearson, 1994; Tullett, 1997). For example, after reviewing the literature on the relationship between divergent thinking and intelligence, Mehdi (1974) concluded that those individuals who are divergent in their thinking are not necessarily those who are highly intelligent. Similarly, Olive's (1972b) research findings indicated a significant but modest relationship between divergent thinking and intelligence as measured by the Otis Quick-Scoring Mental Ability Test. More recently, results from Armstrong's (2000) study suggest that cognitive style is unrelated to overall ability among business and management students.

Other studies have identified unique contributions of styles to human performance, over and above abilities. In the academic setting, for example, when studying the interrelationships among intelligence, field independence, spatial ability, and achievement in mathematics and haptic perception among 201 school boys, Satterly (1976) found that although intelligence and field independence were related, field independence made a unique contribution to students' achievement in the two subject matters beyond that of intelligence. Furthermore, principal-components factor analysis supported the independence of cognitive style from factors representing general ability and spatial ability. Similarly, when he compared the functions of learning style and intelligence in predicting academic performance of 100 kindergartners, McDermott (1984) found that although intelligence was the better predictor for these children's academic performance, learning styles explained significant portions of the variance in later performance.

Still other studies suggest that abilities/intelligence and styles interact. For example, Brooks, Simutis, and O'Neil (1985) argued that research on abilities and styles in map reading indicates that abilities may play a role in an individual's selection of a particular style and of how effectively the style is used. Similarly, Schroder (1989) illustrated how two managers of the same competence level may make different kinds of contributions to their organization by using different styles. Finally, Messer (1976) reviewed studies reporting correlations between the Matching Familiar Figures Test (MFFT; Kagan, Rosman, Day, Albert, & Philips, 1964) and intelligence tests. He concluded that conceptual tempo is moderately correlated with IQ when IQ falls within the normal range. Furthermore, the relationship tends to be higher for errors than for response time and slightly stronger for girls than for boys. Messer cautioned, however, that the order of presenting the MFFT and IQ tests may have affected the MFFT scores and size of the correlations between reflectivity–impulsivity and IQ.

Today, the idea that styles play an important role in human performance has been widely although not universally accepted. A quick survey of existing studies with the aim of disentangling abilities and styles shows that the majority of the studies were conducted more than two decades ago. Scholars no longer seem to question the legitimacy of styles as an important individual-difference variable in human performance. However, the debate over the utility of the field dependence/independence (FDI) construct as a style variable has never ceased. As noted earlier, some scholars (e.g., Jones, 1997b; Richardson & Turner, 2000; Shipman, 1990) contend that the FDI construct primarily represents individual variations in perceptual/spatial/visual preference patterns based on the repeated empirical evidence that (Group) Embedded Figures Test performance is only related to intellectual tasks that require disembedding, especially visual disembedding.

Other scholars (e.g., Kogan, 1980; Saracho, 1991a, 2001; Witkin & Goodenough, 1977), however, have argued that field dependence/independence can be used to describe individual differences in a broadly defined intellectual (behavioral) style. This argument is based on the overall empirical finding that FDI plays an important role in people's intellectual activities in a wide array of areas. For example, Dyk and Witkin (1965) reported that when parents encouraged their children to act independently, children tended to be field independent. They also suggested that when children are encouraged to conform to authority, children tend to be more field dependent. In the study of the role of FDI in secondary school students' reenrollments in vocational education and their attitudes toward teachers and programs, Fritz (1981) found that reenrolled drafting students were statistically more field independent than were students in three home-economics programs. Furthermore, he concluded that field-independent students were less concerned about interpersonal relations with their teachers. Woodward and Kalyan-Masih (1990) reported significant relationships of field dependence/independence to loneliness as well as to coping strategies among gifted rural adolescents. They found that field-independent adolescents in rural environments tended to seek individual pursuits and demonstrated more autonomy and self-reliance. In his study of middle-school students, Dulin (1993) found that field-independent students showed a significantly lower preference for cooperative learning. In his book *Cognitive Styles and Classroom Learning*, Morgan (1997) noted that studies had reported that field-independent students from higher education institutions tend to select areas of study associated with the sciences and field-dependent students are more likely to choose fields of human services, such as teaching and social work. More recently, Saracho (2001) noted that previous research had shown that field dependence/independence characterizes an individual's perceptual style, personality, intelligence, and social behavior.

Still, other work (e.g., Streufert & Nogami, 1989; Widiger, Knudson, & Porter, 1980) points to the possibility that Witkin's Group Embedded Figures Test may measure an aspect of intelligence—spatial ability—as well as cognitive style. The same statement could be made about Kagan's (1965c) Matching Familiar Figures Test (e.g., Streufert & Nogami, 1989).

Then, the question is: If there is evidence that styles and abilities/general intelligence are related, is it still worthwhile to study the role of styles in human performance and behaviors? In particular, if there is evidence that the field dependence/independence construct represents spatial ability, should the FDI construct still be included in the styles literature?

We would argue that it makes sense to study intellectual styles as a source of individual differences in human performance and behavior, given the ample evidence that (a) styles contribute to human performance over and above abilities, (b) styles and abilities are generally orthogonal, and (c) there are fundamental differences between styles and abilities at the conceptual level. Furthermore, as the pioneer work in the field of intellectual styles and the most widely researched style construct, Witkin's notion of field dependence/independence has demonstrated its undeniable importance in the styles literature. Moreover, the FDI construct has proven to be more than simply indicative of perceptual ability. In addition, it has been empirically shown to be related to many other style constructs (e.g., Holland's career personality types, the Myers–Briggs personality types, and Kagan's reflectivity–impulsivity). Thus, undoubtedly, the field dependence/independence construct remains one of the most viable style constructs. As Davis (1991) argued, the very source of power and attraction of the FDI construct as an integrative variable comes from the fact that it sometimes acts as an ability and sometimes as a style.

Style and Personality.   In literature, there also are relationships between styles and abilities at the conceptual (e.g., Adorno, Frenkel-Brunswick, Levinson, & Sanford, 1950; Eysenck, 1978; Hashway, 1998; Messick, 1996) and empirical levels (e.g., Busato, Prins, Elshout, & Hamaker, 1999; Furnham, 1992, 1996a, 1996b; Furnham, Jackson, & Miller, 1999; Gadzella, 1999; Jackson & Lawty-Jones, 1996; Pacini & Epstein, 1999; Riding & Wigley, 1997). Conceptually, various arguments have been made about the relationships between styles and personalities. In the 1960s and 1970s, some authors (e.g., Berg, 1967; Cattell, 1973) argued that from an individual-difference perspective, styles are inseparable from personality. For example, after reviewing then-existing research work on psychological theories of cognitive styles, Cattell (1973) announced: "the inevitable conclusion is that the styles are the effect of the personality factors" (p. 396). In the 1980s and 1990s, scholars tended to emphasize the interrelationship between the two constructs. For example, Kirton and De Ciantis (1986) maintained that cognitive styles should be related to personality traits because both constructs are known for their tendency to be stable across time and contexts (Goldstein & Blackman, 1981; McKenna, 1983).

Messick (1994) acknowledged the link between the two constructs by pointing out the need to organize styles within the broader personality system. Indeed, several such attempts to connect the two constructs have been made, the most noteworthy of which may be Royce and Powell's (1983). The authors depicted a multifaceted three-level style hierarchy under which a hierarchy of intellectual abilities and a hierarchy of affective factors (e.g., emotionality and temperament) are subsumed. To achieve the goals for various tasks, the style system shares a common space and works concordantly with various cognitive or affective factors.

Moreover, styles have also been perceived as being moderated by personality in affecting human performance. For instance, Furnham (1995) asserted that the contribution of personalities to styles seems to be "implicit in the writings of many educational and psychological researchers" (p. 398), although the relationship is seldom described as such.

Empirically, with some exceptions (e.g., Elder, 1989; Getreu, 1997; Kirton, 1976; Kubes, 1992; Tullett & Davies, 1997), the majority of studies obtained significant relationships between styles and personalities. In all but the final chapter of this book, empirical evidence demonstrating this relationship will be provided. The interest of the relevant studies presented in the following chapters lies in exploring the precise relationships between the styles and personality traits measured, under the assumption that style is a legitimate individual-difference construct to examine.

In the present chapter, we intend to review only those studies designed to clarify the relationship between the style and personality constructs—studies that intend to make a statement about the legitimacy (or illegitimacy) of style as an individual-difference variable in human performance. Although significant relationships are invariably obtained between measures of the two constructs, there is disagreement regarding the necessity for measuring the two constructs separately in the realm of empirical research. For example, Busato, Prins, Elshout, and Hamaker (1999) examined the relationships between learning styles and the Big Five personality traits among 900 university students. The authors employed Vermunt's (1992) inventory of learning styles and Elshout and Akkerman's (1975) "vijf persoonlijkheids-factoren test, 5PFT," the first published questionnaire specially designed to measure the personality traits known as the Big Five. They concluded that although there was some systematic overlap between the learning styles and personality traits assessed, it certainly makes sense to measure learning styles and personality separately. Similarly, findings of the relationships between the two style dimensions (wholist–analytic and verbal–imagery) and a few personality dimensions (e.g., extraversion, neuroticism, psychoticism, impulsiveness, empathy, and so on) led Riding and Wigley (1997) to conclude that understanding each of the two constructs is critical for teachers, lecturers, and trainers to become more effective teachers and learners.

By contrast, after studying the relationships between learning styles as assessed by the Learning Styles Questionnaire (Honey & Mumford, 1982) and personality traits as measured by the Eysenck Personality Questionnaire (Eysenck & Eysenck, 1975) among 166 volunteers and psychology students, Jackson and Lawty-Jones (1996) concluded that learning style is a subset of personality and need not be measured independently, unless learning style is of interest in its own right. In a similar vein, Furnham (1992, 1996a, 1996b) concluded that in the interest of parsimony, personality tests could be used to examine learning styles.

Where do we stand on this dispute? We would say that, although it seems undeniable that personality and styles have a strong relationship, there are at least four reasons for measuring styles in addition to personality. First, in the empirical literature on the relationship between personality and styles, conclusions about the necessity of measuring styles separately have been subjective. Some writers (e.g., Busato et al., 1999) conclude that personality and styles are two different constructs (and thus need to be measured separately) even when a strong relationship has been found, whereas other scholars (e.g., Furnham, Jackson, & Miller, 1999) assert that styles are a subset of personality (and thus do not need to be measured separately), when only a moderately significant relationship was found. To this end, findings about the extent to which styles and personality correlate have been inconsistent. For example, Furnham, one of the strong advocates for parsimony of measurement, identified different degrees of relationships in different investigations. Whereas he found substantial overlap between the two constructs in his 1992 study, he identified only moderate correlations in one of his 1996 studies (Furnham, 1996b). In their 1999 study, Furnham and colleagues found no significant relationship between learning styles and neuroticism, one of the major personality dimensions.

Second, there is no evidence that personality determines intellectual styles. Instead, it could be argued that personality and styles are inextricably entwined. Thus, the fact that a personality measure and a style measure overlap should not warrant the futility of the assessment of either of the two constructs. Knowledge about intellectual styles as well as about personality contributes to our understanding of individual differences in human performance and behaviors.

Third, whether or not (or the degree to which) relationships were found between the two constructs is highly contingent upon the inventories used to assess styles. For example, a style inventory such as the Educational Cognitive Style Inventory developed at Fitchburg State College contains questions that appear to address latent personality domains, as it does in a personality measure. Inevitably, a study that employs such a style inventory in testing the relationship between styles and personalities would lead one to conclude that styles and personalities are inseparable (Hashway, 1998). On the other hand, a style inventory that is not personality-oriented would tend to have low or no correlation with measures of personality. For example, the Kirton Adaption–Innovation Inventory (Kirton, 1976), a cognition-rooted style inventory, has been found to have either low or no correlation with a number of personality measures, including the Eysenck Personality Inventory (Eysenck & Eysenck, 1964; e.g., study by Kirton, 1976) and the Spielberger Anxiety Trait Inventory (Spielberger, Gorsuch, Lushene, Vagg, & Jacobs, 1983; e.g., study by Elder, 1989).

Finally, other variables (e.g., age, education, and gender) often serve as moderators of style–personality relations. For example, in studying the relationships between Holland's career personality types (as measured by the Self-Directed Search, SDS, Holland, 1985) and the Big Five personality traits (as measured by the NEO-Personality Inventory, NEO-PI, Costa & McCrae, 1985), Tokar (1995) found that gender affected the relationships under investigation. For females, a significant overlap between the SDS and NEO-PI scales was characterized by an avoidance of others dimension and a dimension considered uninterpretable. For males, however, a significant overlap between the two inventories was represented by openness and extraversion (see also Tokar, Vaux, & Swanson, 1995). Thus, the issue is not whether or not styles should be measured in addition to measuring personalities. Instead, the issue is how styles can be measured more validly.

Summary. Both conceptual arguments and empirical evidence suggest that styles are related to abilities and personalities in a complex fashion. Like abilities and personalities, styles make a difference in human performance. Moreover, styles contribute to individual differences in performance beyond what can be accounted for by abilities and personalities. At present, it seems that the distinctions between styles and abilities have been well articulated. The number of empirical studies aimed at separating styles from abilities has apparently decreased in the last two decades. However, the distinction of styles from personalities seems to be difficult to conceptualize. No compelling attempt has been made to distinguish the two constructs at a conceptual level, although the link between the two has been discussed extensively. Fortunately, there is much empirical evidence supporting the unique contribution made by styles to individual differences in human performance. Perhaps because the distinction between styles and personalities has not been clearly spelled out, scholars in the field continue their effort in empirically testing this relationship. However, regardless of what has been found in the past, as an individual-difference variable in human performance, styles have established their unique position in field of psychology.

CHAPTER SUMMARY

In this chapter, we outlined the major historical events in the field of intellectual styles. The role of intellectual styles in human performance is as critical as that of abilities and personality traits. However, in looking back to the history of the field as well as in examining the current published works on styles, one cannot help but notice that the three controversial issues we mentioned in the first chapter remain largely unaddressed. Although several scholars (e.g., Goldstein & Blackman, 1981; Kogan, 1989; McKenna, 1983; Messick, 1996; Sternberg, 1997) alluded to one of the three issues in different contexts, and although the results of numerous studies (see the following chapters) can be used to address these controversial issues, not a single piece of work has explicitly discussed the three issues in a systematic way. The remaining chapters of the book deal with the three issues at both the conceptual and empirical levels.

Part II

EMPIRICAL STUDIES: INDIVIDUAL MODELS

Chapter 3

Styles Research: Student Oriented

In this chapter, we explore the nature of intellectual styles, centering our discussion on the three controversial issues mentioned in chapter 1. To re-capitulate, the three issues are: (1) the overlap issue—whether different style labels represent different style constructs or whether they are similar constructs with different root words for styles; (2) the value issue—whether styles are value-laden or value-free; and (3) the malleability issue—whether styles represent traits (and thus are stable and unchangeable) or states (and thus are flexible and modifiable). The exploration is done through system-atically examining empirical findings obtained among students at various educational levels.

To accomplish this goal, we propose five questions to be answered. First, do styles overlap with one another? Second, how do students' intellectual styles relate to their personality traits? Third, what are the roles of students' intellectual styles in their academic performance? Fourth, how do students' intellectual styles relate to socialization factors in their backgrounds and can students' styles be trained? Finally, what are the roles of students' intel-lectual styles in their behaviors? The overlap issue will be dealt with in the context of answering the first question; the value and malleability issues will be addressed in the process of answering the remaining four questions.

STYLE OVERLAP

In chapter 1, we stated that one of the major arguments of this book is that style constructs overlap with one another; but simultaneously, each style construct has its own unique characteristics. Would this assertion hold with research findings based on the study of student populations? The answer is affirmative.

The literature shows that the majority of research on the relationships among different styles was conducted in the last decade or so. Results from many studies are supportive of our claim about the style overlap issue. This research is characterized by the large number of style inventories involved and by the inclusion of a great variety of student populations from different parts of the world, ranging from primary school students to university students, and from nursing students to business students. Some examples of the inventories employed are Cantwell and Moore's (1996) Strategic Flexibility Questionnaire; Pask and Scott's (1972) original testing materials designed to suit holist and serialist learning strategies; Entwistle's (1981) Approaches to Studying Inventory; Entwistle and Tait's (1994) Revised Approaches to Studying Inventory; Riechmann and Grasha's (1974) Learning Preferences Inventory; Honey and Mumford's (1992) Learning Styles Questionnaire; Allinson and Hayes's (1996) Cognitive Style Index; Kolb's (1976) Learning Style Inventory; Dunn, Dunn, and Price's (1979) Learning Styles Inventory; and Renzulli and Smith's (1978) Learning Style Inventory.

Many of these style inventories appear to have very similar names. The apparent use of similar inventories for assessing the relationships among styles would, undoubtedly, give rise to some people's questioning of the uniqueness, and therefore, the value of, the existence of each individual inventory. This kind of concern, although seemingly legitimate, is misplaced. Even when some inventories have exactly the same names, each inventory is unique. For example, the last three inventories mentioned are all called the Learning Style Inventory (LSI). However, each of them assesses quite different styles. Kolb's LSI measures an individual's preference for perceiving and processing information. Kolb identified four adaptive learning modes that can be organized along two continua. One continuum (with one end representing concrete experience and the other abstract conceptualization) represents how one prefers to perceive the environment; and the other continuum (with one end representing reflective observation and the other active experience) represents how one processes the incoming information. Dunn, Dunn, and Price's (1979) LSI, however, assesses an individual's preferred modes of concentration and for learning difficult information. The learning styles considered by these authors are multidimensional in nature—emotional (motivation, persistence, responsibility, structure), environmental (sound, light, temperature, design), physical (perceptual, intake, time, mobility), and sociological (peers, self, pair, team, adult, varied). Finally, Renzulli and Smith's (1978) LSI identifies an individual's preferred ways of dealing with learning tasks, with each corresponding to a method of teaching, such as projects, discussion, and drill and recitation.

Empirically, investigations have shown the significant overlap among these styles inventories. For example, Fourqurean, Meisgeier, and Swank (1990) investigated the relationship between the Jungian psychological types as measured by the Murphy–Meisgeier Type Indicator for Children (MMTIC, Meisgeier & Murphy, 1987), which is constructed based on the Myers–Briggs Type Indicator (MBTI, Myers, 1962), and learning styles as measured by Dunn et al.'s (1979) Learning Style Inventory (Dunn LSI) as well as by Renzulli and Smith's (1978) Learning Style Inventory (Renzulli LSI). Research participants were 492 ninth graders enrolled in a large metropolitan high school. Results indicated that styles from the MMTIC were related to the learning styles from both the Dunn LSI and the Renzulli LSI. For example, regarding the relationships between the MMTIC and the Dunn LSI scales, students identified as introverted intuitive tended to indicate a strong preference for both auditory and visual presentations of information but did not prefer to learn by using a variety of learning methods. Students identified as sensing perceiving types indicated a dislike for learning by touching and manipulating concrete objects. Also, with regard to the relationships between the MMTIC and the Renzulli scales, introverted students indicated a dislike for working on projects, simulations, or group learning, but they indicated a stronger preference for learning through lectures. The judging type of students revealed a preference for learning by repetition and drill, teaching games, and independent study.

In fact, with the exception of one study (i.e., Sadler-Smith, 1997), all studies in the literature demonstrated significant relationships between or among the styles investigated. For example, in a study of 207 Australian final-year nursing students, Cantwell and Moore (1998) identified "theoretically consistent associations" (p. 100) between the scales in Biggs's (1987) Study Process Questionnaire (SPQ) and those in Cantwell and Moore's (1996) Strategic Flexibility Questionnaire. The adaptive control strategy was positively correlated with both the deep and the achieving approaches. Similarly, a surface approach was positively correlated with the inflexible and irresolute control strategies.

Sadler-Smith (1999) conducted a study aimed at exploring the relationships between two style constructs: the intuition-analysis style as assessed by the Cognitive Style Index (Allinson & Hayes, 1996) and the three study approaches (achieving, reproducing, and meaning) as assessed by a short version of Entwistle's (1988) Approaches to Studying Inventory constructed by Gibbs, Habeshaw, and Habeshaw (1988). Furthermore, Sadler-Smith also added a collaborative scale. The research participants for this study were 130 second-year undergraduates taking a range of business-related degree programs. Results revealed significant relationships between the two style constructs. The analysts scored significantly higher on the meaning approach than did the intuitives, whereas the intuitives indicated a stronger preference for a collaborative approach than did the analysts.

As a final example, Atkinson, Murrell, and Winters (1990) investigated the relationships between Holland's (1973) career personality types and Kolb's (1976) learning styles among 169 first-year college students. Results indicate that scales from the two measures are significantly related. From the perspective of Holland's codes, three major relationships were found. First, Holland's investigative students tended to be predominantly assimilators (40.5%), followed by divergers (23.8%) and convergers (21.4%). Second, Holland's artistic students tended to be divergers (57.1%) and assimilators (25%). Third, Holland's social type of students tended to be divergers (41.5%) and accommodators (24.6%).

However, as mentioned earlier, we also have identified a study that involved an inventory (Riding's Cognitive Styles Analysis) that did not result in any significant relationship with any of the other three style inventories administered. In a sample of 245 university undergraduates in business studies, Sadler-Smith (1997) tested the relationships among the styles measured four instruments: Riding's (1991) Cognitive Styles Analysis, the Learning Preferences Inventory (LPI, Riechmann & Grasha, 1974), the Learning Styles Questionnaire (LSQ, Honey & Mumford, 1986, 1992), and the Revised Approaches to Studying Inventory (RASI, Entwistle & Tait, 1994). After examining the correlation coefficients among the scales of the different instruments, the authors concluded that the data suggested some overlap between the dimensions measured by the LSQ and the RASI. However, no statistically significant relationships were identified between cognitive styles (as measured by the CSA) and any of the other "style" constructs investigated.

Yet, the lack of relationship of the CSA to the other styles assessed in the aforementioned study does not mean that the CSA is not associated with styles measured by other style inventories. For instance, in Ford's (1995) study, 38 university students were tested for field dependence/independence using Riding's (1991) computer-administered Cognitive Styles Analysis (CSA). Students were also taught the computerized version of Pask and Scott's (1972) original testing materials designed to suit holist and serialist learning strategies. A computerized test was used for assessing learning performance. It was found that students' holist and serialist competencies could be predicted by the CSA scores.

Why are the results obtained for the CSA inconsistent? The CSA assesses the two style dimensions (i.e., wholistic–analytic and verbal–imagery), whereas all the other three inventories used in Sadler-Smith's (1997) study are from the family of learning strategies, as would have been classified by Riding and Cheema (1991). Nevertheless, the study of the relationships of the styles in CSA with other style construct is rather limited. Further investigation should be conducted to determine the relationships between the CSA and other style inventories.

Given that almost all existing styles resulted in significant overlaps among intellectual styles, we would argue that the various intellectual styles as measured by different inventories are intricately entwined. They invariably overlap with one another to varying degrees. Yet, the degree of overlap is such that each style construct has unique value in explaining individual differences in performance and behaviors in academic settings.

STYLES AND PERSONALITY TRAITS

To address the controversial issue over whether intellectual styles are value-laden or value-free, we thoroughly examined the studies that focus on the relationships between students' intellectual styles and their personality traits. This research indicated that some styles (e.g., field-independent style and reflective style) are consistently associated with personality traits that are normally perceived to be positive (e.g., higher levels of assertiveness, self-esteem, and moral maturity). Their polar opposite styles (e.g., field-dependent style and impulsive style) are consistently associated with the kinds of personality traits that are typically perceived to be negative (e.g., lower levels of assertiveness, self-esteem, and moral maturity). Thus, these styles are more value-laden. Still, the adaptive value of other styles (e.g., analytic and wholist) is more situation-specific, which makes these styles be more value-differentiated. Findings from this review indicate that while some intellectual styles are essentially value-laden, other styles are more value-differentiated. However, intellectual styles are not value-free.

Research evidence for significant relationships between intellectual styles and personality traits is abundant. In reading this literature, we found that several intellectual style constructs are frequently involved in this research: field dependence/independence, reflectivity–impulsivity, learning approach, and brain dominance (also called "mode of thinking"; see Zhang, 2002b). Moreover, we began to see studies that are based on an integrative style model, such as Riding and Cheema's (1991) model comprising two style dimensions—verbal–imagery and wholistic–analytic. Additionally, we discovered that several personality traits have maintained the interest of scholars in the context of their examining the nature of intellectual styles. These are the Big Five personality traits (Costa & McCrae, 1985—neuroticism, extraversion, openness to experience, agreeableness, and conscientiousness), the Big Three personality traits (Eysenck & Eysenck, 1964—Extraversion, Neuroticism, and Psychoticism), personality traits that relate to the self (e.g., self-esteem, self-confidence, self-control, and sense of identity), personality traits as they relate to dealing with the world (e.g., assertiveness and shyness), as well as a whole range of other personality traits. These traits include anxiety, response to threat of frustration and tolerance of ambiguity, locus of control, moral maturity, and sense of responsibility.

Findings from the studies that we identified in the literature suggest that field dependence/independence, reflectivity–impulsivity, learning approaches, and brain dominance are largely value-laden, whereas the two stylistic dimensions as assessed by the Cognitive Styles Analysis are value-differentiated in the context of the relationships between styles and personality traits.

The field-dependence/independence construct has been found to be significantly related to a number of personality traits, including assertiveness (e.g., Deng, Li, & Zhang, 2000), locus of control (e.g., Leventhal & Sisco, 1996), moral maturity (e.g., Schleifer & Douglas, 1973), responses to the threat of frustration (e.g., Campbell & Douglas, 1972), self-esteem (e.g., Bosacki, Innerd, & Towson, 1997), and sense of identity (e.g., Bhatnager & Rastogi, 1986). Except in the case of the variable of self-esteem, in which an interaction effect of gender was found with the field-dependence/independence style dimension, for all the other personal traits, the relationships of field dependence/independence to other personality traits are straightforward. That is, field independence was associated with the kinds of personality traits that are conventionally perceived to be positive (e.g., higher level of assertiveness, internal locus of control, higher level of moral maturity, optimistic in the face of threat of frustration, and a better developed sense of identity). On the contrary, field dependence was associated with the kinds of personality traits that are typically perceived to be negative (e.g., lower levels of assertiveness, external locus of control, lower levels of moral maturity, pessimism, and a poorly developed sense of identity). Therefore, the results of this group of studies indicate that field independence is likely to be more positively valued than field dependence.

The relationship between field dependence/independence and self-esteem is not as straightforward. There is a gender effect. In a study of 63 sixth-grade students in a southwestern Ontario city, Bosacki, Innerd, and Towson (1997) found that field independence and self-esteem were correlated negatively for girls and positively for boys.

Reflectivity–impulsivity has been tested with children's responses to the threat of frustration and with their moral maturity. Campbell and Douglas (1972) found that children who scored higher on impulsivity displayed higher levels of pessimism in the face of threatened frustration than did children who scored higher on reflectivity. By the same token, Schleifer and Douglas (1973) found that children who scored higher on reflectivity tended to have a higher level of moral maturity, whereas children who scored higher on impulsivity tended to show a lower level of moral maturity. Collectively, these two studies suggest that the reflective style is typically superior to the impulsive style in terms of its adaptive value.

Learning approaches have been found to be significantly related to students' self-confidence, their self-esteem, and to the Big Five personality traits. Research evidence has indicated that the deep approach to learning as well as the meaning- and application-directed learning approaches are correlated with higher levels of self-confidence (e.g., Watkins, Biggs, & Regmi, 1991), higher levels of self-esteem (e.g., Watkins & Dahlin, 1997), and openness to experience and conscientiousness (e.g., Busato et al., 1999)—the kinds of personality traits that are traditionally perceived as being positive human traits. On the contrary, the surface approach to learning and a reproductively-directed learning approach have been proved to be significantly correlated with lower levels of self-confidence, lower levels of self-esteem, and neuroticism, all of which are widely regarded as being relatively less adaptive human traits. In other words, results from these studies consistently suggest that the learning approach construct is value-laden. The deep and meaning and application-directed approaches are generally adaptive; the surface and the reproduction-directed approaches are generally not as adaptive.

Mode of thinking (i.e., brain dominance) also has been studied in relation to personality traits. Although there is a tendency for the holistic mode of thinking (i.e., right-brain dominance) to show superiority over the analytic mode of thinking (i.e., left-brain dominance), mode of thinking can be value-differentiated. From a conventional perspective, the holistic mode of thinking is generally adaptive, in part because it is highly related to creative behaviors (e.g., Harnad, 1972; Kim & Michael, 1995; Krueger, 1976; Okabayashi & Torrance, 1984; Tan-Willman, 1981; Torrance & Reynolds, 1978). Moreover, there is empirical evidence suggesting that the holistic mode of thinking is associated with higher levels of tolerance of ambiguity and the analytic mode of thinking with lower levels of tolerance of ambiguity (e.g., Saleh, 1998).

However, several studies of the relationships between mode of thinking and personality traits have resulted in findings that do not support the superiority of the holistic mode of thinking over the analytic mode. For example, in examining the relationships between information-processing styles and personality traits, Gadzella (1999) administered the Human Information Processing Survey (Torrance, Taggart, & Taggart, 1984) and the 16 Personality Factor Questionnaire (Cattell, Cattell, & Cattell, 1978) to 55 students enrolled in undergraduate psychology classes in a Midwestern state university in the United States. The investigator found that students with an analytic mode of thinking tended to display higher levels of self-control than did students with a holistic mode of thinking, and that students comfortable with both the analytic and the holistic modes of thinking tended to score higher on the anxiety scale than did students with an integrative mode of thinking. When studying 70 undergraduate students in The Netherlands, Jong, Merckelbach, and Nijman (1995) also found that the holistic mode of thinking was related to higher levels of anxiety. Thus, in general, these studies seem to indicate that the holistic mode of thinking is related to lower levels of self-control, but to higher levels of anxiety. On average, both lower levels of self-control and higher levels of anxiety are considered less adaptive personality traits. Furthermore, the holistic mode of thinking carries negative value because it is related to undesirable personality traits such as lack of self-control and high levels of anxiety. We cannot completely agree, especially in the case of people's anxiety levels: The adaptive value of a person's anxiety level depends on the situation. A proximal level of anxiety can be very conducive to one's creative behaviors. Therefore, the construct of mode of thinking is largely value-laden, with the holistic mode of thinking generally viewed as more desirable than the analytic mode of thinking. Meanwhile, these modes of thinking can be value-differentiated at times.

Riding and Cheema's (1991) two stylistic dimensions (verbal–imagery and analytic–wholistic) have been found to be significantly related to a range of personality traits, including neuroticism, impulsiveness, psychoticism, shyness, assertiveness, and sense of responsibility. Although there is certain indication that the wholist and the verbal styles carry negative value, the styles in Riding and Cheema's framework are primarily value-differentiated.

The wholist style has been found to be highly associated with psychoticism (Riding & Wigley, 1997), whereas the verbal style has been linked to lower levels of sense of responsibility (Riding, Burton, Rees, & Sharratt, 1995). Students with the wholist and verbal combined styles tended to be more susceptible to neuroticism. These findings suggest that the wholist and verbal styles tend to carry undesirable value because they are significantly related to personality traits generally viewed as undesirable.

However, some research findings do not yield a clear indication of the nature of the two style dimensions regarding their value. For example, like the analytic style, the wholist style also was found to be associated with low scores on impulsiveness. Furthermore, like students with the wholist–verbal combined styles, students with the analytic–imagery combined styles also tend to be high on the neuroticism scale (Riding & Wigley, 1997).

In a similar vein, other findings also reveal that the two style dimensions are essentially value-differentiated. Riding and Wright (1995) found that students who were high on the analytic style tended to be perceived as more shy by their housemates, whereas students who were high on the wholist style tended to be perceived as less shy by their housemates. Given that the desirability of shyness could vary greatly from situation to situation, and from culture to culture, the styles (in this case, analytic and wholist) that are associated with shyness can be perceived as being desirable at times and undesirable at others. That is, these styles are value-differentiated.

Across all studies considered in this section, it is easily discernible that several intellectual styles have been consistently related to personality traits that are deemed desirable in most societies. For example, the deep approach to learning as well as the meaning-directed and application-directed learning styles are related to such personality traits as openness to experience, higher levels of self-esteem, and higher levels of self-confidence, whereas the opposite has been found for the surface approach to learning and reproducing-directed learning. A second example relates to the field-dependence/independence construct. Studies in this section suggest that, compared with field-dependent students, field-independent students exhibit significantly higher levels of assertiveness, higher levels of moral maturity, lower levels of pessimism, and more positive and psychologically better developed senses of identity. Similarly, compared with students with an impulsive style, students with a reflective style tend to display higher levels of moral maturity and lower levels of pessimism. Moreover, it has been demonstrated that the modes of thinking and the wholistic–analytic and verbal–imagery style dimensions are mainly value-differentiated.

Therefore, together, these findings indicate that some intellectual styles are better than others. That is, intellectual styles are mainly value-laden, or at least value-differentiated. However, styles are not value-free.

STYLES AND ACADEMIC PERFORMANCE

In examining the nature of intellectual styles, and in particular the value issue of styles, we have looked closely into the manner in which intellectual styles relate to students' academic performance. This research indicates that styles are not value-free because some styles are consistently associated with better academic performance, whereas their opposite styles are consistently associated with poor academic performance (e.g., field-independent style over field-dependent style; reflective style over impulsive style; deep approach to learning over surface approach to learning; divergent thinking over convergent thinking, and so forth).

For example, the FDI construct was investigated in relation to various kinds of academic achievement (e.g., problem solving, laboratory tasks, language learning, tasks involving disembedding skill, organizing information, etc.) and to job performance (see chap. 5 for job performance). In general, field-independent people are higher in their academic achievement than are field-dependent people (e.g., Bagley & Mallick, 1998; Mansfield, 1998; see also Jonassen & Grabowski, 1993 for a comprehensive review). Since the late 1970s and early 1980s, the FDI construct has become more and more widely examined in the context of learners' achievement under computer-assisted instructional conditions. In general, field-independent learners achieve more in computer-based learning environments. For example, compared with field-dependent learners, field-independent learners do better on problem-solving performance (e.g., Williams, 2001) and programming performance (e.g., Clements, 1986; Johnson & Kane, 1992; Wilson, Mundy-Castle, & Sibanda, 1990). Field-independent and field-dependent learners use different learning strategies in a computer-assisted learning environment (e.g., Ford & Chen, 2000; Liu & Reed, 1994). For example, field-dependent learners made less use of Back/Forward buttons, whereas field-independent learners made greater use of Back/Forward buttons. Field-dependent learners spent less time exploring the "detailed techniques" section of the tutorial, whereas field-independent learners made greater use of the "detailed techniques" section. (See chap. 8 for findings about relations of other styles to achievement.)

Further examination of the literature shows that some of the usually value-laden intellectual styles can become value-differentiated in the context of students' academic performance. This change in the nature of styles (from value-laden to value-differentiated) can be attributed to a number of learning-environment-relevant factors, including the nature of an academic discipline, performance tasks, and instructional materials. We also have come to the realization that some other styles (e.g., Kolb's learning styles, Allinson and Hayes's cognitive styles, and French et al.'s cognitive styles) are essentially value-differentiated, as the relationships between these styles and achievement vary as a function of the aforementioned learning environment factors.

The field-dependence/independence construct and the learning approach construct, which both are essentially value-laden, have been discovered in some studies to be value-differentiated. For example, in examining the relationships between the field-dependent/independent styles and students' achievement in introductory psychology, Feij (1976) found contrasting results between art-trained and math-trained undergraduate students in The Netherlands. For art-trained students, there was a significantly positive relationship between field independence and achievement in introductory psychology. By contrast, for the math-trained students, there was a negative relationship between the two variables. Similarly, Varma and Thakur (1992) assessed whether field-independent and field-dependent school children differ in their academic performance in different subject matters. Results showed that field-independent students achieved at higher levels in mathematics and physical sciences and that field-dependent students had higher achievement in social sciences and literature. Thus, both studies indicated that field-independent and field-dependent styles have adaptive value, with one or the other style more functional, depending on the academic disciplines.

The adaptive value (or value-differentiation) of the field-dependent and field-independent styles also can manifest itself when students are instructed with different teaching materials. For instance, Ford (1995) conducted a study that examined students' achievement under matched and mismatched learning environments among 38 university students in the United Kingdom. Students were assessed for field dependence/independence as determined by their response to the wholist/analytic scale on Riding's (1991) Cognitive Styles Analysis. Computerized teaching materials were designed to suit holist and serialist learners as defined by Pask and Scott (1972). Based on the nature of the field-dependence/independence construct and that of the holist/serialist construct, it was hypothesized that the holist teaching materials would be more suitable for field-dependent students and that the serialist teaching materials would better suited to field-independent students. As expected, in the holist learning environment, field-dependent students achieved significantly better test scores, demonstrated greater learning efficiency, and spent more time on learning than did students with a field-independent style. Conversely, in the serialist learning environment, field-independent students performed significantly better than did field-dependent students.

The learning approaches assessed by Biggs's Study Process Questionnaire have also been found on occasion to be value-differentiated. For example, Zhang (2000a) investigated the relationships between learning approaches and academic performance among 652 university students in Hong Kong. The investigator found that the unique contribution of students' learning approaches to their achievement beyond abilities was subject-specific. In general, the surface learning approach contributed positively to students' achievement in chemistry and geography. However, the deep and achieving learning approaches contributed positively to students' achievement in the remaining subjects examined, including mathematics, Chinese language and culture, Chinese history, history, and English.

The adaptive value of learning approaches can also be observed when students are provided with different learning materials. For example, Kirby and Pedwell (1991) investigated undergraduate students' performance on summarizing text passages relating to the content of an introductory psychology course in two different summarization conditions: text present and text absent. Students were randomly assigned to the two summarization conditions and their learning approaches were assessed by Biggs' (1987) Study Process Questionnaire. All students read two texts and were reminded that they would be asked questions about the texts. Students were also aware whether or not they would have access to the texts when writing the summaries. Students' scores on summary and recall were the dependent variables. The investigators found that students with different learning approaches performed significantly differently under the two conditions. Under the text present condition, surface learners wrote more extensive summaries. Under the text absent condition, the deep learners produced more extensive summaries.

We also have identified empirical evidence for the styles that normally appear to be value-differentiated in the context of students' academic achievement. For example, results from Davies, Rutledge, and Davies' (1997) study revealed that the styles defined in Kolb's Learning Style Inventory have adaptive value in the context of student achievement in different performance tasks. Two hundred and one first-year medical students responded to Kolb's Learning Style Inventory and were assessed on their academic performance in physiology and on a series of interview skills (i.e., questioning techniques, listening, ability to develop a rapport, and nonverbal skills). Results indicated that accommodators did better in all the interviewing categories, whereas convergers scored the lowest in all interviewing skills except for listening. For academic achievement in physiology, however, the reverse performance level was found for the accommodators and the convergers. Convergers achieved the higher scores in physiology, whereas accommodators' achievement in physiology was lower.

Similarly, Armstrong (2000) investigated whether students would do better on tasks that were deemed to be consonant with their styles. Four hundred and twelve final-year undergraduate students majoring in management and business administration were administered Allinson and Hayes' (1996) Cognitive Style Index. Students were also assessed on several types of tasks. Although Armstrong did not find support for the hypothesis that wholist students would perform better on tasks relevant to business policy and strategy formulation, Armstrong did find that students with an analytic cognitive style performed significantly better than did those whose cognitive style was predominantly wholistic, as hypothesized.

Finally, the adaptive value of styles in the context of students' academic achievement also can be highlighted by students' age differences. For example, French, Ekstron, and Price (1963) investigated the relationships between the analytic/holistic styles and achievement in computer programming. Whereas a significant relationship between the holistic style and computer programming achievement scores was found among young children (Bradley, 1985), a significant relationship between the analytic style and computer programming achievement scores was discovered among college students (Cheney, 1980).

To summarize, we have attempted in this section to discuss some value issue of intellectual styles in the context of students' academic achievement. We have demonstrated that some styles are primarily value-laden; at times, they become value-differentiated. Other styles are largely value-differentiated, displaying adaptive value in different situations. However, intellectual styles are not value-free.

STYLES AND SOCIALIZATION

There are many ways of joining the debate over the issue of malleability of styles. In this section, we argue for the modifiability of intellectual styles by taking two approaches. First, we demonstrate that styles vary as a function of socialization factors. Second, we show that styles can be deliberately trained and modified.

Styles and Socialization Factors

Witkin and Goodenough (1981) asserted that how children are socialized is a critical factor to their performance on any test of intellectual styles (see also Messick, 1994). This claim finds empirical support in the significant relationships of intellectual styles to many socialization factors, three of which are culture, gender, and age.

Styles and Culture. Research findings indicated that culture is an important socialization factor in student differences in intellectual styles. These studies have involved many different intellectual styles such as reflective/impulsive styles (e.g., Salkind, Kojima, & Zelniker, 1978), Dunn et al.'s (1979) learning styles (e.g., Dunn, Gemake, Jalali, Zenhausern, Quinn, & Spriridakis, 1990; Dunn & Griggs, 1990), modes of thinking, Myers–Briggs's personality styles, and field-dependent/independent styles. For example, Saleh (1998) studied the relationship between styles and culture among a group of university students in the United States. The author found that cultural individualism was related to the holistic mode of thinking and that cultural collectivism was associated with the analytic mode of thinking. In their study of the learning styles of African American school boys, Melear and Alcock (1999) discovered that the learning styles of African American boys differed from those of White American male students. Compared with White American males, African American males were more likely to fall in the extraverted-sensing-thinking-perceiving (ESTP) and the extraverted-intuitive-thinking-perceiving (ENTP) types of the Myers–Briggs Types Indicator. Moreover, among the African American group, there were fewer extraverted-sensing-thinking-judging (ESTJ) and extraverted-intuitive-feeling-judging (ENFJ) types.

Interestingly enough, the socialization of intellectual styles has also been demonstrated by the diminishing effect of culture. For instance, Volet, Renshaw, and Tietzel (1994) conducted a short-term longitudinal investigation of cross-cultural differences in learning approaches using Biggs's model of learning approaches. The authors examined the change in students' approaches to learning between the beginning and the end of a semester. The research participants were a group of local Australian students and a group of Southeast Asian students enrolled in a Western Australian university. Results indicated that by the end of the semester, the differences in learning approaches between the two cultural groups found at the beginning of the semester had disappeared. It was concluded that the similarity in learning approaches between the two groups was attributable to the adaptation of the Southeast Asian students to the demands of the academic course and the learning environments.

Several review articles relevant to the relationships between intellectual styles and culture also have supported the modifiability of styles. In reviewing research about the role of culture and ethnic orientation in the intellectual styles among Mexican-Americans, Saracho (1983) concluded that different socialization patterns resulted in Mexican-American students tending to be more field-dependent than their Anglo-American peers. Based on Saracho's review, other studies have suggested that Mexican-American students' cognitive style could partially result from their contact with the Mexican culture.

Similarly, in reviewing studies of field dependence/independence in various cultural contexts, Bagley and Mallick (1998) noted the unique cognitive styles of school children from many different cultures, including Jamaica, Canada, Japan, India, the United Kingdom, the United States, and China. The authors concluded that there is enough empirical evidence to conclude that field dependence/independence is highly contingent upon cultural setting and socialization experiences.

Thus, existing empirical evidence clearly indicates that students from different cultures tend to have different intellectual styles as a result of different cultural influences. However, by no means do cross-cultural differences in intellectual styles restrict the modifiability of styles. Students' intellectual styles change as a result of their socialization. Students adapt their intellectual styles to the demands of the nature of tasks and those of new learning contexts, including cultural environments.

Styles and Gender. Findings about the relationships between styles and gender have been characterized by their "irregularities" (Vernon, 1972, p. 370). Whereas some studies (e.g., Ginter, Brown, Scalise, & Ripley, 1989; Hilliard, 1995; Wilson, Smart, & Watson, 1996) did not identify any significant gender difference in intellectual styles, other studies revealed straightforward gender differences in styles (e.g., Thompson, Finkler, & Walker, 1979; Witkin, 1954; Witkin, Dyk, Faterson, Goodenough, & Karp, 1962; Zelazek, 1986). Additionally, still other studies indicated the effects of an interaction between age and gender upon intellectual styles (e.g., Bosacki, Innerd, & Towson, 1997; Ogunyemi, 1973; Sadler-Smith & Tsang, 1998). Yet others produced inconsistent or even contradictory results (e.g., Coles, 1985; Miller, Finley, & McKinley, 1990; Richardson, 1990; Severiens & Ten Dam, 1994; Watkins & Hattie, 1981). Nevertheless, gender clearly plays an important role in students' intellectual styles.

Several studies examining different intellectual styles have detected clear gender differences. For example, in their original study of field dependent/independent styles, Witkin and colleagues (Witkin, 1954; Witkin et al., 1962) concluded that males are generally more field independent than are females. On Riechmann and Grasha's (1974) Learning Preferences Inventory scales, males exhibited more avoidance and competitiveness, but less collaboration and participation than did their female counterparts (e.g., Thompson et al., 1979; Zelazek, 1986). In investigating Kolb's (1976) learning styles among students, Titus (1990) found that females tended to be more concrete than their male counterparts. After examining gender difference in Gregorc's (1979) learning styles, Davenport (1986) reported that males showed a stronger preference for the abstract sequential learning style and females a stronger preference for the abstract random style.

The interactive effects of age and gender upon intellectual styles also have been well documented. Sadler-Smith and Tsang (1998) compared learning approaches between undergraduates in Hong Kong and those in the United Kingdom. Whereas straightforward gender differences were observed in learning approaches in the U.K. sample, an interaction between age and gender effect on learning approaches was identified in the Hong Kong sample. In the U.K. group, male students reported a deeper learning approach than did female students, and female students scored significantly higher on the surface learning approach scales than did their male counterparts. In the Hong Kong group, it was established that older male students scored higher on the deep learning approach scales than did younger male students. However, for the female students, this pattern was reversed. That is, older female students scored significantly lower on the deep learning approach scales than did younger female students.

When Bosacki, Innerd, and Towson (1997) studied the relationship between field dependence/independence and self-esteem in a group of 63 preadolescents (aged 11 and 12); they found that field independence and self-esteem was positively correlated for boys, but negatively for girls. Similarly, in studying the relationship between cognitive styles as defined by Kagan and Moss (1963) and science achievement among a group of 170 school children in Nigeria, Ogunyemi (1973) discovered that whereas results did not indicate any relationship for girls, they revealed a significant relationship between styles and achievement in science for boys. High science-achieving boys were more inferential–categorical and less analytic–descriptive in their styles than were low science-achieving boys.

Contradictory findings have been observed in studies of different samples responding to the same inventory. For example, Severiens and Ten Dam (1994) conducted a quantitative meta-analysis of 19 studies involving the test of gender differences in Kolb's learning styles as assessed by the Learning Style Inventory and in Entwistle's learning approaches as measured by the Approaches to Studying Inventory. On Kolb's inventory, a relatively small but consistent gender difference was identified across studies. However, on Entwistle's inventory, although gender differences in learning styles also are small across studies, between-studies gender differences vary dramatically and are sometimes even contradictory. The authors note, for example, that whereas male students scored higher on the deep approach to learning scale in studies by Miller, Finley, and McKinley (1990) and by Richardson (1990), females scored higher on the deep approach to learning scale in the studies by Watkins and Hattie (1981) and by Coles (1985).

The question arises of how these irregular findings can be explained. Severiens and Ten Dam (1997) attributed these mixed and even contradictory findings of the relationships between styles and gender to the various contexts (e.g., different countries and different subject matters) in which the empirical studies were conducted. Additionally, we would argue that the mixed results could be due to the varying age levels of the students who responded to the items in the inventory. For some intellectual styles, gender difference may not be apparent at a young age (say, at early childhood). Yet, for the same styles, gender difference may become more apparent at an older age (say, by adolescence). Or, the reverse pattern could be true. Indeed, when Vernon (1972, p. 370) summarized the relationships between field dependence/independence and gender, he observed that females tend to score lower than males on visual/spatial tasks. However, this gender difference disappears in old age.

Gender differences in styles, like differences in most other human performance and behaviors, have been attributed to two major sources: genetic endowments and environmental factors. For example, when discussing gender differences in field dependence/independence, Sherman (1967) pointed out that girls talk earlier and therefore tend to find satisfaction in verbal forms, whereas boys make better use of their superior musculature. Other scholars have also noted evidence of hereditary determination of gender differences in field dependence/independence (e.g., Bieri & Messerley, 1957; Hartlage, 1970; Stafford, 1961; Stuart & Breslow, 1965). However, as Vernon (1972) noted, most scholars tend to attribute gender differences in styles to socialization factors. For example, boys are expected to be more active and independent, whereas girls are expected to be more passive and conforming (e.g., Vaught, 1965; see also Reis, 1987; Tavris,

1992). These differing expectations and socializations cultivate different levels of psychological differentiation between males and females. Vernon (1972) argued that both genetic and socialization factors are involved in the development of field dependence/independence.

To take Vernon's argument a step further, we would contend that the development of all intellectual styles can be ascribed to both genetic endowment and environmental influence work together. This argument is, of course, nothing new. However, it is clear that gender does matter in students' intellectual styles.

Styles and Age. Age is another factor in determining students' intellectual styles. Evidence for the significant relationships between intellectual styles and age is rich. Several authors have noted a general change in styles with maturation. For example, putting Gurley's (1984) and Witkin, Oltman, Raskin, and Karp's (1971) work together, Jonassen and Grabowski (1993) portrayed the following picture of the growth curve of field dependence/independence: In general, children are more field dependent and their field independence increases as they grow into adulthood. Adults, especially adult learners, are the most field independent. From that point in time on, people's field independence decreases throughout the rest of their lives, with older people the most field dependent. Titus (1990) remarked that from adolescence to adulthood, the level of abstraction (based on Kolb's learning style scales) increases. Jonassen and Grabowski (1993) also observed that, with maturation, people's conceptual differentiation changes from leveling to sharpening (Holzman & Klein, 1954).

In the context of student learning, two groups of studies of the relationships between styles and age clearly stand out. The first has Biggs' (1978) learning approach construct as its theoretical foundation. For example, Hilliard (1995) administered the Study Process Questionnaire to 339 third- and fourth-year medical students at the University of Toronto. Although no significant age difference was found in the deep learning approach, a significant age difference was identified in the surface and achieving learning scales: Older students scored significantly lower on both the surface and the achieving learning approaches than did younger students.

As a matter of fact, the findings regarding the relationships between learning approaches and age have been found to be fairly consistent across a number of studies in the existing literature. In general, compared with younger students, older students tend to take a deeper approach to learning. Meanwhile, older students tend to be less surface- and achievement-oriented toward learning. For example, in a study conducted among 99 students (majoring in psychology, sociology, and social anthropology) in a first-year course in research methods, Richardson (1995) found that older students reported a deeper approach to learning than did younger students and that younger students reported a more reproducing-oriented approach (including surface approach, syllabus-bound, fear of failure, and improvidence scales) to learning than did their older counterparts. In a study of 153 first-, third-, and fifth-year students in the Faculty of Medicine at the University of Newcastle, Clarke (1986) found a decline in the achieving approach on Entwistle and Ramsden's (1983) Approaches to Studying Inventory (ASI) among older students. Similarly, Biggs (1988) discovered that among ordinary degree students (as opposed to mature-age students), the deep and achieving scores decreased with institutional exposure, a finding also obtained by Watkins and Hattie (1985). Moreover, Biggs found that mature-age students scored significantly higher on the deep learning approach scales than did university students of traditional age. Similarly, Sadler-Smith (1996) established that mature-age business studies students scored significantly higher on the deep approach scales than did the traditional-age group of students. Complementarily, traditional-age business students scored significantly higher on the surface approach scales than did the mature-age students.

The second group of studies of the relationships between styles and age focused on students' perceptual styles. For example, Kim (1996) compared the levels of field dependence/independence between young students (college, high school, and junior high school) and adults. It was discovered that the adult research participants were significantly more field dependent than were the younger student participants. Ginter et al. (1989) examined the relationships of age to a variety of perceptual learning styles among students studying in two universities in the southern United States. Students were categorized into one of the five style groups: print, visual, interactive, split (representing students who were divided between two style categories), and no preference. It was found that older students preferred a print style or a split style, whereas younger students indicated a stronger preference for a visual style.

In summary, empirical studies reviewed in this subsection have demonstrated that age is another important socialization variable in determining students' intellectual styles. In the previous two subsections, it has been demonstrated that culture and gender are two of the important socialization factors in students' intellectual styles. There are many other socialization factors (e.g., learning environmental factors, parental styles, extracurricular experience, interaction with teachers, teaching styles, teacher expectations, and so on) that have been empirically demonstrated to be influential on students' intellectual styles. We address the importance of some of these factors (e.g., extracurricular experience, interaction with teachers, teaching styles, and teacher expectations) in relation to students' intellectual styles in other contexts (see chaps. 5 and 8). In the following subsection, we provide empirical evidence supporting the view that intellectual styles can be trained, and thus are malleable.

Styles Training and Modification

When one reads the literature, one can easily recognize the dynamic nature of intellectual styles. Two types of evidence in the context of research on students' intellectual styles are (1) style modification as a result of adaptation to the stylistic demands of learning environments, and (2) style modification as a result of deliberate training.

Empirical studies suggest that students adapt their learning styles to the requirements of their learning environments. For example, Jones (2001), with the intention of examining the sensitivity of students' learning styles to subject areas, administered Kolb's Learning Style Inventory (LSI) twice to the same group of 105 students studying at a small community college in the Midwestern United States. Whereas the students were not given instruction outside of the general instruction for the LSI when completing the first administration, they were instructed to keep four target disciplines (English, math, science, and social studies) in mind while completing the inventory at the second administration. Results indicated that 81% of the students demonstrated a shift in at least two of the four different learning style quadrants on the LSI. The investigators concluded that, regardless of gender differences, students were able to adapt their learning styles to the stylistic demands of the target academic discipline. Similarly, in the context of discussing the relationships between styles and culture, we introduced the study carried out by Volet et al. (1994), in which the investigators found that over the course of a semester, Southeast Asian students adapted to using the learning styles demanded by the nature of their learning tasks and their new learning environments.

Styles modification can also result from direct training. For example, Nunn (1995) conducted a year-long learning styles intervention course with 103 middle school students. The aim of the study was to determine if systematic application of learning styles instruction enhances students' school success as measured by students' academic achievement and their locus of control. The intervention began with assessing, profiling, and interpreting students' learning styles as determined by Canfield's (1988) Learning Styles Inventory. Major intervention involved experienced schoolteachers helping students to apply their learning styles to facilitating positive adjustment to school life. Over the course of one year, students met with the teachers for one class session every other day during the 6-day school cycle. Results indicated that within the at-risk student group, significant improvement in students' GPA and their locus of control could be attributed to the effects of the intervention course. Research results from Reynolds' (1991) study confirmed Nunn's finding. Reynolds' research involved conducting a workshop for a group of college students that introduced knowledge in such areas as cognitive styles, perceptual preferences, physical or social environmental needs, and motivation. It was concluded that by gaining insight into their own learning characteristics, the research participants became more successful learners (see also Beck, 1992; Matson, 1980).

In this subsection, we have provided empirical evidence supporting the malleability of styles. Students' intellectual styles vary as a function of different socialization experiences due to culture, gender, and age. Students' intellectual styles are adaptive to different learning environments, and they change as a result of direct training.

STYLES AND BEHAVIORS

Because intellectual styles affect the way students think about and represent situations in the real world, it is only natural that styles tend to affect their behaviors. In this section, we explore the nature of intellectual styles by examining the effects of learning styles on students' behaviors, including learning, career/educational choice, and conduct/social behaviors. Findings on the relationships of styles to learning behavior and career/educational choice behavior lead us to conclude that styles are at least partially socialized. Moreover, findings on the relationships between styles and students' conduct/social behavior enable us to assert, again, that styles are value-laden and that styles are likely to be socialized.

Styles and Learning Behavior/Preferences

Many studies (e.g., Dulin, 1993; Fourqurean, Meisgeier, & Swank, 1990; Reed, Oughton, Ayersman, Ervin Jr., & Giessler, 2000; Sadler-Smith, 1999, 2001) have revealed that students with different intellectual styles exhibit different learning behaviors (or preferences). For example, McCaulley and Natter (1974) investigated the relationships between students' scores on the Myers–Briggs Type Indicator and learning activities. They found that although introversion was not related to any of the learning preference scales, extraversion was significantly related to a preference for group projects, oral presentations, and social contacts. Intuitive students indicated a preference for working on their own initiative and for being engaged in extra reading, but had trouble managing their time. Sensing students revealed a strong like for films, audiovisual aids, and for following a predetermined schedule; they also tended to pursue their set goals in an orderly fashion. Perceiving types showed difficulty with time management and tended to procrastinate when trying to complete assignments. Judging type of students indicated a preference for planning their work and they also indicated a stronger preference for schoolwork than did any other types of students. The thinking type students had a predilection for a serious, business-like approach and they enjoyed lectures. The feeling type students demonstrated a preference for group projects as well as for nontechnical subject matters.

Ford and Chen (2000) conducted an empirical study focusing on the relationships between the field-dependence/independence construct and strategic differences in hypermedia navigation among 65 postgraduate students in the United Kingdom. They found that field-independent students made significantly greater use of the index in the hypermedia environment than did field-dependent students. This result is in accord with that obtained by Liu and Reed (1994) in their study of international university students pursuing their degrees in the United States.

Clearly, the above empirical findings indicate that there is a significant relationship between intellectual styles and learning behaviors. It is widely recognized that results obtained from correlational methods do not imply causal relationships. Thus, it is possible that students with particular intellectual styles tend to display certain learning behaviors. However, it is also possible that, after being required to perform their learning tasks in certain ways in a particular environment for a relatively long period of time (e.g., students are often required to do group projects, or they are predominantly lectured to, and so forth), students have acquired the intellectual styles that are necessary for being successful in that learning environment. That is, students have been socialized into dealing with their learning tasks in certain ways.

Styles and Educational/Career Choice

A large number of studies (e.g., Biggs, 1988; Hilliard, 1995; Morgan, 1997; Wieseman, Portis, & Simpson, 1992; Witkin, Moore, Goodenough, & Cox, 1977) have yielded significant findings about the relationships between students' intellectual styles and their educational and career choices. For example, in Canada, Hilliard (1995) found significant relationships between learning approaches as measured by Biggs' Study Process Questionnaire and career choice among undergraduate medical students. In particular, students who had committed themselves to a career in a medical specialty tended to have higher scores in the deep approach to learning than did those who had chosen family medicine. Students who had chosen their career in a surgical specialty scored significantly higher on the achieving learning approach than did students who had chosen family medicine (see also Plovnick, 1974).

In Wieseman, Portis, and Simpson's (1992) study, 537 students in an introductory education program were required to complete the Group Embedded Figures Test. The aim of the study was to test the hypothesis that students seeking a career in education would be generally more field dependent in their cognitive style. The hypothesis was supported. Similarly, as mentioned earlier, Morgan (1997) observed that empirical research had largely shown that field-independent students from higher education institutions are likely to select areas of study in the science arena and that field-dependent students tend toward choosing fields of human services such as teaching and social work.

Styles and Conduct/Social Behaviors

Thus far, empirical research on the relationships of intellectual styles to both conduct and social behaviors is limited. Findings from this research indicate that styles are, by and large, value-laden, and thus, could affect conduct and behavior.

Empirical studies examining the relationships of styles to conduct behaviors have been carried out only by Riding and his colleagues using Riding's Cognitive Styles Analysis (CSA). Their research revealed that students with a wholist style, especially those with a wholist style in combination with a verbal style, tended to display problem behaviors.

A first study was conducted by Riding and Wigley (1997) among a group of 340 postsecondary students. Apart from responding to the CSA, the students completed several personality questionnaires measuring various personality dimensions, including extraversion, neuroticism, and psychoticism. Results indicated that, among male students, students with a wholist style scored significantly higher on psychoticism than did students with an analytic style. Borrowing Cook's (1993) observation, the authors remarked that being high on the psychoticism scale could be an indicator of being socially deviant.

Two studies conducted by Riding and his colleagues used teacher ratings of students' classroom behavior. In both studies, a 5-point Likert scale was used, with 1 representing *poor classroom behavior*, and 5 representing *very good behavior*. The first study (Riding & Burton, 1998) was done among secondary school students, and the second (Riding & Fairhurst, 2001) among primary school students. In both studies, apart from finding that girls behaved better than boys, the authors identified that, among boys, students with a wholist style behaved the worst. It was also found that verbalizers misbehaved more than did imagers.

Finally, Riding and his colleague carried out two studies that focused on examining the relationships of cognitive styles to behavioral problems among boys in special education schools. In the first study (Riding & Craig, 1998), research participants were schoolboys studying in two residential special schools because of behavioral problems. The students were assessed on Riding's (1991) Cognitive Styles Analysis. It was found that, on the wholist–analytic style dimension, these boys were higher on the wholist end of the continuum. Furthermore, when compared with a group of boys from ordinary secondary schools, the boys from the special schools scored significantly higher on the wholist style. In addition, it was once again found that verbalizers misbehaved more than did imagers. These results were confirmed by those obtained from a similar study by the same authors in 1999 (Riding & Craig, 1999). Therefore, collectively, these studies suggest that students with wholist and verbal cognitive styles tend to exhibit problem behaviors.

Research on the relationships between styles and social behaviors is equally limited. All existing studies identified in the literature were based on the field-dependence/independence construct. Furthermore, all studies have been carried out in young children. In one such study, Saracho (1996) examined the cognitive style (field dependence/independence) and social play behaviors of 2,400 three- to five-year-olds. It was found that field-independent children engaged in more play than did field-dependent children. In an earlier study, Saracho (1992) found that the field-dependent children tended to communicate ideas in physical and block play more than did the field-independent children. This finding concurred with the results obtained by Coates, Lord, and Jakabovics (1975). Although these research results are obtained from young children, they still speak to the issue of style malleability. Again, it is possible that children with different styles (field dependent or field independent) have a tendency to engage in different play behaviors. It is also possible that at a young age, these children have been exposed to different play situations, which has, directly or indirectly, led to the development of different styles.

When Witkin and Goodenough (1977) reviewed the studies of the relationships between field dependence/independence and interpersonal behaviors, they mentioned a number of studies (e.g., Coates, 1972; Crandall & Sinkeldam, 1964; Jakabovics, 1974; Schleifer & Douglas, 1973) focusing on the relationships between field dependence/independence and social dependency. In these studies, preschoolers were tested for their field dependence/independence and were rated for autonomous achievement striving and dependence. Whereas no significant relationship was found between field dependence/independence and interpersonal dependence (e.g., frequently seeking help, attention, recognition, physical contact, and nearness to adults), field independence was significantly associated with autonomous achievement striving behaviors (e.g., trying to initiate activities, to overcome obstacles, to complete activities, and to obtain satisfaction from work). These studies suggest that field independence is superior to field dependence as the former is significantly associated with desirable social behaviors.

CONCLUSIONS AND FUTURE RESEARCH

In this chapter, we discussed the nature of intellectual styles based on existing empirical evidence obtained as a result of investigating various student populations. Findings from the five lines of research (each addressing a question proposed at the beginning of the chapter) have not only portrayed a current picture of the research endeavors of scholars in the field among different student populations, but also have enabled us to state our position on each of the three controversial issues regarding the nature of intellectual styles. We believe that intellectual styles are fundamentally value-laden, although at times they can be value-differentiated. They can be socialized and modified. Moreover, style constructs overlap with one another; but simultaneously, each style construct has its own unique characteristics.

No doubt, findings presented in this chapter have demonstrated that there is strong evidence supporting the impact of intellectual styles in various domains of student life as well as supporting our positions with regard to the three relevant controversial issues. Thus, as an important individual-difference variable in students' performance and behaviors, intellectual styles certainly deserve the attention that they have received from scholars over the past few decades, and they should continue to be widely researched.

Chapter 4

Styles Research and Applications: Teacher Oriented

In the previous chapter, we discussed the nature of intellectual styles as they relate to three of the major controversial issues in the field by introducing some of the major research on the intellectual styles of students. In this chapter, we focus on the styles literature as it pertains to teachers. In particular, we explore the nature of intellectual styles by answering four main questions regarding teachers' intellectual styles. First, are teachers' intellectual styles affected by personal and situational characteristics? Second, are some intellectual styles more conducive to teachers' psychological well-being than are other styles? Third, how do teachers' intellectual styles relate to their teaching behavior? Finally, does the match/mismatch between teachers' and students' intellectual styles matter in the teaching–learning process and/or student-learning outcome? Answers to these questions will facilitate an understanding of two of the three controversial issues: styles as stable versus malleable; and styles as value-laden (or value-differentiated) versus value-free.

ARE TEACHERS' INTELLECTUAL STYLES AFFECTED BY PERSONAL AND SITUATIONAL CHARACTERISTICS?

Background Information

To address the malleability issue of intellectual styles, we examined studies of teachers' styles in relation to their personal and situational characteristics. As they have in the study of other theoretical constructs, scholars have

51

also explored the nature of intellectual styles by examining how teachers' intellectual styles relate to a range of basic socialization variables, both personal and situational. It should be noted, however, that for historical reasons, research focusing on teachers' intellectual styles and their socialization variables is rather limited. As a target research population, teachers generally came to the scene of educational research much later than did students and the content of student learning (see Henson & Borthwick, 1984). The study of teachers' intellectual styles was motivated by the belief that student learning outcome could be enhanced by matching teaching styles with learning styles (or vice versa). Thus, from the very beginning, the research focus has not been on teachers' intellectual styles as they relate to teachers' characteristics, but rather, on the impact of the match/mismatch between teachers' and students' styles on classroom interaction, student learning outcome, and the subjective evaluations teachers and students make of each other.

Empirical Evidence

Limited as it may be, the research on intellectual styles as they relate to teachers' personal and situational characteristics has revealed the dynamic nature of teachers' styles. It has been found that teachers' intellectual styles vary as a function of subject area taught, gender, grade level taught, and length of teaching experience.

The dynamic nature of intellectual styles has been found in the significant relationships between teachers' intellectual styles and the subject areas that they teach. For example, Robinson (1982) studied the relationship between teachers' learning styles as assessed by Kolb's Learning Style Inventory and the subject areas they taught. It was found that the abstract/concrete style dimension was significantly related to teaching in art, English, and mathematics (see also Crookes, 1977).

Lawrence (1997) examined learning-style preferences and subject areas taught based on data collected from 353 teachers and lecturers in further education colleges. The style inventory employed was the Learning Style Questionnaire (Honey & Mumford, 1986), which identifies four learning style preferences: Activist, Reflector, Theorist, and Pragmatist. An activist prefers learning that is action- and experience-oriented. A reflector prefers to learn through data gathering and analysis. A theorist prefers learning that focuses on analyzing and synthesizing information. A pragmatist prefers learning that can provide practical solutions to his or her problems. Teachers in 12 subject areas participated in the study. The author found that the teachers in the majority of the subject areas (9 out of 12) had a dominant style preference of Reflector, or Reflector–Theorist in combination. The particular subject areas were biology, business studies and information technology, chemistry, geography, mathematics, modern foreign languages, physics, social sciences, and technology. A number of other specific findings were obtained. For example, teachers of chemistry, physics, technology, and geography tended to have a dominant style preference of Reflector and a back-up style of Theorist. Teachers of English and history tended to have a dominant style preference of Activist and a back-up style of Reflector.

Early in 1974, Tines examined the learning styles (with the scanner style on one end of the continuum and the focuser style on the other) of teachers of English, social studies, foreign languages, mathematics, and science. The author found that English and social studies teachers tended to fall on the scanning extreme, while the foreign language teachers and mathematics teachers were clustered at the focuser end. The science teachers fell in the middle of the continuum.

The dynamic nature of styles also has been manifested in the strong association between intellectual styles and gender among teachers. For example, in investigating the relationships between teacher stress and cognitive style, Borg and Riding (1993) found that male teachers with an imagery style and female teachers with a verbal style reported more stress than did male verbal teachers and female imagery teachers. Robinson (1982) discovered a significant relationship between teachers' learning styles (measured by Kolb's Learning Style Inventory) and gender.

Similarly, the dynamic nature of styles has also gained empirical support from existing studies of the relationships of teachers' intellectual styles to their teaching experience and the grade level they taught. For example, Robinson's (1982) study showed a negative relationship between teachers' scores on Kolb's active/reflective dimension and their years of teaching experience. Stone (1976) found that teachers of lower grades tended to be field dependent in their cognitive style.

Accounting for the Lack of Research

Obviously, research on the relationships between teachers' intellectual styles and socialization factors is fairly narrow. This lack of research, however, is not an indication of the triviality of such studies. As we noted earlier, this shortage of research stems from the fact that, from its inception, research related to teachers' intellectual styles has been inseparable from the notion of style match/mismatch between teachers and students.

Relevance to the Issue of Style Malleability

Then, a question regarding the validity of using findings from such existing research arose in the context of discussing the issue of style malleability. That is, could empirical findings from this limited body of research on

teachers' intellectual styles and socialization factors still play a role in facilitating an understanding of the nature of styles as related to the issue of the
malleability of styles? The answer is affirmative. We maintain our position
that intellectual styles are dynamic for two reasons. First, the findings on
the relationships between intellectual styles and socialization factors, although limited, are consistent with empirical evidence found in student
populations. Second, we believe that it makes sense that teachers' intellectual styles vary as a function of their socialization experiences. Take the significant relationship between teachers' intellectual styles and the subject areas they teach, for example. No causal relationship can be inferred between
the two variables. Thus, it is possible that teachers with certain intellectual
styles tend to gravitate toward teaching in particular academic disciplines.
Yet, it is equally possible that teaching in a particular discipline has
strengthened their dormant intellectual styles, or changed their predominant intellectual styles to become more in accordance with what is essential
for pursuing a successful career in a particular academic discipline. That is
to say, teachers' intellectual styles might have been modified as a result of
socialization in that academic discipline.

INTELLECTUAL STYLES AND PSYCHOLOGICAL
WELL-BEING

Introduction

To address the value issue of intellectual styles, we also examined studies of
teachers' styles in relation to their psychological well-being. The assumption is that styles that are typically superior in terms of their adaptive value
should positively contribute to the development of teachers' psychological
well-being. In this context, psychological well-being is loosely defined as a
mental state that may directly or indirectly be caused by one's subjective
evaluations of his or her surroundings. In the styles literature, several such
variables have been investigated with teachers' intellectual styles: teachers'
attitude toward or perceptions about their work environment, job satisfaction, and occupational stress. We put these variables under the more encompassing term of *psychological well-being* because they are all psychological
in nature and they all contribute to the development and maintenance of
mental health. The majority of the existing studies suggest that teachers' intellectual styles matter in their psychological well-being. Moreover, this research indicates that some intellectual styles are more conducive to the development of healthier psychological well-being than are their opposing
styles. That is to say, some intellectual styles are superior to their opposing

styles in the context of psychological well-being. Thus, intellectual styles are primarily value-laden.

Value of Styles: Research Evidence

The value-laden nature of intellectual styles has been demonstrated in the study of relationships of teachers' intellectual styles to their attitudes toward science and science teaching, their perceptions of their teaching environment, job satisfaction, and occupational stress. For example, in investigating the relationship between field dependence/independence and attitudes toward science and science teaching among elementary school teachers, Devore (1984) found that field independence was significantly associated with the development of positive attitudes toward science and science teaching.

Prosser and Trigwell (1997) studied the relationships between teaching approaches and perceptions of teaching environment among 46 teachers of first-year university physics and chemistry subjects. The Approaches to Teaching Inventory (Trigwell & Prosser, 1996) was used to assess two approaches to teaching: conceptual change (parallel to students' deep approach to learning) and information transmission (parallel to students' surface approach to learning). Results indicated that teachers who took a conceptual-change approach to teaching perceived their teaching environment more positively than did those who took a knowledge-transmission approach to teaching. The former believed that they had a sense of control (over their teaching), that their class sizes were appropriate, and that they had departmental support, whereas the latter had the opposite feeling about their work environment. Given that the conceptual-change teaching approach is related to better psychological well-being (i.e., positive feelings about one's work environment in this context), the conceptual-change teaching approach may be considered to carry a more positive value, whereas the knowledge-transmission can be regarded as carrying a more negative value.

Banks (1978) studied the relationship between Kolb's learning styles and satisfaction with principals' performance (an aspect of job satisfaction) among 621 secondary school teachers in the United States. It was concluded that, in general, when teachers were allowed to use their reflective and experimental styles, they were more likely to be satisfied with their principals' job performance, and thus indicated more satisfaction with their school environment as a whole.

Finally, the value-laden nature of styles was also manifested in Kagan's (1989) study of 70 elementary school teachers' cognitive styles and their occupational stress. It was established that teachers with nonanalytical styles tended to report less occupational stress, whereas teachers who were more analytical and realistic tended to report higher levels of occupational stress (e.g., lack of administrative support, problems working with students, difficult relationships with teachers, task overload, and financial insecurity).

Thus, according to the foregoing research findings, intellectual styles are value-laden. Some styles (e.g., field-independent cognitive style, conceptual-change teaching approach, and reflective and experimental styles) can be perceived as possessing positive characteristics, in that they are useful in helping teachers take a positive view of their surroundings. Other styles (e.g., field-dependent cognitive style, knowledge-transmission teaching approach, and concrete and abstract styles), however, have been found to be significantly associated with teachers' negative views of their surroundings.

INTELLECTUAL STYLES AND TEACHING BEHAVIORS

General Information

There is an increasing body of literature focusing on the investigation of the relationships between teachers' intellectual styles and their teaching behaviors. The investigations have been conducted among teachers teaching at various levels of educational institutions, including kindergartens, elementary schools, middle schools, community colleges, and universities. Moreover, in this literature, a large number of intellectual styles are involved. Among them are the styles measured by the Myers–Briggs Type Indicator (Myers & McCaulley, 1988) and the field-dependent/independent styles. Other styles that have been investigated are Gregorc's (1979) mind styles, Kolb's (1976) learning styles, Kagan et al.'s (1964) reflective and impulsive styles, Pask's (1972) serialist and holist styles, and Harrison and Bramson's (1977) modes of thinking. Moreover, teaching behaviors examined are of a wide range—from verbal to nonverbal, and from teacher planning to classroom interaction. It is true that several studies (e.g., Hansen, 1981; Packer & Bain, 1978) did not find significant relationships between teachers' intellectual styles and their teaching behaviors. However, there are many possible reasons for researchers' not having found a significant relationship between the two variables. For example, it could be that the styles measured do not directly affect teaching behaviors. Instead, the styles may have an indirect impact on teaching behaviors through a mediating variable that had not been taken into account in the studies. It could also be that the teaching behaviors assessed were not clearly defined and thus had not been observed or been measured in a valid fashion. Moreover, results from the great majority of the studies have indicated that teachers' intellectual styles make a difference in their teaching behaviors. This research has suggested that teachers tend to teach in ways that are congruent with their own intellectual styles (e.g., Harrison, 1997; Mehdikhani, 1983; Stensrud & Stensrud, 1983). In Table 4.1, some of the major research findings are summarized. Like most of the research on styles, research on the relationships between teachers' intellectual styles and their teaching behaviors has also shed light on the nature of intellectual styles, in particular, with regard to the malleability and value issues of styles.

Malleability of Styles

No doubt, an argument can easily be made for the malleable nature of styles in the context of the significant relationships between teachers' intellectual styles and their teaching behaviors. We believe so because the two variables involved in this relationship are in a chicken-and-egg situation. On the one hand, because teachers' intellectual styles affect the way they perceive the world and interact in their environment, it is only logical that their intellectual styles affect their teaching behaviors. On the other hand, it is also possible that when teachers are rewarded for displaying certain teaching behaviors, they tend to repeat the same behaviors. The repeated use of the same teaching behaviors may bring out teachers' dormant intellectual styles or even change their previously dominant styles. That is, teachers' intellectual styles can be modified through their educational practices.

Value of Styles

As for the value issue of styles, existing studies (e.g., Caverni & Drozda-Senkowska, 1984; Koppelman, 1980; Mahlios, 1981; Moore, 1973; Quinn, 1988; Serafino, 1979) seem to suggest that intellectual styles, in particular, the field dependent/independent styles and the reflective/impulsive styles, are value-laden. In general, these studies have indicated that field-independent teachers tend to exhibit teaching behaviors that are more conducive to effective student learning and development. For example, field-independent teachers tended to ask more reason-seeking questions (Koppelman, 1980; Serafino, 1979), make more reliable judgments of students' essays (Caverni & Drozda-Senkowska, 1984), and use more positive techniques for classroom management (Koppelman, 1980; Quinn, 1988). They also tended to be less critical of, but more nurturing toward, students (Koppelman, 1980). However, the field-dependent teachers use less positive techniques for classroom management; they tend to be more critical of, but less nurturing toward, students; their judgments of students' essays are less reliable. On a similar note, Pavlovich (1971) discovered that reflective teachers tended to be engaged in very different verbal behaviors from impulsive teachers. The former tended to praise and encourage students and to accept and adopt

TABLE 4.1
Relationships Between Teachers' Intellectual Styles and Teaching Behaviors

Styles	Major Findings		References
Myers–Briggs Personality Styles	Introverted teachers were more approving	Extraverted teachers were more disapproving	Stuber, 1997
	Extraverted, Thinking, and Judging teachers used more nonverbal behaviors, group-oriented instruction, and analytical teaching approaches	Introverted, Feeling, and Perceiving teachers used more verbal behaviors, individual-oriented instruction, and global teaching approaches	Kim, 1993
	Judging, Thinking, and Sensing teachers tended to display less child-centered behaviors	Perceiving, Feeling, and Intuitive teachers tended to display more child-centered behaviors	Kagan & Smith, 1988
	Judging and Thinking teachers had a stronger preference to teach in structured format and tended to be controlling	Intuitive and Feeling teachers were more flexible and spontaneous in their teaching and tended to be student-centered	Carlyn, 1976; Jonassen, 1981; Rudisill, 1973
	Introverted teachers demonstrated better classroom management behaviors	Extraverted teachers demonstrated fewer good class management behavior	Quinn, 1988
Field dependent/ independent	FI teachers asked significantly more reason-seeking questions	FD teachers asked significantly less reason-seeking questions	Koppelman, 1980; Serafino, 1979
	FI teachers made more reliable judgments on students' essays	FD teachers made less reliable judgments on students' essays	Caverni & Drozda-Senkowska, 1984
	FI teachers: more analytical in their teaching styles, more nurturing toward students as learners; less critical than FD teachers; used more impersonal or positive techniques for classroom management	FD teachers: showed more warmth toward students; engaged in more physical contact; more directive, more critical; used criticism of student behavior as a primary means of classroom control	Koppelman, 1980

	FI teachers: more academic interactions with a whole class; asked more academic questions; asked more questions at the analytical level; provided more corrective feedback; more elaborative in corrective feedback	FD teachers: more academic interaction in small group settings; more interaction in private settings; asked more factual questions	Mahlios, 1981
	FI teachers: use questions as instructional tools	FD teachers: use questions primarily as a method of assessing student learning outcome	Moore, 1973
	FI teachers: tended to be better classroom managers in special education setting	FD teachers: tended to be poorer at classroom management in special education setting	Quinn, 1988
	FI teachers: prefer teaching situations that are impersonal in nature	FD teachers: prefer teaching situations that allow more interaction with students	Wu, 1968
Mind Styles	Teachers with abstract learning styles used analogies, modeled with their voices, and used illustrators more frequently	Teachers with concrete learning styles displayed fewer teacher behaviors shown in teachers with abstract styles	Stuber, 1997
Reflective/Impulsive	Reflective teachers tended to praise and encourage students and to accept and adopt students' ideas	Impulsive teachers tended to ask questions, lecture, and to give directions	Pavlovich, 1971
Mode of Thinking	Teachers who are idealistic and realistic tended to direct questions and comments to individual students	Teachers who are pragmatic tended to direct questions and comments to a whole class	Kagan & Smith, 1988

the ideas of students, whereas the latter tended to ask questions, lecture, and give directions. It was concluded that reflective teachers tended to cause students to change in a favorable direction, whereas impulsive teachers tended to influence students in a more negative way, resulting in student changes in an unfavorable direction. Therefore, according to this research evidence, intellectual styles are value-laden.

Consistent with the previous research findings that we have discussed, empirical results emerging from the relationships between teachers' styles and their teaching behaviors suggest that intellectual styles are value-laden. There is no empirical evidence supporting the view that styles are wholly value-free.

DOES MATCH/MISMATCH BETWEEN TEACHERS' AND STUDENTS' STYLES MATTER?

General Information

To understand the nature of intellectual styles, we have also examined the influence of teacher–student style match on student learning and development as well as on student–teacher interaction. As previously mentioned, the motivation for studying teachers' intellectual styles was to establish whether the match of teachers' teaching styles to students' learning styles would improve student learning (Henson & Borthwick, 1984). For this reason, studies of the degree of match between teachers' and students' styles are important in the literature on teachers' intellectual styles. Furthermore, the literature shows that although the initial advocacy for the study of the match/mismatch hypothesis was advanced as early as 1965 by Kagan (see Henson & Borthwick, 1984, p. 6), no empirical research effort was completed until the early 1970s (e.g., see Lange, 1973; Packer & Bain, 1978; Saracho, 1978; Spindell, 1976; Tines, 1974). In the last three decades, the study of this match/mismatch has been gaining increasing momentum. To date, more than 100 research articles and dissertations (with the great majority, doctoral dissertations) have been produced and documented in the literature. After more than three decades of investigation, what have researchers found? Does the match/mismatch between teachers' and students' intellectual styles matter in enhancing student learning and development as well as in teacher–student interaction? Through this body of literature, what have we learned about the nature of intellectual styles? The remainder of this section attempts to answer these questions in the order in which the questions have been raised.

When reading the literature on the match/mismatch between teachers' and students' intellectual styles, one can hardly miss two recurrent themes in the existing studies. The first is the effects of match (or mismatch) between teachers' and students' intellectual styles on students' affective development and academic achievement. The second is the effects of this match on interpersonal attraction between teachers and students, including teachers' evaluation (and expectation) of students' academic performance, and students' evaluation of teachers. Furthermore, among these studies, Witkin's field dependent/independent styles are the most frequently investigated. Other style constructs, however, have also been involved in these matching/mismatching studies. This research seems to have created the most ambiguous findings in the styles literature. A large number of studies have supported the positive effects of the match of teachers' and students' intellectual styles on the areas mentioned above (e.g., students' affective development, academic achievement, and interpersonal attraction between teachers and students). Yet, the number of studies that have suggested a null effect seems to be even larger, especially regarding the impact of style match on students' academic performance. Table 4.2 lists some of the major studies. These mixed findings pervade both themes of studies.

Style Match/Mismatch and Academic Achievement

Results from studies of the impact of the degree of match or mismatch between teacher and student intellectual styles on student academic achievement, for example, yielded quite different results. Many scholars (e.g., Adderley, 1987; Block, 1981; Cafferty, 1981) have recognized that a match of student–teacher dyads in their intellectual styles is beneficial for students' academic achievement, others (e.g., Blanch, 2001; Foley, 1999; Stone, 1982) have found that this match does not make a difference.

Block (1981) tested the field dependent/independent styles among a group of 200 (66 Black and 134 White) students and their teachers. Students were also assessed on the Comprehensive Test of Basic Skills to determine their achievement in mathematics and reading. Results indicated that a teacher–student style match had a significantly positive impact on student achievement in reading, although not on achievement in mathematics. Furthermore, there was a significant two-way interaction between the match of teacher–student styles and socially defined race: When teacher and student styles were better matched, the achievement gap in reading was reduced between Black and White students. Using the test for Cognitive Style Mapping (Hill, 1976), Cafferty (1981) assessed the cognitive styles of 1,689 teacher–student dyads in a high school. The grades students received from their respective teachers were also used. It was found that, in general, the greater the degree of teacher–student style match, the higher were students' grade point averages. Using the Gregorc Style Delineator, Grout (1991) examined the relationship of the compatibility of English teachers'

TABLE 4.2

Selected Studies of Teachers' and Students' Style Match/Mismatch

	Matching/Mismatching Has Significant Effects	Matching/Mismatching Has No Significant Effects
Student Academic Achievement	Adderley, 1987; Block, 1981; Cafferty, 1981; Grout, 1991; Lange, 1973; Murray, 1979; Packer & Bain, 1978	Allinson, Hayes, & Davis, 1994; Avery, 1986; Blanch, 2001; Compagnone, 1980; Cooper & Miller, 1991; Cupkie, 1980; Foley, 1999; Giunta, 1984; Jolly, 1981; Jones, 1982; MacNeil, 1980; Malinsky, 2001; Mehdikhani, 1983; O'Neill, 1990; Paradise & Block, 1984; Saracho & Dayton, 1980; Schenker, 1982; Smutz, 2003; Stone, 1982; Susabda, 1993; Tines, 1974; Tymms & Gallacher, 1995
Students' Affects	Copenhaver, 1979; Grout, 1991; Lange, 1973	Haldeman, 1979; Schenker, 1982; Tines, 1976
Teachers' Ratings of Students	DiStefano, 1969; James, 1973; Saracho, 1978, 1991b; Saracho & Spodek, 1994; Strout, 1986	Packer & Bain, 1978; Renninger & Snyder, 1983; Spindell, 1976
Students' Ratings of Teachers	Cooper & Miller, 1991; DiStefano, 1969; James, 1973; Kagan, 1989; Lange, 1973; Packer & Bain, 1978; Renninger & Snyder, 1983	Kim, 1993; Pettigrew, Bayless, Zakrajsek, & Goc-Karp, 1985; Parisi, 1980; Pozzi, 1979; Saracho, 1991a; Taylor, 1980

styles and their students' learning styles to student achievement in English. It was once again discovered that the congruence between teacher and student learning styles significantly contributed to student achievement in English.

However, as previously stated, many empirical studies have suggested that the congruence between teachers' and students' styles does not always help student academic achievement. Results of these studies provided alternative explanations for significant individual differences in academic achievement. In general, it can be argued that intellectual styles, both teachers' and students', do play an important role in student academic achievement. However, the match (or mismatch) of the styles between students and teachers is not critical. For example, Saracho and Dayton (1980) examined the relationships of schoolchildren's (second and fifth graders) academic gains to the congruence between teacher–student cognitive styles as measured by the Embedded Figures Test. Results indicated that it was not the match/mismatch of cognitive styles between teachers and students that significantly affected students' academic gains; rather, it was teachers' cognitive styles that proved to be one of the most critical factors in student achievement. Schoolchildren whose teachers were field independent showed significantly greater academic gains than did children whose teachers were field dependent. Similarly, Foley (1999) investigated the possible effects of teacher and student (third graders) learning style preferences on student achievement in reading. Learning styles were assessed by Dunn, Dunn, and Price's (1975, 1979, 1981, 1986) Learning Style Inventory, and reading achievement was measured by the Texas Assessment of Academic Skills (TAAS). Although the authors found that both teacher and student learning style preferences had a significant impact on student achievement in reading, the match/mismatch of learning styles did not play a role.

Style Match/Mismatch and Affective Development

Studies of the effects of teacher–student style matches on students' affective development have also produced mixed findings, with some indicating that a teacher–student style match has significant effects on students' affective development and others suggesting that the match does not make a difference in the affective domain of students. In the case of the former, for example, Grout (1991) found that students whose styles (as assessed by the Gregorc Style Delineator) were more similar to those of their English teachers reported a higher degree of enjoyment in their English class and attended their lessons more frequently. On the contrary, students whose styles did not match their teachers' reported a lower degree of enjoyment and a lower attendance rate. Similarly, Copenhaver (1979) reported that high school students showed significantly more positive attitudes toward learning if their learning styles were congruent with those of their teachers than if their styles did not match.

Other researchers, however, did not find significant association between teacher–student style match and students' affective development. For example, Haldeman (1979) studied the possible influence of the match (or mismatch) between student and teacher styles on students' change in self-concept in a period of 8 months. Teachers and students were assessed for their reflective/impulsive styles on the appropriate form of the Matching Familiar Figures Test; and students' self-concept was measured by the Piers–Harris Children's Self Concept Scale (Piers, 1984). Results did not reveal any significant correlation between style match and change in student self-concept. The author postulated that competing or more dominant variables might have diminished the possible effects of teacher–student style match on students' change in self-concept. In a similar vein, Schenker (1982) did not identify any significant relationships of the degree of teacher–student style match (mismatch) to students' attitudes toward learning in English, mathematics, social studies, and science, nor to students' level of self-esteem.

Style Match/Mismatch and Teachers' Evaluations of Students

Substantial research has been undertaken on the impact of the congruence (or lack thereof) of intellectual styles of teacher–student dyads on teachers' subjective evaluations of student academic competence/performance. As one can predict, findings on this research are also inconclusive. For example, Saracho (1978, 1983) has found that the effects of match/mismatch involve a great deal of complexity. In her first study (Saracho, 1978) of the relationship between the match/mismatch of teacher–student cognitive styles (measured by the Embedded Figures Test and the Articulation-Body-Concept Scale) and teachers' perceptions of student academic performance, she found the two variables to be significantly correlated. She established that teachers (both field dependent and field independent) ranked students who matched their styles similarly to students' actual rankings on a standardized achievement test. However, teachers (both field dependent and field independent) tended to underestimate children with whom their styles did not match. Furthermore, the field-dependent teachers tended to underestimate mismatched children more than did the field-independent teachers. Five years later, in a similar study, Saracho (1983) found that there was only one case of accurate rating. That is, the field-independent teachers accurately estimated the achievement of female students who were also field independent. The field-independent teachers did not make an accurate estimation of their mismatched female students, nor did they accurately estimate the achievement of boys (matched and mismatched). As for the field-dependent teachers, they failed in making an accurate evaluation of any students (boys or girls, matched or mismatched).

A more comprehensive study was conducted by Spindell (1976), who examined the effects of teacher–student cognitive style match on teachers' subjective evaluations of students' on-task performance, intelligence, and predicted school performance. Cognitive styles were assessed with the Embedded Figures Test. No significant results were found in any of the relationships investigated.

Style Match/Mismatch and Students' Evaluation of Teachers

Still, given that some studies have indicated that teachers evaluate students more positively when their intellectual styles match, it seems plausible to think that students' evaluations of teachers also are affected by such a match. Various studies have examined the possible effects of teacher–student style match on students' evaluations of their teachers. Again, one can find both studies that suggest a significant influence of style match and studies that indicate a null effect of style match in student evaluations of teachers. For example, using the Myers–Briggs Type Indicator, Cooper and Miller (1991) studied the relationship of congruence/incongruence between teacher–student styles to student evaluations of business courses and their professors. Results indicated that the level of teacher–student style match had a significant impact on students' evaluations of both their courses and their professors. By the same token, when Lange (1973) investigated this relationship among students and professors in nursing education, she found that, to a significant degree, students whose styles matched their teachers' perceived their professors more positively than did students whose styles were mismatched with their professors' (see Table 4.2 for other studies).

Research findings that indicate no significant relationship between teacher–student style match and students' evaluations of teachers also abound. For example, Pettigrew, Bayless, Zakrajsek, and Goc-Karp (1985) conducted a study among 117 students in physical education majors and 21 professors, using Canfield's (1976) Learning Styles Inventory to assess students' preferred learning styles and Canfield and Canfield's (1976) Instructional Styles Inventory to measure teachers' preferred teaching styles. Students also rated teachers on a number of factors related to teaching effectiveness. Results indicated that the style match/mismatch between teachers and students did not have a significant effect on students' evaluations of their teachers. Similarly, in a study of 55 teachers and 856 undergraduate students from a small, 4-year liberal arts college, Parisi (1980) did not find any significant influence of teacher–student style match on the field dependent/independent styles on students' evaluations of their teachers (see Table 4.2 for other studies).

Accounting for the Mixed Findings

To summarize, findings of the impact of teacher–student style match (or mismatch) on student learning and development are mixed, as they are for teachers' and students' mutual evaluations. Yet, the question that remains is: How could we account for why some studies would show significant effects of teacher-style matches and others would not. There could be many reasons for these inconsistent findings. For example, it may depend on the style constructs studied and the particular measures used to assess the style constructs. It may depend on how and what achievement and affective measures were used. It may be contingent upon the sample size in a particular study. It may also depend on the duration and intensity of the interaction between teachers and students, in particular, with regard to the effects of student–teacher interaction on student–teacher mutual evaluations.

Relevance to the Malleability and Value of Styles

A further question to be answered is: How have these findings facilitated our understanding of the nature of intellectual styles, particularly in relation to the controversial issues over styles we have been discussing? We would argue that the findings obtained from these matching studies can be used to further elucidate our earlier position on at least two of the three controversial issues over the nature of intellectual styles: malleability and value. From our viewpoint, this research denotes that styles are at least somewhat modifiable. Furthermore, to us, this research also signifies that intellectual styles are both value-laden and value-differentiated. However, they cannot be value-free. In the remainder of this section, we substantiate our positions.

Style Malleability. The issue of malleability of intellectual styles penetrates this body of research at two different levels. At a general level, the evidence that the match between student and teacher styles enhances student academic achievement gives us good reason to believe that styles are modifiable. One could argue that to some degree the match between the two parties' styles could be coincidental. However, it is also conceivable that this match could very well be a result of mutual adaptation of intellectual styles between teachers and students. In other words, the final product (i.e., the degree of match in styles) that researchers identified may be attributable to the dynamic interaction between teachers and students. After repeated interaction and adaptation, both parties may change (consciously or unconsciously) their original predominant intellectual styles to achieve a state of style match.

At a more specific level, we have identified a great deal of work in the style-matching literature that suggests the flexible nature of intellectual styles. To begin with, the very fact that advocates call for style matching between teachers and students conveys their belief that styles (both students' and teachers') can be changed. Early in 1984, Henson and Borthwick stated that "since it is readily recognized that the majority of humans are capable of changing, both teaching and learning styles can therefore be manipulated" (p. 6). Indeed, many studies have shown that teachers and students do intentionally adapt to each other's intellectual styles. For example, Stone (1982) found that teachers adapted their teaching behaviors based on students' learning styles. Blanch (2001) concluded that at the collegiate level, students are better able to adapt to a variety of teaching styles, even if their teachers' styles are incongruent with their own. Similarly, Chang (1988) discovered that students did adapt their learning styles to their teachers' teaching styles. Adaptations were significantly influenced not only by students' own learning styles but also by their perceptions of teachers' teaching behaviors. Although these studies did not measure the stylistic changes of students and teachers, they did address the issue of adaptation. The empirical evidence that students and teachers are able to adapt to each other's styles implies that styles are modifiable. Whether or not the adaptive styles eventually become their predominant styles presumably is contingent upon the environment in which they operate. If people (in this case, students and/or teachers) stay in an environment that requires them to use particular styles for a prolonged period of time, it is very likely that they will form new ways of dealing with their environment, that is, new styles. Otherwise, the adaptive styles that people use might be more transient. In both cases, however, the aforementioned studies suggest that people's intellectual styles are at least somewhat flexible and thus modifiable. For example, Lange (1973) concluded that after they took a nursing course, students changed in their cognitive style maps in the direction of the instructor's cognitive style.

Style Value

That intellectual styles are value-laden and value-differentiated also can be easily discerned in this research on style matching/mismatching. Interestingly enough, we noticed that it was the studies that resulted in significant relationships between style match and teacher–student mutual subjective evaluations that revealed the value-differentiation of styles, while the studies that indicated no significant effect between the two variables showed the value-laden aspect of styles.

Styles Being Value-Differentiated.   We discuss the former situation first. As has been previously argued, although the match of styles between teachers and students could happen by chance, it is also possible that the match is the result of the intentional adaptation of styles between teachers and students. If that were the case, it would mean that in order to obtain favorable ratings from each other, teachers and students would try to adapt to each other's styles without judging the value of the styles they were trying to acquire. Take the field dependent/independent styles, for example—students/teachers may intentionally adapt themselves to using either the field-independent style or the field-dependent style, depending on one's judgment of which style the other party uses. Under this circumstance, field dependence and field independence can be considered value-differentiated. In other words, because the use of the same style (either field dependent or field independent) can be associated with either positive or negative evaluation, contingent upon the match (or mismatch) of one's own style with that of the evaluator(s), one cannot say that one style is better than the other. In a like vein, when it comes to the situation of evaluating someone else, one does not put emphasis on what styles the other party has, but rather on whether or not the other party's styles match with his or her own. In this case, styles are also value-differentiated, because either style (field dependent or field independent) can win the appreciation of some people, if not that of others. For example, some people see positive value in the field-dependent style, while others see positive value in the field-independent style.

Styles Being Value-Laden.   The value-laden aspect of styles can be detected in findings showing no significant effect of style match on student academic achievement or on students' evaluations of teachers. For example, when Saracho and Dayton (1980) investigated the relationship of teacher and student cognitive styles to student academic achievement gains, they found that style match between teachers and students did not matter for student achievement gains. Instead, students, regardless of their own cognitive styles, showed greater achievement gains if they were taught by field-independent teachers. At the same time, those children who were taught by field-dependent teachers demonstrated significantly lesser gains in academic achievement. In other words, the field-independent style manifested more positive value in facilitating teachers in their efforts at enhancing student academic achievement than did the field-dependent style.

Better student achievement under field-independent teachers might be related to the fact that field-independent teachers have higher expectations for their students than do field-dependent teachers (see Saracho, 1991b). Having realistically high expectations for students is perceived as being a positive characteristic of teachers because it tends to produce positive teacher-expectations effect in the form of better student academic achievement (see

Brophy & Good, 1970; Rosenthal & Jacobson, 1968; Rubovits & Maehr, 1971). Indeed, Saracho (1991b) proposed that field-dependent teachers ought to be trained to become field independent. However, the case for training field-independent teachers to become field dependent has yet to be made. Thus, once again, it can be argued that there is a general perception that field independence is more positively valued than field dependence.

The superiority of field independence over field dependence has also been identified in other similar studies. Taylor's (1980) research, for example, was intended to explore whether or not students would rate their teachers significantly higher if their teachers' styles matched their own. The answer was no. Regardless of their styles (field dependent or field independent), students rated field-independent teachers much more favorably than they did the field-dependent teachers. This was found in both secondary school settings and higher educational institutions. The preference for field-dependent teachers by students of both styles is, again, yet to be demonstrated.

Value Issue in Summary. At present, the evidence for the value-laden nature of styles in the context of style-matching studies is limited to investigations involving field dependence/independence. This is due mainly to the fact that research on style match itself has been dominated by studies of field dependence/independence. Nonetheless, the research evidence identified in the context of style match studies is consistent with findings obtained in other areas of the study of styles. Thus, we are confident in asserting once more that styles are largely value-laden (or value-differentiated) and that styles are not value-free.

Practical Implications for Teachers

There is a further question one would naturally ask: "Given these conflicting findings, what should classroom teachers do to promote student learning and development and, perhaps, to receive favorable evaluations from their students?" We would say that because styles do make a difference in student learning and development and in student–teacher interaction, it is beneficial for teachers to become aware of their own teaching styles and their students' learning styles. Because research findings on the effects of style match are mixed, teachers ought to recognize that students are diverse in their styles of learning. Some students may learn better and appreciate their teachers more when their styles match their teachers' styles. Other students may not be affected by this match. Still other students may prefer that their teachers' styles are completely different from those of their own. Therefore, teachers should ensure effective teaching and learning by expanding the repertoire of their teaching styles and by being flexible. By utilizing a wide range of teaching styles and by being flexible in their teaching, teachers automatically accommodate the learning styles of the majority, if not all, of their students. This procedure will not only accommodate students' various learning styles, but also provide them an opportunity to challenge themselves to develop styles that they normally would not use. Obviously, this recommendation aligns with our belief that styles are malleable.

CONCLUSIONS AND FUTURE RESEARCH

In this chapter, we explored the nature of intellectual styles within the context of research centered on teachers. We described four lines of research. Like the findings obtained from student populations, findings from teacher-oriented research allowed us to further elucidate our positions on two of the three major controversial issues over styles: styles as traits versus states and styles as value-laden or value-differentiated versus value-free. Once again, research results from this chapter have led us to maintain our positions: that styles are malleable and thus represent states; and that styles are essentially value-laden or value-differentiated.

In reading this literature, we have also identified some areas related to teachers' intellectual styles that need to be further investigated. First, given that teachers' intellectual styles play such an important role in student learning and development, a deeper understanding should be obtained regarding what contributes to the formation and the development of teacher styles. Presently, there is a lack of knowledge of the relationships of teacher styles to the basic socialization variables as well as to multiple psychological variables. Even more important is research on how teachers' personality traits relate to their intellectual styles. Presently, there is little to no research on the topic.

Second, although studies on the style match/mismatch hypothesis are abundant, none of the studies has taken students' ability levels into account. It is widely recognized that students' abilities play a paramount role in their academic performance as well as in their perceptions about their learning environment (including their teachers' teaching). Therefore, the results of the match/mismatch studies might have, to some extent, been confounded by students' abilities.

Finally, compared with the research methods employed among the student populations, the research methods used to study teachers are more varied (e.g., using interviews and observations apart from self-reports). Nevertheless, as with the existing research among students, current teacher-centered research needs to be expanded to include longitudinal and more qualitative studies so that we achieve a better understanding about the nature of intellectual styles.

Chapter 5

Styles Research and Applications in Nonacademic Settings

In the previous two chapters, we explored the nature of intellectual styles as they relate to three of the major controversial issues in the field by presenting some of the major research on the intellectual styles of students and teachers. In this chapter, we focus on the styles literature as it pertains to people in nonacademic settings. Our review of this part of the literature also indicates that styles are malleable, that they are either value-laden or value-differentiated but not value-free, and that different style constructs share certain degrees of similarities, while each possesses its own uniqueness.

The argument that styles are malleable is supported by empirical studies suggesting that people's intellectual styles vary as a function of such socialization factors as demographic characteristics, occupational groups, job functions, and cultures. The issue of the value of styles is addressed by empirical evidence revealing the relationships of intellectual styles to personality traits and to task performance. We also address the value issue by presenting research evidence reflecting people's perceptions about intellectual styles. Finally, we present empirical studies demonstrating significant overlaps among different style constructs.

ARE INTELLECTUAL STYLES MALLEABLE?

To address the issue of the malleability of intellectual styles, we examined studies that investigated the relationships of intellectual styles to several socialization factors: demographic characteristics, occupational groups, job

71

functions, and cultures. This research indicates that people's styles differ based on these socialization factors.

Styles and Demographic Characteristics

At the outset, it should be pointed out that there is a general lack of studies on the relationships between intellectual styles and demographic characteristics in nonacademic settings. Nonetheless, existing studies uniformly indicate that demographic characteristics play an important role in people's intellectual styles. These demographics include age, gender, education, work position, and length of service.

Styles and Age. Style differences as a function of age have been empirically shown in several studies. For example, in studying 203 telephone sales agents in the insurance industry, Furnham, Jackson, and Miller (1999) found that the research participants differed in styles as assessed by Honey and Mumford's (1982) Learning Styles Questionnaire (LSQ) depending on their age. Older participants tended to score higher on the reflector and theorist styles than did their younger counterparts, whereas younger participants tended to score higher on the activist style. People with an activist style tend to seek sensations and to be impulsive and extraverted. People with a reflector style are described as introverted and cautious. People with a theorist style tend to be intellectual, rational, and objective in their thinking. Another style assessed by the LSQ is the pragmatist style. Pragmatists tended to be expedient, realistic, and practical. These results are consistent with our common-sense notion that older people are more reflective and take more factors into account in their decision making and that younger people tend to be impulsive and speak their mind without much forethought, perhaps because of a lack of experience and knowledge.

Hill, Puurula, Sitko-Lutek, and Rakowska (2000) investigated the relationships between age and styles assessed by Allinson and Hayes' (1996) Cognitive Style Index (CSI) among a heterogeneous group of management-related personnel from Finland, Poland, and the United Kingdom. They concluded that there was a general trend toward more intuitive scores as participants grew older. The intuition–analysis style dimension underlying the CSI represents the conceptual tempo dimension investigated by Kagan (1966b), which concerns individuals' tendency for postponing cognitive closure pending consideration of the accuracy of an answer achieved. People who are more intuitive tend to reach closure sooner and with less information than do analytical people. The finding in Hill et al.'s (2000) study also makes sense. In an organizational context, older people normally have experienced much more than younger people. As a result of the rich experiences gained with age, they could simply have "a feeling of 'knowing without knowing how,' having a 'hunch' or 'just knowing' " (p. 287).

Three studies have examined the relationship of age to Kirton's (1976) adaption–innovation cognitive style dimension, which produced conflicting findings. Among 55 U.S. service-sector managers, Jacobson (1993) found a positive relationship between age and the innovative style. However, in his initial testing of the Kirton Adaption–Innovation Inventory among a heterogeneous sample of 532 research participants (business leaders, lower level employees, housewives, and students) and a replication sample of 276 participants, Kirton (1976) found that older people obtained lower innovative scores than did their younger counterparts. Similarly, in their study of 67 professional staff within a local authority in the United Kingdom, Hayward and Everett (1983) also found that older participants were more adaptive in their style than were younger participants.

We have no way of knowing exactly why the first study resulted in findings that were contradictory to those of the latter two studies. However, there are at least two factors that might have contributed to the different findings. First, the samples involved in each study were different. They were from different occupational fields. Therefore, it could be possible that the nature of their occupations has interacted with age in exerting impact on the socialization process of styles. The second factor contributing to the differing findings could be related to the fact that the ranges of ages of participants from each study were not the same. Third, the first study was among managers, whereas the latter two studies were conducted among nonmanagerial staff. It is conceivable that, among managers, the ones who are more innovative tend to be older. Age has enabled the managers to accumulate much more experience. To meet the challenges of an ever-changing society, managers with more experience would have more resources to draw from to be innovative. In the nonmanagerial staff members, however, those who are older would tend to be more adaptive. Older people would have known their work routines very well. Perhaps some of them have stopped trying to be innovative.

Regardless of the conflicts among the results, all studies suggested a significant relationship between intellectual styles and age. Therefore, age reflects a socialization effect on intellectual styles. Yet, the question arises as to how we explain why age makes a difference in people's intellectual styles in nonacademic settings. The ages of people working in organizations are usually highly related to their length of service in an organization. People who work in the same work environment for a longer period of time would have more exposure to their organizational culture. They thus may have become more in tune with the climate of their organization. Thus, age may have directly or indirectly played a crucial role in the socialization process of one's intellectual styles. Conner, Kinicki, and Keats (1994) argued that age and organizational tenure are important individual characteristics that influence people's characteristic ways of information processing (i.e., intellectual styles). They contended that because members of a similar age would have shared the same social, economic, and political environment, they would have a common understanding of many events. By the same token, Conner et al. believe that because people with similar lengths of organizational tenure would have experienced a common organizational history, they may develop a similar understanding of the organizational environment (see also Hayes & Allinson, 1998).

Styles and Gender. In chapter 3, we pointed out that research on the relationships between intellectual styles and gender in academic settings is abundant and that findings are far from unequivocal. Research on the same topic in nonacademic settings, however, is a completely different story. Like research on the relationship of styles with any other demographic characteristic in nonacademic settings, research examining the relationships between styles and gender is sparse. However, unlike findings in academic settings, findings in nonacademic settings have been quite consistent. All existing studies using the Kirton Adaption–Innovation Inventory (Kirton, 1976) indicate that, among the general population, women are, on average, more adaptive and that men are more innovative, on average (e.g., Goldsmith, 1985; Jacobson, 1993; Jorde, 1984; Kirton, 1976; Kirton & Kubes, 1992; Kubes, 1989; Prato Previde, 1984, 1991). However, women in leadership positions are more innovative than are their male counterparts (e.g., Dewan, 1982; Kirton, 1993; McCarthy, 1993; Tullett, 1995). We also located a study that involved the use of a different style inventory. Hill et al. (2000) administered the Cognitive Style Index (Allinson & Hayes, 1996) to 200 managers in Finland, Poland, and the United Kingdom and found that female managers were more intuitive than male managers

Literally in all the general population studies, females had means about half a standard deviation more adaptive than did their male counterparts. It should be noted that the theoretical mean for the Kirton inventory is 96. General population samples in the United Kingdom, United States, Italy, and Slovakia have resulted in means of 95 +/−.5, and scores are roughly normally distributed within a range of 45 to 146, with a standard deviation of 17.9 (see Clapp & De Ciantis, 1989). The lower an individual scores on the inventory, the more adaptive one's style is; the higher an individual scores, the more innovative one's style is. For example, in Kirton's (1976) study of a U.K. sample, the mean for females was 90.8, whereas the mean for males was 98.1. Similar findings have been obtained among samples in the United States, Italy, and Slovakia.

This finding on gender difference in styles among the general population is largely the result of socialization. Traditionally, being innovative has been more acceptable in males than in females. Both at home and work situations, men were expected to come up with new ideas and make the rules and decisions, and women to follow the rules and carry out tasks according to what was prescribed by men. Although today, more and more women are getting into the positions of rule- and decision-making, the number of men in these positions is far larger. Therefore, by virtue of socialization, women may become less innovative, on average, than men.

The socialization effects of gender on styles, however, are confounded by the occupational status that women have. As was briefly mentioned earlier, research indicates that females in leadership positions tend to be more innovative, on average, than their male counterparts. For example, Dewan (1982) found that Indian female entrepreneurial managers were more innovative than their male counterparts. This finding supported Kirton's (1978b, 1980, 1994) hypothesis that those who cross certain boundaries, professional or social, are more likely to be innovative than their norm groups. Further evidence was provided by Kirton (1993), McCarthy (1993), and Tullett (1995). Kirton (1993) found that male engineering managers had a mean KAI score of 96.7 (SD = 16.0), which is 14 points below the U.K. male norm group mean. However, McCarthy's (1993) study indicated that female engineering managers had a mean of 102.3 (SD = 15.6), which is 11.5 points above the U.K. female norm group mean. By the same token, Tullett (1995) found that although both male and female project managers were more innovative than the general U.K. population, the extent to which female project managers were more innovative than the female general population was greater than it was for the male comparison group.

The effect of gender combined with occupational status on people's intellectual styles has also been supported by Hill et al.'s (2000) study of managers in Finland, Poland, and the United Kingdom, using the Cognitive Style Index (Allinson & Hayes, 1996). It was found that across the three national groups, female managers were more intuitive than male managers.

In summary, existing studies show that women who have nontraditional occupational status (by virtue of being in a leadership position or of being in a male-dominated profession) tend to use creativity-generating intellectual styles such as being innovative or intuitive. This general finding indicates that styles can be changed. As discussed previously, in the general population, women are socialized to be obedient and adaptive. However, women can become creative in their thinking after they are socialized in a nontraditional work setting. Furthermore, they are more innovative than their male counterparts. These women are socialized to think more creatively not only because they take leadership positions (such as managers) but also because they sometimes enter an occupation that is largely dominated by males (e.g., engineering). Obviously, it is also possible that more innovative women tend to enter nontraditional occupations and/or take leadership positions.

Finally, as a socialization factor, gender was also found to be the mediator of the relationship between two different style constructs. In studying the relationship between the Myers–Briggs Type Indicator and the Kirton Adaption–Innovation Inventory among 55 U.S. service-sector managers, Jacobson (1993) obtained different relationships for men and women. For women, extraverted managers were more innovative. However, for men, no significant relationship was found. Thus, for women to be innovative, it may be important that they be extraverted. Women who take leadership positions and who work in a "nontraditional" field tended to be innovative and intuitive. It is also feasible that to cross boundaries—social and professional—women would also need to reach out to the world around them and interact with other people. These female managers' extraverted style may have been a result of their work environments. Or, of course, it may be that extraverted women are the ones who gravitate to positions of leadership.

Styles and Education. In the limited studies that have been carried out, education also has manifested itself as a socialization variable for intellectual styles. Two studies examined Kirton's adaption–innovation style dimension. Keller and Holland (1978a) investigated the relationship between KAI scores and levels of education among 256 professional employees working for three applied research and development organizations in the United States. Data indicated that employees with higher levels of education tended to be more innovative than those with lower levels of education. Similarly, in testing the correlations between the KAI scores and the levels of educational attainment, Cutright (1990) found that higher adaptive scores were related to lower educational attainment and that higher innovative scores were related to higher educational attainment.

Obviously, research on the relationships between styles and education is very limited. Although results from this limited research preclude us from making any definitive conclusion about the socialization effect of education on intellectual styles, it is not difficult to imagine that education can make a difference in one's intellectual styles.

Styles and Work Position. Work position has evidenced itself as another socialization factor that has to do with people's intellectual styles. For example, Keller and Holland (1978a) found a positive relationship between innovation scores and employees' work positions. This relationship makes sense. People in higher positions in an organization would necessarily find themselves confronted with more situations in which they need to think in a novel way that facilitates new ways of doing things. People higher in the organizational hierarchy are expected to make decisions that meet the needs of an ever-changing work environment. On the contrary, employees working in lower positions in an organization are often expected to take orders from their supervisors. Carrying out orders is essentially their job responsibility. People in lower positions are seldom expected to be innovative in their thinking. With the passage of time, people in higher positions may become more and more innovative in their cognitive style, and people in lower positions may grow more and more adaptive in their cognitive style, as defined in the Kirton adaption–innovation style dimension.

Similarly, Hill et al. (2000) concluded that the difference in managers and nonmanagers' scores on the Cognitive Style Index was highly significant for the Finland and U.K. groups, although not for the Polish group. Yet, statistically significant or not, in all three groups, the direction of the correlation is identical: Managers were more intuitive than nonmanagers. Usually, people in leadership positions would have gained relatively more work experience in their occupation. As noted earlier, rich experiences tend to facilitate intuitive—the "simply know how"—type of thinking (Hill et al., 2000).

The difference in intellectual styles between people in leadership and nonleadership positions has been found in many empirical studies (e.g., Barrie, 2002; Hardy, 1997). Results of Powell and Butterfield's (1978) review suggest that within organizational climates, there are subclimates formed by the perceptions of people of the same position in the organizational hierarchy. That is, people in the same position tend to perceive their work environment in a similar fashion. Capitalizing on Powell and Butterfield's conclusion drawn from the available studies at the time, and based on the research evidence mentioned earlier, we argue that people who are socialized in the same work environment in the same position often tend to develop similar intellectual styles. That is, people's intellectual styles can be socialized in the workplace.

Length of Service/Seniority. Length of service/seniority is yet another variable that has been examined in relation to people's intellectual styles. All existing studies assessed employees' KAI scores and all studies were conducted in work settings that primarily required an adaptive style, rather than an innovative style. This research has consistently indicated that longer serving and senior-level employees are more adaptive than innovative in their cognitive style.

For example, Hayward and Everett (1983) studied the styles of managers within a local authority in the United Kingdom. They found that staff who served more than 5 years were much more adaptive, as opposed to innovative, than were those who served less than 5 years in the local authority. Holland's (1987) study of managers working in branches of U.K. clearing banks suggested that established managers (who also served in the bank industry for a longer period of time) were more adaptive than were trainee managers (who served for a shorter period of time). Likewise, Holland, Bowskill, and Bailey's (1991) investigation of employees from a large British pharmaceutical company revealed a significant difference in KAI scores between the newest entrants (under 1 year of service) and those with more than 3 years service in the two adaptive departments (line managers and programmers).

In accounting for this phenomenon of the "narrowing gap" (i.e., as one stays longer in an organization, one's cognitive style becomes more like that of the established group) between the newest entrant groups and the more established groups in these adaptive departments, Hayward and Everett (1983; see also Lindsay, 1985; Thomson, 1985) resorted to studying labor turnover in organizations. It is imaginable that people whose styles mismatch with those of their organizations tend to leave their jobs; as a result, the ones who stay in the organizations are those whose styles tend to fit in better with the styles of their workplace. However, for at least two reasons, labor turnover in the context of these studies should not be the sole factor used to account for the finding. First, none of the studies provided any data for labor turnover, nor was there any information about the cognitive styles of those who left the organizations. Second, none of the studies was longitudinal.

Holland and his colleagues (Holland, 1987; Holland et al., 1991) believed that cognitive style is not the only factor at work in labor turnover; individuals may leave for reasons other than a mismatch of cognitive style. However, these authors did not fully emphasize the importance of the socialization effect of the experiences associated with people's length of service in an organization. We believe that the more adaptive style found in longer serving and more senior staff is at least in part the result of socialization. There was a high correlation between age and seniority (which is associated with length of service) in Holland's study, whereas there was a higher correlation between age and length of service in Hayward and Everett's study. The tendency for being adaptive among the senior/longer-serving employees, therefore, could be simply a result of socialization effect due to age and/or length of service. As people grow older and serve an organization for a longer period of time, their way of thinking becomes more in tune with the cognitive climate of their organization. The organizations involved in these studies (e.g., local government, branch banks, programming development, and line management departments) are adaptively oriented organizations. Therefore, people who worked in such organizations for a longer period of time would become more adaptive. In fact, in an organization such as the local authority investigated in Hayward and Everett's study, employees at the junior and intermediate levels (those with less than 5 years of service) scored much higher ($M = 110.8$) than the general population. That is, compared with the general population, the junior- and intermediate-level employees were much more innovative. Yet, they were still working in the organization. Such data indicate that the argument for "labor turnover due to style mismatch" is ill grounded. Holland, Bowskill, and Bailey (1987) concluded that there was no direct link between the KAI and job satisfaction (see Ettlie & O'Keefe, 1982; Goldsmith, McNeilly, & Russ, 1989). Job satisfaction can be conversely related to labor turnover. If there is no direct link between the KAI and job satisfaction, there should not be any direct link between the KAI and labor turnover. Again, the socialization effects of age and length of service seem to be a more plausible explanation for the finding than is labor turnover.

Summary. Although investigations of the relationships between intellectual styles and demographic characteristics are meager, existing empirical evidence indicates that a number of variables are likely to play an important role in the socialization process of people's intellectual styles. These are age, gender, education, work position, and length of service.

Occupational Groups

Substantial research has been done investigating characteristic intellectual styles that particular occupational groups tend to have. In general, the available results indicate that people's intellectual styles differ as a function of their occupations. In the following, we summarize some of the major findings and explain why this research supports our argument that intellectual styles are socialized.

Research on intellectual styles characteristic of occupational groups is grounded in Kirton's adaption–innovation style dimension. The two exceptions identified in the literature are Hardy (1997) and Kanske's (1999) studies. The former found that the dominant learning style of middle managers employed in the banking industry was visual, whereas the latter revealed that convergence is the predominant learning style of pilots of U.S. Air Force aircraft.

Much research on the Kirton adaption–innovation dimension has been devoted to the distribution of different occupational groups on the KAI. As mentioned earlier, data from several cultures indicate that among the general population, KAI scores form a normal distribution, with a mean of 96 and a standard deviation of 17.9. However, when people's styles are studied within the context of occupational groups, their mean KAI scores tended to fall either above or below the KAI theoretical mean, depending on their occupations. Accountants, bank employees, nurses, and occupational groups involved in various forms of production tended to fall on the adaptive end of the Kirton continuum (e.g., Foxall, 1986a; Hayward & Everett, 1983;

Kirton & Pender, 1982; Thomson, 1980). On the contrary, employees working in such organizations as research and development, marketing, personnel, and planning tended to fall on the innovative end of the continuum (e.g., Foxall, 1986a; Foxall & Payne, 1989; Keller & Holland, 1978a; Lowe & Taylor, 1986; Thomson, 1980). These findings are not surprising. Those occupational groups (mentioned above) whose Kirton means fall on the adaptive side are those who usually deal with tasks that are more stable and structured in nature. Working on these tasks requires people to be more adaptive than innovative. However, the nature of the tasks dealt with in the latter occupational groups is such that people who work in these occupations are required to be more innovative rather than adaptive.

Indeed, when Foxall, Payne, and Walters (1992) discussed the adaptors and innovators in organizations, they explained how the nature of an organization determines employees' cognitive styles. Organizations that operate in relatively more stable and predictable environments tend to be more mechanistically structured (Burns & Stalker, 1961). Such organizations (e.g., banks and local authorities) put strong emphasis on continuity and efficiency. Managers working in these organizations, therefore, tended to be more adaptive (e.g., Foxall, 1986a; Gryskiewicz, Hills, Holt, & Hills, 1986; Hayward & Everett, 1983; P. Holland, 1985; Kirton & Pender, 1982; Thomson, 1980). At the same time, other organizations (e.g., research and development agencies and market-oriented industries) tend to operate in relatively more dynamic and unpredictable environments and are likely to be more organically structured (Burns & Stalker, 1961). Rendering good management in such organizations often requires managers to be innovative in dealing with constant change in the outside world. Therefore, it should not be surprising that managers working in these organizations have been found to be more innovative (e.g., Foxall, 1986b; Gryskiewicz et al., 1986; Keller & Holland, 1978a; Kirton & McCarthy, 1988; Kirton & Pender, 1982; Lowe & Taylor, 1986; Thomson, 1980).

The socialization effect of occupational groups on people's intellectual styles is further evidenced by research findings indicating that employees of specific departments in an organization tended to have similar intellectual styles. For example, Pettigrew and King's (1997) study of 266 staff nurses working in 13 regional acute-care hospitals revealed that nurses working in different settings tended to have different cognitive styles. Nurses in pediatric, psychiatric, critical care, and medical–surgical settings obtained higher innovative scores, whereas nurses working in maternity, ambulatory, operating room, and postanesthesia settings obtained higher adaptive scores. Evidently, if a nurse works for a long time in a setting (such as any one of the former group) that requires generation of innovative ways of dealing with unpredictable situations, that nurse would develop a more innovative cognitive style. By contrast, a nurse who works in relatively more predictable hospital settings that require more routine work would tend to develop an adaptive style over a reasonable period of time.

Of course, one could always argue that the reason that people in the same occupations tend to have similar intellectual styles is largely because people with similar intellectual styles have chosen to enter the same occupations. Indeed, in his theory of career interest, Holland (1973) noted that people deliberately search for work environments that allow them to use their abilities, exercise their skills, and express their values (see also Osipow, 1969). To this, we add that people would also gravitate toward work environments that accommodate their intellectual styles.

However, this preselection of work environment does not mean that people's intellectual styles cannot be changed after they have worked in an organization for some time, at least for most people. An individual may enter an organization with somewhat similar styles as the climate/style of an organization. After working on tasks that require using a particular style(s) that is/are consistent with that/those of the organization, and after one interacts with people in that organization, one's intellectual style(s) tend(s) to be modified. It would be either the case that one's predominant intellectual style is strengthened, or that one is socialized to use a different style. According to Baker's (1968) theory of behavior settings, human environments (including work environments) often inadvertently have a coercive effect on the behaviors of people who inhabit them. Intellectual styles are manifested in behaviors. Therefore, intellectual styles can also be influenced by environments, including by occupational group settings. Torbit's (1981) research found that although counselor trainees had a general preference for divergent learning, practicing counselors were perceived to have a stronger preference for divergent learning. Such a finding signifies that people choose careers that are congruent with their learning styles and that they are further shaped to fit the learning norms of the career after they enter it.

Styles and Job Functions

Intellectual styles of people in nonacademic settings have also been examined against people's job functions. Broadly speaking, two dimensions of job functions have been studied in the context of intellectual styles. The first concerns internally oriented or externally oriented job functions. The second concerns job functions across boundaries (functional, professional, or social) or within boundaries.

Styles and Internally/Externally Oriented Job Functions. Based on his study of engineers in a firm, Kirton (1980) concluded that, regardless of the overall orientation of an organization, the tasks of specific departments can be divided into two major subfunctions: internally oriented and externally oriented. Furthermore, managers working for internally oriented departments tend to be more adaptive; managers working for externally oriented departments tend to be more innovative. These findings have subsequently been confirmed by Foxall and his colleagues' empirical work (e.g., Foxall, 1990; Foxall & Payne, 1989; Foxall, Payne, & Walters, 1992).

For example, Foxall (1990) supported Kirton's findings when investigating the Kirton styles among a group of 78 marketing managers working for a large pan-European business organization. Participants were divided into two subfunctional groups (a subfunctional group refers to a group that serves one of the key functions integral to the major function of an organization), depending on brief career details and resumes. The internally oriented group included participants whose work required an awareness of the firm's external environment (because they worked for a marketing department). However, these participants' day-to-day interactions were essentially internally directed. They were marketing administrators, brand/product managers, marketing services managers, market forecasters and analysts. The participants in the externally oriented group were engaged in tasks that required a predominantly external orientation. These tasks demanded that they frequently, if not constantly, interact with external agencies, normally on behalf of the whole organization. This subgroup was composed of marketing strategists and planners, marketing directors, and marketing and sales managers. The mean of the internally oriented subgroup was significantly more adaptive ($M = 100.21$, $SD = 8.21$, $n = 34$) than that of the externally oriented subgroup ($M = 112.66$, $SD = 9.88$, $n = 44$; $t = 6.64$, $p < .001$).

In a second study, Foxall, Payne, and Walters (1992) investigated the Kirton styles of 123 midcareer managers attending Master of Business Administration (MBA) programs at three Australian business schools. Results showed that three (general management, engineering, and accounting/finance) of the five broadly defined managerial functions were divisible into internally and externally oriented subfunctions. The failure to divide the other two broadly defined functions (marketing and operations/production) into internally and externally oriented subfunctions was attributed to the small number of participants in each group. Furthermore, the Kirton means of each pair of the subfunctions were different, with that for the externally oriented subfunctional group being higher (i.e., more innovative) than that for the internally oriented subfunctional group. A final study was conducted among samples of British and Australian midcareer managers who were also undertaking MBA programs. Results again supported the previous findings (see also Kirton & Pender, 1982).

How then do we account for the difference in the cognitive styles between the internally oriented and externally oriented functional groups? Again, one could argue that this difference is attributable to people's preselection of careers. One could also argue that this difference is partially a result of labor turnover. We believe that this difference is also attributable to the socialization effects of job functions (task orientations). Regardless of the overall orientation of an organization, when one's primary job function concerns the maintenance of existing operations, and when one interacts mainly with one's immediate supervisors or coworkers (i.e., internally oriented), one works within the confines of the existing system. The tasks they deal with tend to require them to promote the continuity and efficiency of an organization. That is, their job functions require them to be adaptive. On the contrary, when one's primary job function concerns tasks such as planning and designing new products, and when one constantly interacts with people outside their immediate work environment, one works beyond the confines of the existing system. The tasks they deal with tend to require them to be more innovative so that their organization can successfully compete against the outside world. Furthermore, for both the internally oriented and externally oriented groups, the more experience they have in dealing with their respective tasks, the higher they score on each respective style: The internally oriented group scores higher on the adaptive style, and the externally oriented group scores higher on the innovative style (see earlier sections on styles and age/length of service).

Styles and Across/Within-Boundaries Job Functions. As early as 1978 (Kirton, 1978a; also Kirton, 1980; Kirton & Pender, 1982), there was empirical evidence indicating that groups whose focus of operations is across boundaries tend to have a more innovative style. These boundaries can be functional (e.g., people dealing with externally oriented tasks), social (e.g., women in leadership positions), or professional (e.g., people of one gender working in an occupation dominated by the opposite gender). Furthermore, the more boundaries one crosses, the more innovative one is in cognitive style. This research evidence was supported by subsequent studies.

Foxall (1990) compared the Kirton mean scores of midcareer managers who were undertaking MBA programs from three different cultural groups: Australia, the United Kingdom, and the United States. The Kirton mean for the American managers was significantly lower than the means of both the Australian and the British groups. Foxall asserted that the finding was not unexpected as, according to Kirton's earlier finding, individuals who engage in activities that are not commonplace for the groups to which they belong tend to be more innovative. In the late 1980s, although MBA programs were commonplace in the United States, they were still relatively rare in the United Kingdom and Australia. Therefore, an advanced managerial education such as an MBA in the United Kingdom or Australia was given relatively higher social status than getting the same degree in the United States. Thus, the finding lent support to Kirton's (1989) argument that divergence from accepted social norms (i.e., crossing social boundaries) is normally carried out by more innovative people. This finding has implications for the nature of style malleability. People who are successful in taking up occupations that deviate from social norms would have run into and overcome many obstacles. Yet, to overcome difficulties, people need to be more innovative. That is, people are challenged to be innovative thinkers in the process of working toward their goals. Because an MBA program was less commonplace in Australia and in the United Kingdom than in the United States, getting into such a program required innovative thinkers. Namely, the British and Australian managers in the MBA programs had more opportunities to be socialized into innovation than did the American managers.

Similarly, Tullett (1995) found that the Kirton mean score for managers of projects that involved the implementation of significant change initiatives in their organizations was significantly higher than that for managers in general. Tullett asserted that this finding was expected because project managers often work across functional boundaries. The nature of the tasks is such that the managers of change projects were often confronted by new situations. These managers became more innovative in the process of taking up the challenges of new situations. That is to say, their cognitive style was socialized to become more innovative.

In the context of discussing the relationship between styles and gender, we have provided research evidence indicating that women with a nontraditional occupational status have a propensity for using intellectual styles that foster creativity (e.g., innovative and intuitive styles; see for example Hill et al., 2000; Tullett, 1995). Research lends support to Kirton's argument that the more boundaries people cross, the more innovative they are in their thinking. For example, female managers in engineering cross all three boundaries: social, professional, and functional. First, these women crossed the social boundary by going outside their homes into the workplace. Second, they crossed the professional boundary of working in a field that is still dominated by men. Third, by taking up leadership positions, these women also crossed the boundary of working within their internal organizational structures. Instead, they often worked with people beyond their own organizations (see Tullett, 1995, 1997).

Styles and Cultures

Culture is yet another variable that has been empirically proved to play an important role in the socialization of people's intellectual styles. In the previous section, we presented Foxall's work (Foxall, 1990), which found that midcareer managers in Australia and the United Kingdom were more innovative than those in the United States. Earlier, we explained this result in light of the degree of novelty that an MBA carries in each culture. The result could also mean that different cultural environments cultivate different degrees of innovative thinking. As a matter of fact, this style difference as a function of national origin is consistent with findings from previous studies using the KAI. It is true that similar Kirton mean scores have been produced in the study of general population samples from many countries, ranging from the United States and Canada (e.g., Ettlie & O'Keefe, 1982; Gryskiewicz et al., 1987; Kirton, 1980) to New Zealand (e.g., Kirton, 1978b), and from the United Kingdom (e.g., Kirton, 1980) to Asian countries such as Singapore and Malaysia (e.g., Thomson, 1980). However, other studies (e.g., Hossaini, 1981; Khaneja, 1982) revealed that Indian and Iranian samples were significantly more adaptive than samples from the other countries mentioned above. Kirton (1988) concluded: "Clearly there may be cultural differences in adaptor–innovator norm" (p. 74).

Studies using other style inventories in nonacademic settings also revealed cross-cultural differences in styles. For example, using Kolb's (1976) Learning Style Inventory, Ahmad and Varghese (1991) found that Indian managers were more concrete and active than were their Western counterparts. Using their (1996) Cognitive Style Index (CSI), Allinson and Hayes (1997) obtained higher scores for intuition in Western countries and lower scores for the Far East, developing countries, and Arab nations. Using both Allinson and Hayes's (1996) CSI and Honey and Mumford's (1986) Learning Styles Questionnaire, Hill, Alker, Houghton, and Kennington (1998) found that managers from former Soviet countries scored higher on the analysis and reflection scales than did their Western counterparts. Also using the Honey and Mumford inventory, Sitko-Lutek, Kennington, and Rakowska (1998) found that Polish managers were more reflective than were their American, British, and Canadian counterparts. As a final example, using Allinson and Hayes's (1996) CSI, Hill and her colleagues (Hill et al., 2000) found that British managers obtained higher intuitive scores than did their Finnish and Polish counterparts.

With the abundant empirical evidence demonstrating people's differences in intellectual styles as a function of their culture, we cannot help but argue for the socialization effects of culture on people's intellectual styles. We believe that culture (cultures being gender culture, socioeconomic culture, organizational culture, and so forth) affect people's way of processing information. Yiu and Saner (2000) contended that nationalities and their respective cultures affect individuals in numerous interconnected ways, including their cognitive schemas (see also Hambrick, Davison, Snell, & Snow, 1998). Similarly, Hofstede (1991) stated that culture is the programming of the mind. From their empirical data, Mesquita and Frijda (1992) concluded that culture not only influences what we know to be true, but also affects how we perceive and process new information. Berry (1976) declared that intellectual style is a cultural phenomenon.

Summary of the Issue of Style Malleability

This section provides empirical evidence indicating that intellectual styles are malleable. Research indicates that people's intellectual styles differ as a function of various factors, including demographic characteristics (e.g., age, gender, and education, work position, and length of service), occupational groups, job functions, and culture. Intellectual styles are far from decontextualized. Instead, people develop particular intellectual styles partially as a result of individual, occupational, and cultural socialization. Furthermore, very often, these factors interact to exert impact on the development of intellectual styles.

ARE STYLES VALUE-FREE?

To address the issue of the value of intellectual styles, we examined studies that fall into three categories. The first category concerns the relationships between intellectual styles and task performance. The second pertains to people's perceptions of particular intellectual styles. The third relates to the relationships between intellectual styles and personality traits. Findings from this body of literature suggest that intellectual styles are essentially value-laden, and that they are, at times, value-differentiated. However, they are not value-free.

Styles and Task Performance

Studies investigating the relationships of intellectual styles with task performance (on the job or on tests) revealed the value-laden nature of styles. Some styles clearly carry more adaptive value than do others.

For example, Sayles-Folks and Harrison (1989) investigated the relationship between the impulsive/reflective styles and rated work behavior among 102 clients with mental retardation or mental illness who were enrolled in work activity programs in a vocational rehabilitation center. Results indicated that, compared with the patients with an impulsive cognitive style, reflective patients were rated as having more positive work abilities, less bizarre behaviors, more appropriate interpersonal behavior, and more positive overall work adjustment.

Wegner (1980) studied the relationship between field dependence/independence and managerial dispositions among 227 first-line foremen working at a heavy industrial manufacturing facility. Wegner concluded that field-independent foremen were the ones who received more education and that their leadership patterns were more in line with the underlying assumptions of Theory Y as defined by McGregor (1960). On the contrary, field-dependent foremen tended to have received less education and their leadership patterns were more in line with the underlying assumptions of Theory X. In his book *The Human Side of Enterprise*, McGregor (1960) examined available theories on behavior of individuals at work at the time and formulated two models that he calls Theory X and Theory Y. Theory X assumes that human beings have an inherent dislike of work and that they are irresponsible. Thus, they need to be given orders at work. Leaders believing in Theory X tend to give their subordinates little autonomy at work. Theory Y assumes that the experience of physical and mental effort in work is as natural as play or rest. The average person learns, under proper conditions, not only to accept but also to seek responsibility. Leaders believing in Theory Y tend to provide much more autonomy to their subordinates. In most cultures and under most circumstances, people prefer to be treated as responsible human beings (i.e., they prefer Theory Y). Being associated with the use of Theory Y, the field-independent style is regarded as carrying more positive value than the field-dependent style.

These findings relevant to the reflectivity/impulsivity and field-dependence/independence constructs are consistent with those obtained in research conducted among populations of academic settings discussed in chapter 3. In academic settings, the reflective and independent styles have been found to be consistently associated with higher achievement and with personality traits that are normally perceived to be positive (e.g., higher levels of assertiveness, self-esteem, and moral maturity), whereas the impulsive and field-dependent styles are consistently associated with the kinds of personality traits that are typically perceived to be negative (e.g., lower levels of assertiveness, self-esteem, and moral maturity).

Studies using the Kirton Adaption–Innovation Inventory indicated that the performance of innovators is superior to that of adaptors. For instance, among 156 administrative and professional staff from British advertising and design industries, Gelade (1995) found that innovators had better performance on Guilford and Guilford's (1980) Consequences and Alternate Uses tests. On the Consequences test, the innovators produced a higher number of uncommon responses than did the adaptors. Meanwhile, on the Alternate Uses test, the innovators also produced more responses than did the adaptors. Similarly, among 34 senior British managers working for a local government planning authority, Foxall and Hackett (1992) found that innovators employed a significantly larger number of software applications. This indicates that the innovators are more willing to adapt to the rapid change in organizations in which the employment of modern technology is required more and more.

Finally, using the Cognitive Style Index (Allinson & Hayes, 1996), Allinson, Armstrong, and Hayes (2001) studied 142 manager–subordinate dyads

in two large British manufacturing organizations. Compared with the analytic leaders, the intuitive leaders were less dominating and more nurturing.

Perceptions of Styles

Empirical work examining people's perceptions about or attitudes toward
particular intellectual styles indicates that although styles are occasionally
viewed as value-differentiated (e.g., Keller & Holland, 1978b), in that the
same style is more valued in one situation than it is in another situation, the
majority of empirical findings point to the value-laden nature of intellectual styles.

For example, in summarizing research on the relationship between psychological differentiation and different forms of pathology, Witkin (1965)
pointed out that field-independent patients were predicted to be better
candidates for change, and that field-dependent patients were not preferred by psychotherapists. Streufert and Nogami (1989) concluded that
even though there are certain tasks where field dependence could be of
greater value, in most employment categories, field independence is more
valued.

In the arena of international human resource management, researchers
have found that successful expatriates differed in cognitive styles from less
successful ones. For example, Avallone (1997) found that the intuitive–
feeler and intuitive–thinker type pairs on the Myers–Briggs Type Indicator
were the most suitable for working as expatriates. Yiu and Saner (2000) proposed that higher level of cognitive complexity distinguishes successful ex-
patriate managers from less successful ones.

Styles and Personality Traits

The value-laden nature of intellectual styles is also evident in the context of
the relationships between styles and personality traits. Some styles (e.g., innovative and field independent) are related to personality traits that are
normally perceived to carry more adaptive value, such as higher levels of
self-confidence and self-esteem, optimism, flexibility, and tolerance of ambiguity, whereas other styles (e.g., adaptive and field dependent) are associated with personality traits that often are considered to carry less adaptive
value, such as lower levels of self-confidence and self-esteem, and higher
levels of pessimism, rigidity, dogmatism, intolerance of ambiguity, and depression.

For example, in a sample of 256 professional employees from three applied research and development organizations, Keller and Holland (1978a,
1978b) found that people who obtained higher innovative scores on the
KAI achieved higher scores on a self-esteem measure and manifested lower

need for clarity and more tolerance of ambiguity (see also Kirton, 1976). Similarly, Hill and her colleagues (Hill et al., 2000) found that managers who were high on Kirton scores indicated a stronger feeling of self-confidence. Positive relationship was also found between employees' innovative scores and their expressed level of self-efficacy for doing creative work (see Tierney, 1997).

Furthermore, Kirton (1976) has suggested that people who obtained higher scores on the KAI scored lower on the Dogmatism Scale of Rokeach (1960). By the same token, Goldsmith (1984) found a negative relationship between the Kirton scores and the Dogmatism Scale by Trodahl and Powell (1965). However, Kirton scores were positively associated with scores on the flexibility scale on the California Psychological Inventory (Gough, 1975; see e.g., Gryskiewicz, 1982; Gryskiewicz et al., 1987; Kirton, 1976).

Research on Witkin's field dependence/independence indicated that the field-independent style generally was more adaptive than the field-dependent style. For example, in a sample of 37 post-cholecystectomy patients, Wise, Hall, and Wong (1978) found a positive relationship between field dependence and depression. Also, for example, when studying the relationship between field dependence/independence and job satisfaction among a sample of 504 registered staff nurses, Hageman (1990) made two hypotheses. First, among nurses working in settings that allowed little autonomy, field-dependent nurses would be more satisfied than field-independent nurses. Second, among nurses working in settings that allowed great autonomy, field-independent nurses would be more satisfied than field-dependent nurses. However, only the second hypothesis was supported.

One would argue that the field-independent style carries more adaptive value than does the field-dependent style because the former is associated with healthier mental states such as lower (or no) depression and higher levels of satisfaction with one's work and coworkers. In fact, Wunderley, Reddy, and Dember (1998) confirmed this positive relationship between a style with more adaptive value (i.e., the innovative style defined by Kirton) and a healthier state of mind: optimism.

Summary of the Issue of Style Value

In this section, we provide empirical evidence suggesting that intellectual styles are value-laden. Cross-examining the findings relevant to the three topics discussed previously, we found that certain styles (e.g., reflective, field independent, intuitive, and innovative) are consistently associated with better performance (on the job or on tests) and more adaptive personality traits. Moreover, they are perceived in a more positive light. By contrast, the opposite of the above styles (i.e., impulsive, field dependent, analytic, and adaptive) are consistently associated with lower performance and less adaptive personality traits. Furthermore, they tend to be perceived more negatively. Therefore, intellectual styles are value-laden.

Finally, we conclude this section with a caveat. Although existing empirical evidence points to the value-laden nature of intellectual styles and none has demonstrated the value-differentiated nature of styles, we would like to acknowledge such value-differentiation. That is, the same style that carries more adaptive value in one setting may have less adaptive value in a different situation. For example, the innovative style may be highly valued by a work setting that requires innovative thinking. However, using the same style in a work setting that requires adaptive thinking can only lead to less than satisfactory results.

DO DIFFERENT STYLE CONSTRUCTS OVERLAP WITH ONE ANOTHER?

Empirical evidence indicting the intertwined relationships among styles is also abundant in nonacademic settings. The most frequently researched style constructs are decision-making styles as measured by the KAI (Kirton, 1976), personality styles as measured by the Myers–Briggs Type Indicator (MBTI, Myers, 1962; Myers & McCaulley, 1988), mind styles as measured by the Gregorc Style Delineator (Gregorc, 1982), perceptual styles as measured by the (Group) Embedded Figures Test (Witkin, Oltman, Raskin, & Karp, 1971), and learning styles as measured by Kolb's (1976) Learning Style Inventory.

As a measure of style construct, the KAI has been tested against the Myers–Briggs Type Indicator, the Gregorc Style Delineator, and the Group Embedded Figures Test. Kirton's adaptive–innovative decision-making style was related to both personality type and mind style. Fleenor and Taylor (1994) examined the relationships between the MBTI Creativity Index (Gough, 1987) and the KAI among 12,115 managers participating in a leadership program. They found that 57% of the variance in the KAI scores was accounted for by the MBTI Creativity Index scores. Carne and Kirton (1982), Goldsmith (1986), Jacobson (1993), and Gryskiewicz and Tullar (1995) independently found that Kirton's adaptors tended to belong to the MBTI sensing and judging personality types. Kirton's innovators were more likely to belong to the MBTI intuitive and perceiving personality types. In studying the relationship between adaption–innovation and field dependence/independence, Robertson, Fournet, Zelhart, and Estes (1987) found that innovators were less field dependent than were adaptors and "average" individuals.

There is also a significant relationship between the MBTI and the Gregorc Style Delineator (GSD). In general, people who are high on the Concrete Sequential scale of the GSD tend to be sensing and judging types in the MBTI, whereas people who score high on the Concrete Random scale of the GSD tend to be intuitive and perceiving types (e.g., Bokoros, Goldstein, & Sweeney, 1992; Stuber, 1997).

Joniak and Isaken (1988) examined the relationship between Gregorc's mind styles and Kirton's decision-making styles. Irrespective of concreteness or abstractness, people of sequential types were adaptors, whereas people of random types were innovators.

Finally, the relationship between personality styles as measured by the MBTI and Kolb's learning styles have also been investigated. After examining this relationship in a sample of middle and upper level civilian managers of the United States Army, Konopka (1999) claimed that strong and consistent relationships existed between Kolb's concrete/abstract style dimension and the MBTI feeling/thinking dimension. The same was claimed for the relationship between Kolb's active/reflective dimension and the MBTI extrovert/introvert dimension. Penn (1991) investigated the relationship between the MBTI and the LSI among 229 army nurses. Significant relationships were found between learning styles and the MBTI introversion–extroversion. Accommodators tended to be extroverted, whereas assimilators tended to be introverted.

Summary of the Issue of Style Overlap

This section reviews studies examining the relationships among several different style constructs. Results clearly point to the interconnections among intellectual styles. Invariably, styles underlying one (style) construct overlap with those underlying another construct. Yet, no two style constructs are exactly the same. Although different style constructs share certain degrees of similarities, each style construct makes its unique contribution.

CONCLUSIONS AND FUTURE RESEARCH

This chapter reviews major investigations of intellectual styles among nonacademic populations. Findings presented in this chapter support the conclusions we made about the nature of intellectual styles as they relate to the three controversial issues in the preceding chapters.

In examining this literature, we noted three major limitations that need to be overcome in future investigation of intellectual styles in nonacademic settings. First, research based on more recent style models does not exist in the literature of styles among nonacademic populations. Second, existing studies are limited to investigating in only a few occupations (e.g., government, human resource management organization, industry, hospital, and army). Third, qualitative research is nonexistent. Thus, there is a need for more recently proposed styles to be studied in nonacademic contexts.

Part III

EMPIRICAL STUDIES: INTEGRATIVE MODELS AND THE THEORY OF MENTAL SELF-GOVERNMENT

Chapter 6

Existing Integrative
Models of Styles

As discussed in chapter 2, motivated by bringing some order to the field of styles, several scholars have attempted to conceptually integrate the massive number of different labels for styles. Among these efforts, four major integrative models of styles particularly stand out. The first is Curry's (1983) "onion" model of learning styles. The second is Miller's (1987) model of cognitive processes and styles. The third is Riding and Cheema's (1991) integrative model of cognitive styles. The fourth and the most recent is Grigorenko and Sternberg's (1995; Sternberg, 1988, 1997) model of style traditions. We consider each in turn and complete the chapter by comparing and contrasting the four models.

CURRY'S "ONION" MODEL

The Model

The Original Model. Based on psychometric evidence and reviews of written documentation about learning style measures, Curry (1983) proposed that nine of the major learning style measures can be organized into three layers resembling those of an onion. The innermost layer of the style onion is composed of measures of personality dimensions, including Witkin's (1962) Embedded Figures Test, Myers' (1962) Myers–Briggs Type Indicator, and Kagan's (1965c) Matching Familiar Figures Test. These measures, according to Curry, assess cognitive personality styles that are defined as an individual's approach to adapting and assimilating information. Cognitive personality styles are believed to be relatively permanent. The middle layer comprises style measures that assess information processing, including Kolb's (1976) Learning Style Inventory, Tamir and Cohen's (1980) Cognitive Preference Inventory (CPI), and Schmeck, Ribich, and Ramaniah's (1977) Inventory of Learning Processes (ILP). An information-processing style represents an individual's way of taking in information as interpreted by the classic information-processing model (i.e., orienting, sensory registering, short-term memory, enhanced associations, coding system, and long-term memory). The outermost layer of the onion consists of measures assessing individuals' instructional preferences, including Friedman and Stritter's (1976) Instructional Preference Questionnaire, Rezler and Rezmovic's (1981) Learning Preference Inventory, and Riechmann and Grasha's (1974) Grasha Riechmann Student Learning Style Scales (SLSS). Instructional preference is defined as an individual's choice of learning environment. Curry (1983) believed that people's instructional preference is modified by person–environment interactions.

The Expanded Model. In her 1987 work, Curry expanded her onion model to include 21 style inventories. In this model, the three style constructs in the innermost layer remain the same. To the outermost layer, such style constructs as Canfield's (1980) learning styles and Dunn, Dunn, and Price's (1986) learning styles were added. To the middle layer, such constructs as Biggs' (1979) learning approaches and Entwistle's (1981) study approaches were added. Hickcox (1995) provided comprehensive information about the psychometric properties of the inventories in the model.

Conceptual Foundation

In defending her model, Curry (1983) maintained that a content analysis of the instruments indicated that, across instruments, there were parallels in focus and subscale content groups. For example, uniting three instruments in the outermost layer of the onion model is the notion of students' preference for working at a pace and on material they select themselves, as opposed to having the teacher or a peer group choose for them. The three instruments also assess how much structure an individual prefers. Central to all three inventories in the middle layer of the model is the learner's predilection either for concrete experience and simple reproduction of facts or for reflection and critical analysis of information. Finally, a common concern shared by all three instruments in the innermost layer of the model is the deep structure of personality.

Testable Structures

In her 1983 article, Curry pointed out that the validity of this model should be supported by data indicating the following two results: First, the three measures in any one layer of this model should assess the same thing, or at least the three measures should be more closely related to one another than they are to measures from the other two layers. Second, the innermost layer (cognitive personality) should be shown psychometrically to be essential to the other two layers. Moreover, in her proposed design for research, Curry (1983) pointed out that all research participants should respond to all nine instruments.

Controversial Issues Over Styles

Style Malleability. Curry's (1983) model has explicitly addressed the issue of malleability of styles. She did so by presenting results from an examination of the test–retest reliability data for the nine inventories. She further hypothesized that styles in the outermost layer of the onion (i.e., instructional preferences) should be the most modifiable and that styles in the innermost layer (i.e., personality styles) should be the most stable. That is to say, the degree of malleability determines where styles are placed in the successive layers. Some empirical evidence confirms this hypothesis. For example, Ingham (1989) validated the concept of nested levels in prediction patterns between learning styles in the middle layer and instructional formats in the outermost layer. The correlations among the styles within each layer were higher than were those among the styles across the two layers. Also using Curry's model, Melear (1989) explained the relationships between a then-new learning style inventory (The Learning Style Profile, Keefe & Monk, 1989) and the Myers–Briggs Type Indicator (MBTI, Myers & McCaulley, 1988). Similarly, Sewall (1989) tested Curry's model by examining the factor structure of three style measures: the Myers–Briggs Type Indictor, the Kolb Learning Style Inventory, and Canfield's (1980) Learning Styles Inventory. Sewall concluded that the issue of style stability (malleability) as hypothesized by Curry was partially confirmed by a general pattern of test–retest reliability coefficients. That is, the reliability coefficients were highest for the MBTI scales (cognitive personality layer), medium for Kolb's scales (information processing layer), and lowest for Canfield's scales (instructional preference layer).

Style Overlap. In addition to the studies just mentioned, several other studies were inspired by Curry's model. These studies, however, did not address the issue of style stability. Instead, they examined the association between different style constructs. For example, Beyler and Schmeck (1992) examined the relationships between Schmeck et al.'s (1977) Inventory of Learning Processes and the MBTI. Greenberg, Goldberg, and Foley (1996) tested the relationships between Rezler and Rezmovic's (1981) Learning Preference Inventory and the MBTI. Evidence from these empirical studies supports the notion that different style constructs significantly overlap with one another. However, these style constructs cannot be replaced by one another because each construct makes a unique contribution to the data.

Evaluation of the "Onion" Model

Curry's (1983, 1987) model pioneered the effort to bring together the massive diversity of style labels in the field. Rayner and Riding (1997) commented that the onion model represents a particularly useful effort to integrate cognition-, personality-, and activity-centered research. The model has served as the theoretical framework for a number of empirical studies, as reviewed earlier.

However, the model itself is not yet well researched. To begin with, in establishing her model, Curry (1983) used test–retest reliability data of the nine models to address the issue of style malleability/stability. Unfortunately, such data were absent for three of the nine inventories (i.e., Friedman and Stritter's IPQ, Riechmann and Grasha's SLSS, and Tamir and Cohen's CPI). Subsequent research has not reported such data either. Furthermore, some of the data provided do not rigorously support the hypothesis of style malleability/stability. For example, the test–retest reliability data for Kagan's inventory (average = .69, range = .46 to .92) from the cognitive personality layer are not, as theoretically argued, higher than the data for Schmeck et al.'s inventory (average = .83; range = .79 to .88) from the information-processing layer. In addition, the length of time between testing and retesting the different inventories varied from 7 days to 7 years.

Finally, thus far, hardly any effort has been made to obtain the two results that, according to Curry, should offer empirical evidence for the validity of the model. The only attempt made to administer all of the nine inventories included in the original model to all participants in the same research was Curry's (1991) study of "patterns of learning style" among professionals across a few selected medical specialties. However, the central goal of this study was merely to observe the style differences among professionals of different medical fields.

MILLER'S MODEL OF COGNITIVE PROCESSES AND STYLES

The second integrative model of intellectual styles is Miller's (1987) model of cognitive processes and styles. The major motivation for this model was to renew the interest in the study of styles among the scholarly community in the 1980s. To achieve this goal, Miller linked the then-waning field of intellectual styles to a more vigorous field of cognitive psychology—cognitive processes. Miller views cognitive styles as comprising individual differences in the various subcomponents of an information-processing model of three main types of cognitive processes: perception, memory, and thought. The two subprocesses of perception are pattern recognition and attention. The three subprocesses of memory are representation, organization, and retrieval. The three subprocesses of thought (also known as inductive reasoning) are classification, analogical reasoning, and judgment.

Miller suggested that all cognitive styles are subordinate to a broad stylistic dimension: analytic–holistic. The analytic style refers to the tendency for breaking down an object into different parts and examining each part as a separate entity, in isolation from its context. The holistic style refers to the propensity for perceiving objects as wholes, and as being integrated with the context in which they occur. According to Miller, at the analytic pole of this organization, there are such styles as field independence, sharpening, converging, and serial information processing; at the holistic pole, there are such styles as field dependence, leveling, diverging, and holistic information processing.

Miller (1987) argued that the analytic–holistic dimension is composed of cognitive styles, each contributing to a consistent individual difference in cognitive processing. For example, the leveling/sharpening styles should be related to pattern cognition. Similarly, the convergent/divergent styles should be associated with retrieval. The specific anticipated relationships between styles and cognitive processes are represented in Fig. 6.1 (in Miller, 1987).

However, as Messick (1994) has rightfully pointed out, this proposed organization of styles is merely a heuristic device, rather than a synthesis of empirical findings. We did a thorough search on the PsycInfo database, covering the empirical work between 1970 and December 2004. Results of this search revealed that there was still no empirical study particularly designed to test any part of this model. In conducting this search, however, we did identify empirical studies suggesting significant relationships between field-dependent/independent styles and two cognitive processes (memory and attention). The majority of these studies indicate a strong association between field-dependent/independent styles and memory. For example, in a sample

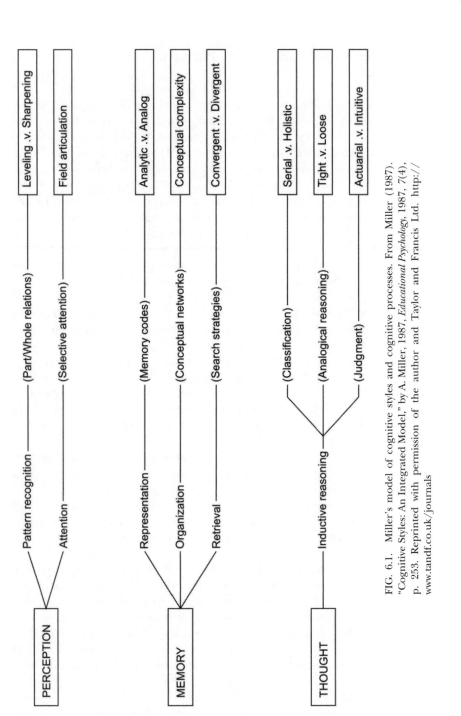

FIG. 6.1. Miller's model of cognitive styles and cognitive processes. From Miller (1987). "Cognitive Styles: An Integrated Model," by A. Miller, 1987, *Educational Psychology*, 7(4), p. 253. Reprinted with permission of the author and Taylor and Francis Ltd. http://www.tandf.co.uk/journals

of undergraduate students, Cochran and Davis (1987) found that working-memory capacity was larger for field-independent students than for field-dependent students. Results from the study of both undergraduate students and school students indicate that memory differences favor field-independent learners over field-dependent learners in memory tasks (e.g., Frank, 1983; Frank & Keene, 1993; Makkar, Malhotra, & Jerath, 1999). Mansfield (1998) concluded that field-independent children obtained better scores than did field-dependent children on all measures of working memory for all five age groups of participants (between ages 11 and 15). Davey's (1990) study of sixth- to eighth-grade readers indicated that field-independent children outperformed field-dependent children on tasks with high memory demands. By the same token, Goode, Goddard, and Pascual-Leone (2002) found that, compared with field-dependent college students, field-independent college students engaged in deeper working memory processing.

We also identified two studies that found significant relationships between field dependence/independence and attention. In one first study, Baillargeon, Pascual-Leone, and Roncadin (1998) administered the Children's Embedded Figures Test and the Figural Intersection Task (which assesses mental-attentional capacity) to 239 nine to 13-year-old children. In general, field-independent children obtained higher scores of mental-attentional capacity than did field-dependent children in the figural intersection task. In a second study, Goode et al. (2002) found that field-independent students had more mental-attentional resources than did field-dependent students.

The empirical studies just mentioned, although not intended for testing Miller's model of styles and cognitive processes, suggest a close relationship between styles (as represented by field dependence/independence) and two cognitive processes: memory and attention. This close relationship indicates a strong likelihood that significant relationships exist between the other styles and cognitive processes proposed in the model. Yet, the manner in which the styles and the cognitive processes are related to one another may not be limited to the way they have been paired in Miller's model. That is, unlike what is illustrated in Fig. 6.1, significant associations may be found between any one of the styles and any one of the cognitive processes (see Fig. 6.2). This prediction, though, also awaits empirical evidence.

Controversial Issues Over Styles

Style Value. Existing findings (all based on the study of field dependence/ independence) uniformly point to the value-laden nature of styles, with field independence carrying more adaptive value than field dependence. Field-independent students outperformed field-dependent students in all memory and attentional tasks.

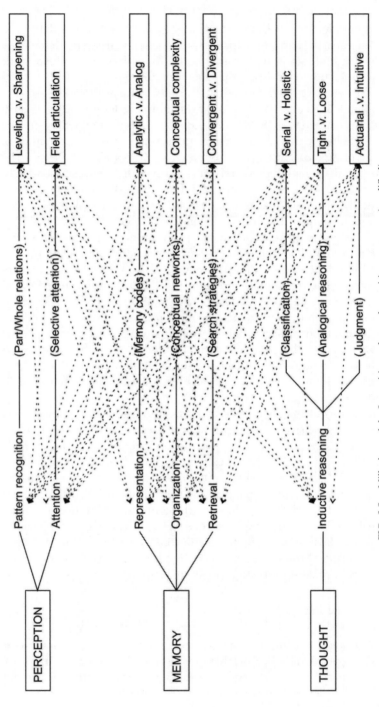

FIG. 6.2. Miller's model of cognitive styles and cognitive processes (modified).

Style Malleability. Miller (1987) believed that cognitive styles represent a way of characterizing stable individual differences. However, Miller did not assert that styles are unchangeable, nor is there any empirical proof suggesting that cognitive styles are nonmodifiable.

Style Overlap. Obviously, because the analytic–holistic dimension is an underlying principle of the styles in Miller's model (Jonassen & Grabowski, 1993), one would expect that the styles at the analytic pole (e.g., field independent, sharpening, convergent, and serial information processing) would overlap with one another, whereas styles at the holistic pole (e.g., field dependent, leveling, divergent, and holistic information processing) would overlap with one another. However, research evidence supporting this prediction has yet to be obtained. For example, existing studies indicate that, contrary to the prediction in which field independence and convergence should be positively related, field independence has been found to be related to the divergent style (e.g., Bloomberg, 1971; Noppe & Gallagher, 1977). Satterly (1979) found no relationship between leveling/sharpening and field dependence/independence.

Evaluation of Miller's Model

The major contribution of Miller's model lies in its attempt to link the field of intellectual styles with a vigorous field of study, that of cognitive psychology. Results from studies examining the relationships between styles and cognitive processes have potential to both cultivate people's tendency for using more adaptive styles and enhance people's ability to engage in more effective cognitive processes in problem solving. As illustrated earlier, initial and "unintended" empirical support has been found for the model. However, more research is needed to prove validity of the model.

Finally, there are two limitations to the model. First, the styles encompassed in the model are restricted to styles that are closely related to cognition. This arose from the fact that Miller intended to examine styles that are closely related to cognitive processes only. Although such a model has merit in allowing for focused investigation of the relationships between one type of styles (cognition-centered) and cognitive processes, it also has set its own limit in that it misses out on the remaining part of a larger picture depicting a much broader field of intellectual styles. Other kinds of styles, such as personality-centered and activity-centered styles (see Grigorenko and Sternberg's model in a later section of this chapter), are left out from this model.

The second limitation of this model lies in its bipolar organization of styles. Miller's integrative model only captures style models with bipolar styles. Models that address more than two styles are automatically excluded from this model.

RIDING AND CHEEMA'S MODEL

The third model is Riding and Cheema's (1991) integrative model of cognitive styles. Based on the descriptions, correlations, methods of assessment, and effects on behavior of more than 30 style labels, Riding and Cheema proposed that styles could be grouped into two principal cognitive-style dimensions (i.e., wholist–analytic and verbal–imagery) and a family of learning strategies. Concerning whether an individual tends to process information in wholes or does so in parts, the wholist–analytic dimension includes such style constructs as Witkin's (1962) field dependence/independence, Kagan's (1965a) impulsivity–reflectivity, Pask's (1972) holist–serialist, Holzman and Klein's (1954) leveler–sharpener, and Guilford's (1959) convergence–divergence. Pertaining to whether an individual has a tendency to represent information by thinking verbally or in terms of mental pictures, the verbalizer–imager dimension is composed of three style constructs: Bartlett's (1932) sensory modality preferences, Riding and Taylor's (1976) verbalizer–imager, and Richardson's (1977) verbalizer–visualizer. Included in the family of learning strategies are such constructs as Myers' (1962) personality types, Dunn, Dunn, and Price's (1975) learning styles, Kolb's (1976) diverger–assimilator–converger–accommodator, and Biggs' (1987) surface-deep learning approaches.

Cognitive Styles Analysis and Its Research

Going beyond theoretical integration of styles, Riding designed the Cognitive Styles Analysis (CSA, Riding, 1991) to measure two style dimensions. The CSA is a computer-based measure comprising three subtests, one assessing the verbal–imagery dimension, and the other two assessing the wholist–analytic dimension. The instrument works on the basis of responses to a series of 48 statements (to be judged true or false) and computes a ratio for both dimensions. No reliability data were reported by Riding (1991). The construct validity of the inventory was supported by the findings that the two style dimensions are independent of each other and that they are unrelated to intelligence (Riding & Pearson, 1994). Recently, Peterson, Deary, and Austin (2003) found that the wholist–analytic dimension reaches a satisfactory level of reliability only if the CSA is doubled in length.

There is good supporting empirical evidence for the two style dimensions. Many of the studies conducted by Riding and his colleagues are documented in Riding (1997) and Riding and Rayner (1998). The research indicates that the two cognitive style dimensions are associated with such elements of learning as learning performance, learning preferences, and subject preferences; with conduct behavior and occupational behavior; and with physical well-being. Furthermore, the two style dimensions have been tested in many empirical studies by other scholars (e.g., Adams, 2001; McKay, 2000; Russell, 1997).

Controversial Issues Over Styles

Style Overlap. In presenting this integrative model of styles, Riding and Cheema (1991) explicitly addressed the issue of style overlap. For example, the authors provided evidence indicating the significant relationships between Kagan's impulsivity–reflectivity and Witkin's field-dependence/independence constructs (see details in chap. 8). They also pointed out the lack of relationships of the convergent–divergent thinking styles and holist–serialist styles to other styles in the wholist–analytic dimension. Furthermore, Riding and Cheema noted that Riding and Dyer's (1983) study found that the leveler–sharpener styles loaded on the same factor as field dependence/independence, suggesting that the two constructs overlap. Finally, based on the descriptions, correlations, and methods of assessment and effects on behavior of relevant styles, Riding and Cheema asserted that the wholist end of the wholist–analytic style dimension should encompass field dependent, impulsive, leveling, divergent, and holist styles, and that the field independent, reflective, sharpening, convergent, and serialist styles should be subsumed under the analytic end of the wholist–analytic style dimension. However, Jones (1997a) countered that from a theoretical perspective, impulsive/reflective styles fit less well in the wholist–analytic style dimension. For example, one of the core criteria for the other styles in the wholist–analytic style dimension is Witkin's perceptual style. Jones (1997a) alleged that although the impulsive/reflective styles are often considered perception-based styles and are assessed through performance differences in perceptual tasks, it is harder to perceive these differences as the sole determinant factors. Thus, the impulsive/reflective styles can be studied independently from the remaining styles in the wholist–analytic style dimension.

Empirical studies that address the issue of style overlap by testing the relationships between the Cognitive Styles Analysis and other style measures are still at the anecdotal level. As reviewed in chapter 3, the CSA was found to be predictive of students' scores on Pask and Scott's (1972) holist–serialist style dimension (Ford, 1995). It was also found, however, that the CSA was not related to any of inventories that assess learning preferences and strategies (Sadler-Smith, 1997). The limited research evidence for the relationships of the CSA to the style constructs supposedly encompassed by the CSA warrants much further investigation.

Style Value.   As discussed in chapter 3, empirical findings on the relationships between the styles as assessed by the Cognitive Styles Analysis and personality traits speak to the issue of value of styles. It was argued that, although there is certain indication that the wholist and verbal styles (especially the two styles in combination) tend to carry undesirable value because they are significantly related to personality traits generally viewed as undesirable (Riding, Burton, Rees, & Sharratt, 1995; Riding & Wigley, 1997), the styles in the CSA are essentially value-differentiated (Riding & Wright, 1995) (see chap. 3 for details). However, these studies are confined to investigations among students. Further understanding of the nature of the styles measured by the CSA as they relate to the issue of value of styles can be achieved by research conducted in a wider range of populations, both academic and nonacademic.

Style Malleability.   Studies that deal with the issue of style malleability based on the Cognitive Styles Analysis barely exist. Based on the results from a study of 12-year-old children (Riding, Burton, Rees, & Sharratt, 1995), Riding and Rayner (1998) noted that there did not seem to be a significant relationship between cognitive styles (as measured by the CSA) and gender. In other words, gender may not be a major socialization factor in people's cognitive styles. Nevertheless, it should be pointed out that there is not enough evidence to draw any conclusion about the malleability of the cognitive styles as measured by the CSA.

Evaluation of Riding and Cheema's Model

As intended, Riding and Cheema's model has brought together various style models. The model has reasonably good empirical foundations. Moreover, as Jones (1997) put it, Riding and Cheema's (1991) work has served as a catalyst for cognitive-styles research. This research, although not designed to address any of the controversial issues over styles, can speak fairly well to the issues of style overlap and style value.

Nonetheless, research on the model itself is limited in several ways. First, evidence for reliability of the Cognitive Styles Analysis inventory is still preliminary, even though the inventory has been used in a reasonably large number of studies. Second, a deeper understanding of the issue of cognitive-style malleability (as assessed by the CSA) requires, at minimum, that the CSA be further examined against basic demographic features. Results from such studies would facilitate our understanding of the nature of cognitive styles measured by the CSA as they relate to the issue of style malleability. Third, studies need to be conducted that submit all styles encompassed by the two style dimensions to factor analysis. Such investigations may provide information on whether the styles in the same style dimension are significantly related to one another and whether the two style dimensions are orthogonal to each other. Finally, as previously mentioned, the CSA should be examined in a wider range of populations.

GRIGORENKO AND STERNBERG'S MODEL

The final and most recent endeavor in integrating works on styles is Grigorenko and Sternberg's (1995; Sternberg, 1997) model of style traditions. According to this model, work on styles takes one of three approaches (i.e., falls into one of three traditions): cognition centered, personality centered, and activity centered.

The Cognition-Centered Tradition

Styles in the cognition-centered tradition, often labeled as cognitive styles, grew out of the cognitive-styles movement in the 1950s and early 1960s. The motivation behind this movement was to provide a link between the study of cognition and the investigation of personality. Cognitive styles are defined as "the characteristic, self-consistent modes of functioning which individuals show in their perceptual and intellectual activities" (Witkin, Oltman, Raskin, & Karp, 1971, p. 3). The styles in this tradition (e.g., conceptual differentiation, Gardner & Schoen, 1962; reflectivity–impulsivity, Kagan, 1965a; leveling–sharpening, Holzman & Klein, 1954; field dependence/independence, Witkin, 1964) closely resemble abilities. Moreover, like abilities, styles in this tradition are measured by tests of maximal performance with "right" and "wrong" answers. Within this tradition, two models have aroused the most interest: Witkin's (1962) field dependence/independence model and Kagan's (1976) reflectivity–impulsivity model (see e.g., chaps. 3, 4, 5, and 8 for details).

The Personality-Centered Tradition

In trying to build a bridge between cognition and personality, scholars also have looked at personality styles as they relate to personality. Styles in the context of this tradition are defined as "deep-seated individual differences exercising a wide, but somewhat loose control over the domains of cognitive function, interest, values, and personality development" (Ross, 1962, p. 76). The personality-centered tradition considers styles as most closely resembling (although different from) personality traits. Furthermore, like personality traits, styles in this tradition are measured by tests of typical, rather than maximal, performance. Myers and McCaulley (1988) have done important work in this tradition, basing their ideas on Jung's (1923) theory of personality types. Holland's (1973, 1994) theory of vocational types and Gregorc's (1979) model of types of styles also fall into this tradition (see chap. 8 for details).

The Activity-Centered Tradition

The activity-centered tradition came into being in the late 1960s and early 1970s, when educators became more and more aware of the notion of styles (see Grigorenko & Sternberg, 1995). Styles in this tradition are often labeled as learning styles. Learning styles, in one common use of the term, are generally viewed as dealing with preferred ways of learning material (e.g., orally, visually, kinesthetically). The existing theories of learning styles vary considerably in their focus, ranging from addressing preferred sensory modalities (Renzulli & Smith, 1978) to delineating personality characteristics that have strong implications for learning behaviors (Bargar & Hoover, 1984). However, a commonality shared by styles in this tradition is that styles are perceived as mediators of activities that arise from both cognition and personality. One major group of works in this tradition is represented by similar theories of deep- and surface-learning approaches proposed by Marton (1976), Biggs (1978), Entwistle (1981), and Schmeck (1983). Moreover, Renzulli and Smith (1978) proposed different learning styles, with each corresponding to a method of teaching, such as discussion, drill and recitation, and lecturing.

Controversial Issues Over Styles

The three controversial issues over styles are not explicitly addressed in Grigorenko and Sternberg's (1995) model of style traditions. However, a careful reading of their work reveals that their model can speak to each of the three issues.

Style Malleability.   In the context of discussing the limitations of the activity-centered style theories, Grigorenko and Sternberg (1995) pointed out that the activity-centered tradition says little about the development of styles. They maintained that the cognition-centered and personality-centered theories do a better job discussing the change of styles in the context of overall intellectual and personality development.

Style Value.   Ideally, a style should not be "good" or "bad" in itself (Sternberg, 1997). However, it is inevitable that some styles are more valued in some contexts and less valued in others, especially in the case of the style constructs in the cognition-centered tradition. Because the styles in the cognition-centered tradition closely resemble abilities, those styles denoting higher ability levels (e.g., field independence and reflectivity) in task performance tend to be considered better than styles that indicate lower ability levels (e.g., field dependence and impulsivity). The issue of value of styles was not addressed in the context of the personality-centered and activity-centered traditions. Thus, one can assume that compared with the styles in the cognition-centered tradition, the styles in the latter two traditions are less value-laden.

Style Overlap. The issue of style overlap has also been implicitly addressed. In discussing the theories in the three traditions, Sternberg (1997) stated that "Although theories of styles differ, they cover a roughly common ground" (p. 147). Guided by this statement and illuminated by Grigorenko and Sternberg's (1995) claim that Sternberg's theory of mental self-government may act as "a wide-angle lens" (p. 207) that combines the thinking of the three approaches to the study of styles, the first author (and later, in collaboration with the coauthor) of this book investigated the relationships of the thinking style construct to style constructs from each of the three style traditions. These are Torrance's (1988) styles of learning and thinking from the cognition-centered tradition, Holland's (1973, 1994) career personality styles from the personality-centered tradition, and Biggs' (1978) learning approaches from the activity-centered approach. This research (see details in chap. 7) suggests that each of the three style constructs shares a common space with thinking styles in the theory of mental self-government. Recently, Zhang (2004d) found that Holland's personality styles and Biggs' learning styles also significantly overlapped.

Evaluation of Grigorenko and Sternberg's Model

Like Riding's model, Grigorenko and Sternberg's model allows for the inclusion of all existing style constructs. Furthermore, the merit of Grigorenko and Sternberg's model lies in the parallelism between two sets of constructs, with ability and personality as one set, and cognition-centered styles and personality-centered styles as the other. Although existing research has provided preliminary evidence for the heuristic value of this model in guiding empirical studies testing the relationships among different styles, the validity of Grigorenko and Sternberg's integrative model addressing three kinds of styles has yet to be systematically tested. Testable predictions for this model can be derived from Grigorenko and Sternberg's definition of each of the three approaches to the study of styles. We predict that any one style construct is more closely related to the other style constructs within the same approach than it is to styles from a different approach. We further predict the following relationships: (a) Cognition-centered styles are more closely related to abilities than are styles of the

other two approaches; (b) personality-centered styles are more closely related to personality traits than are styles from the other two approaches;
and (c) activity-centered styles are more closely related to learning activities
than are styles from the other two approaches.

COMPARING AND CONTRASTING THE FOUR
INTEGRATIVE MODELS

Obviously, although each has its limitations, all four integrative models
have achieved the goal of integrating existing style constructs to varying degrees. The four models are created by two different approaches: a systems
approach and an information-processing approach. Curry's and Grigorenko and Sternberg's models take the former approach; Miller's and
Riding and Cheema's models take the latter.

Both Curry's and Grigorenko and Sternberg's models classify existing
style constructs into three systems: personality dimensions, mental processes, and behavior-oriented dimensions. However, there are differences
between the two models. First, whereas personality dimensions are the core
of Curry's model, the three systems are viewed as parallel systems in Grigorenko and Sternberg's model. Second, whereas Curry believes that the degree of style malleability varies among the three systems, with the innermost
system the most stable and the outermost system the most modifiable,
Grigorenko and Sternberg do not make such a distinction. Sternberg
(1997) believes that styles are malleable, depending on the stylistic demands of a given task.

Similarly, both Miller's and Riding and Cheema's models put emphasis
on mental processes. Yet, the two models stress mental processes from
rather different perspectives. In Miller's model, under one stylistic dimension (analytic–holistic), three specific kinds of cognitive processes (perception, memory, and thought) are at the core of investigation. Riding and
Cheema's model, however, stresses two stylistic dimensions. The wholist–
analytic dimension concerns how one processes information, and the verbal–imagery dimension addresses how one represents information.

THE NEED FOR A NEW INTEGRATIVE MODEL

The limitations of the four existing models dictate that a new integrative
model be constructed. Such a new model should not only overcome some
of the limitations of the existing models, but should also achieve the following three goals. First, the model should be given a name with a term broad
enough to cover various style labels, rather than a narrow and thus mislead-
ing term like *cognitive style* or *learning style*. Second, the model should ad-

dress more explicitly all three controversial issues over styles. Finally, the new model should take an "open system" approach. That is, the model should be ready to encompass any style construct that meets the criteria for being part of the model. In chapter 8, we propose the *Threefold Model of Intellectual Styles,* which accomplishes such a mission.

Chapter 7

The Theory of Mental
Self-Government and Its Research

This chapter focuses on Sternberg's (1988, 1997) theory of mental self-government and the research supporting it. We spend an entire chapter on this theory for three reasons. First, it is among the most recent theories of intellectual styles. Second, it is the most general theory of intellectual styles. Third, and most importantly, it is the research findings based on this theory that have served as the catalyst for the creation of our new integrative model of intellectual styles, which is introduced in the next chapter. The remainder of this chapter is composed of three parts. The first part describes the theory of mental self-government and assessment tools based on it. The second part reviews and analyzes three lines of investigation based on the theory, each revolving around two of the three controversial issues over intellectual styles. The final part evaluates the existing research on the theory of mental self-government and concludes the chapter.

THE THEORY OF MENTAL SELF-GOVERNMENT
AND ITS ASSESSMENT TOOLS

The Theory of Mental Self-Government

Using the word "government" metaphorically, Sternberg (1988, 1997) contended that just as there are many ways of governing a society, so are there many ways of governing or managing our activities. These different ways of managing our activities can be construed as our thinking styles. In managing our activities, we choose styles with which we feel comfortable. Still, people are at least somewhat flexible in their use of styles and try, with varying degrees of success, to adapt themselves to the stylistic demands of a given situation. Thus, an individual with one preference in one situation may have a different preference in another situation. Moreover, styles may change with time and with life demands. Thinking styles are socialized, at least in part (Sternberg, 1994, 1997), suggesting they can to some extent be modified by the environment in which people live. The theory of mental self-government includes 13 thinking styles that fall along five dimensions of mental self-government: (a) functions, (b) forms, (c) levels, (d) scopes, and (e) leanings of government as applied to individuals.

Functions. As in government, there are three functions in human beings' mental self-government: legislative, executive, and judicial. An individual with a *legislative* style enjoys being engaged in tasks that require creative strategies—that is, seeing or doing things in a new way. An individual with an *executive* style is more concerned with implementation of tasks with set guidelines—that is, getting things done in a way that is clearly specified for him or her. An individual with a *judicial* style focuses attention on evaluating others and the products of their activities.

Forms. Also as in government, a human being's mental self-government can take any of four different forms: monarchic, hierarchical, oligarchic, and anarchic. An individual with a *monarchic* style enjoys engaging in tasks that allow complete focus on one thing at a time. An individual with a *hierarchical* style prefers to distribute attention across several tasks that are prioritized. An individual with an *oligarchic* style also likes to work toward multiple objectives during the same period of time, but without setting clear priorities. Finally, an individual with an *anarchic* style enjoys working on tasks that require no system at all.

Levels. People's mental self-government takes place at two levels: local and global. An individual with a *local* style enjoys being engaged in tasks that require one to work with details. An individual with a *global* style will pay more attention to the overall picture regarding an issue.

Scopes. There are two scopes of mental self-government: internal and external. An individual with an *internal* style enjoys being engaged in tasks that allow that individual to work independently. In contrast, an individual with an *external* style likes to be engaged in tasks that provide opportunities for developing interpersonal relationships.

Leanings. Finally, in mental self-government, there are two leanings: liberal and conservative. An individual with a *liberal* style enjoys being engaged in tasks that involve novelty and ambiguity, whereas a *conservative* person tends to adhere to existing rules and procedures in performing tasks.

The theory of mental self-government is viewed as a more general model of styles not only because the theory can be applied to various settings—academic and nonacademic—but also because it embraces all three traditions of the study of styles. The styles in this theory are cognitive in their way of looking at things (e.g., judicial style, global style, and so forth) and correspond to preferences in the use of abilities. But the styles are typical-performance rather than maximal-performance. Therefore, they resemble the personality-centered tradition. Finally, the styles resemble the activity-centered tradition in that they can be measured in the context of activities.

Apart from being general, the theory of mental self-government also possesses two differentiating characteristics when compared with the majority of previous style models. First, the styles it specifies fall along five dimensions, rather than along one. Second, the theory yields a profile of styles for each individual, rather than merely the identification of a single style.

Assessment Tools

The theory of mental self-government has been operationalized through several instruments. These include the Thinking Styles Inventory (TSI, Sternberg & Wagner, 1992), the Thinking Styles in Teaching Inventory (TSTI, Grigorenko & Sternberg, 1993c), the Set of Thinking Styles Tasks for Students (Grigorenko & Sternberg, 1993a), Students' Thinking Styles Evaluated by Teachers (Grigorenko & Sternberg, 1993b), and the Preferred Thinking Styles in Teaching Inventory (PTSTI, Zhang, 2003b). The TSI and the TSTI are two of the most frequently used inventories. Therefore, we elaborate on these two inventories.

The Thinking Styles Inventory. The TSI is a 65-item self-report measure in which respondents rate themselves on a 7-point scale ranging from 1 (*low*) to 7 (*high*) on a number of preferences. Examples of items from the inventory are: (1) "I like tasks that allow me to do things my own way" (legislative), (2) "I like situations in which it is clear what role I must play or in what way I should participate" (executive), and (3) "I like to evaluate and compare different points of view on issues that interest me" (judicial). Psychometric properties of the TSI have been assessed in many studies in various cultures. Although Cronbach's alpha coefficients were generally satisfactory, lower scale reliabilities were usually obtained with three of the 13 scales: local, monarchic, and anarchic. Thus, an effort was made to revise some of the items in the three scales. A careful examination of the item-scale reliabilities from previous data sets indicated that seven items needed to be rewritten: two from the local scale, three from the monarchic scale, and two from the anarchic scale. Results from the three revised scales showed that Cronbach's alphas for the local and the monarchic scales improved dramatically. The alpha coefficients increased from the previously low .50s to the low .70s. The alpha coefficient for the anarchic scale did not show obvious improvement. The revised inventory is available in two languages: Chinese and English (Sternberg, Wagner, & Zhang, 2003). For the revised inventory, with the exception of that for the anarchic scale, Cronbach's alpha coefficients for the scales range from the low .70s to the high .80s. Cronbach's alpha coefficient for the anarchic scale is in the mid .50s.

Internal validity of the inventory was assessed through factor analysis. Although a few studies generally support the dimensions of the thinking styles described in the theory, many more studies suggest a three- or four-factor solution. Based on diverse research evidence, Zhang and her colleagues (e.g., Zhang, 2000a, 2001a, 2002a, 2002b, 2002c, 2002d, 2002e; Zhang & Huang, 2001; Zhang & Postiglione, 2001; Zhang & Sternberg, 2000) have classified the 13 thinking styles into three groups. The first group, known as Type I thinking styles, is composed of thinking styles that are more creativity-generating and that denote higher levels of cognitive complexity, including the legislative, judicial, hierarchical, global, and liberal styles. The second group, known as Type II thinking styles, consists of thinking styles that suggest a norm-favoring tendency and that denote lower levels of cognitive complexity, including the executive, local, monarchic, and conservative styles.

The remaining four thinking styles (i.e., anarchic, oligarchic, internal, and external) belong to neither the Type I group nor the Type II group. However, they may manifest the characteristics of the styles from both groups, depending on the stylistic demands of a specific task. For example, whether one prefers to work alone (internal style) or one prefers to work with others (external style), one can work on tasks that require either Type I or Type II thinking styles. Also for instance, one could use the anarchic style in a sophisticated way—such as dealing with different tasks as they arise, but without losing sight of the central issue. Under this circumstance, the anarchic style manifests the characteristics of Type I thinking styles. On the contrary, one also could use the anarchic style in a simple-minded way—such as dealing with tasks as they come along without knowing how each task contributes to his or her ultimate goal. Under this circumstance, the anarchic style manifests the characteristics of Type II thinking styles. These four thinking styles have recently been labeled as "Type III thinking styles" (Zhang, 2003a).

External validity of the inventory was assessed by testing thinking styles not only against a number of constructs that belong to the family of styles but also against a few constructs that are predicted to be related to thinking styles (see the next part for details). Research findings support the convergent and discriminant validity of the TSI (e.g., Dai & Feldhusen, 1999; Sternberg, 1994; Zhang, 1999a).

The Thinking Styles in Teaching Inventory. The Thinking Styles in Teaching Inventory is a 49-item self-report questionnaire in which respondents rate themselves on a 7-point scale, with 1 denoting that the item *does not describe* them *at all*, and 7 denoting that the item *describes* them *extremely well*. The inventory was designed to assess seven thinking styles as manifested in teaching: legislative, executive, judicial, global, local, liberal, and conservative styles. Each seven items constitute one scale that assesses one thinking style in teaching. Examples of items in the inventory are: "I like students to plan an investigation of a topic that they believe is important" (legislative), "I like to give my students tests that require exacting and highly detailed work" (local), and "Each year I like to select new and original materials to teach my subject" (liberal).

The psychometric properties of the TSTI have been tested in several different studies (e.g., Sternberg & Grigorenko, 1995; Lam, 2000; Lee, 2002; Zhang & Sternberg, 2002). Cronbach's alpha coefficients generally fall between the low .60s and the mid .70s. Internal validity of the inventory has been assessed by factor analysis. Existing studies consistently suggest a distinct two-factor solution for the internal structure of the inventory. One factor is dominated by the judicial, liberal, legislative, and global styles (i.e., Type I styles). The other factor is featured by the executive, conservative, and local styles (i.e., Type II styles). External validity has been assessed by testing the relationship of the TSTI with another style construct—the teaching approach construct as measured by Trigwell and Prosser's (1996) Approaches to Teaching Inventory (ATI). The ATI assesses two approaches to teaching. One is information transmission. Teachers adopting this approach to teaching tend to be content-oriented and to emphasize the reproduction of correct information. The other teaching approach is conceptual change. Teachers adopting this approach are learning-oriented and concerned with students' conceptual change.

Research Using TSI and TSTI: An Overview

In their original forms, the TSI and the TSTI, along with other inventories, have been tested in the United States (Grigorenko & Sternberg, 1997; Sternberg & Grigorenko, 1995). Since 1996, we and our colleagues have been conducting three main lines of research based on the theory of mental self-government. Research participants are from several cultures, including Hong Kong, mainland China, the Philippines, and the United States. The first and also the most basic line of research focuses on exploring the relationships of thinking styles to various personal variables (e.g., age, gender, birth-order, and socioeconomic status) and environmental characteristics (e.g., teaching/learning/work settings, school cultures, residential locations, school types, extracurricular activities, perceived learning or teaching environment, and parental thinking styles). The second line of research investigates the role of thinking styles in various aspects of student learning and development, including academic achievement, self-esteem/self-rated abilities, cognitive development, personality traits, psychosocial development, and students' preferred teaching styles. The third line of research has its focus on understanding the nature of the relationships between thinking styles and style constructs proposed by other theorists, including Biggs' (1978, 1992) learning approaches and its parallel concept "teaching approaches" proposed by Trigwell and Prosser (1996) (from the activity-centered tradition), Holland's (1973, 1994) career personality types and Myers and McCaulley's (1988) personality types (from the personality-centered tradition), as well as Torrance's (1988) modes of thinking (from the cognition-centered tradition).

Meanwhile, the theory of mental self-government has also generated considerable research interest among scholars from other parts of the world, including Australia, Egypt, France, Germany, India, Israel, Italy, Poland, South Africa, and the United Kingdom. Research has been conducted at various levels, ranging from secondary school to college, and from academic to nonacademic settings. These studies fit well into our three lines of investigation. For example, consistent with the first line of our research, several studies examined the relationships of thinking styles to student characteristics (e.g., Tucker, 1999; Verman, 2001; Yang & Lin, 2004) and to environmental characteristics (e.g., Hommerding, 2003). Other studies have investigated the relationships of students' thinking styles to academic achievement (e.g., E. Cheung, 2002; F. Cheung, 2002; Kwan, 2002; Nachmias & Shany, 2002) and to creative and critical thinking (Yang & Lin, 2004), which fits in our second line of research. Still other studies examined the statistical overlaps between thinking styles and other style constructs such as Myers–Briggs's personality types (e.g., Yang & Lin, 2004), Biggs' learning approaches (e.g., Tse, 2003), Trigwell and Prosser's teaching approaches (Lee, 2002), and Kolb's (1976) learning style preferences (e.g., Cano-Garcia & Hughes, 2000), research which falls into our third line of investigation. Along with our own research, these studies have produced numerous research articles and more than three dozen dissertations, both at the master's degree level and at the PhD level. In the following part of this chapter, we illustrate the main findings from this research and discuss the implications of these findings for understanding the nature of thinking styles as they relate to the three controversial issues over intellectual styles.

WHAT DO RESEARCH FINDINGS SAY
ABOUT THE NATURE OF THINKING STYLES?

Findings from each of the three lines of research can be used to address the three controversial issues to which we have returned again and again in our discussion of intellectual styles: the malleability issue, the value issue, and the overlap issue. The rest of this part is divided into three sections. Each section introduces the major findings in one of the three lines of research. It also elucidates our views about the three issues, based on relevant research evidence.

The First Line of Investigation: Thinking Styles
With Personal and Environmental Characteristics

Sternberg (1988, 1997) contended that styles are at least partially socialized. He proposed that at least seven socialization variables are likely to affect the development of thinking and learning styles. These are culture, gender, age, parental style, religious upbringing, schooling, and occupation. The assumption underlying his hypothesis is that, from early on, we perceive certain modes of interaction with others and with things in the environment to be more rewarded than others. We then gravitate toward those modes. At the same time, we have built-in predispositions that place constraints on how much and how well we are able to adopt these rewarded styles. To some extent, society structures tasks along lines that benefit one style or another in a given situation. We therefore need to learn when to be what if we wish to adapt.

Many empirical studies have tested and confirmed Sternberg's hypothesis. As noted earlier, these studies have examined the relationships of thinking styles to a wide range of personal and environmental characteristics. Results suggest that thinking styles represent states and that they are malleable. Meanwhile, these results also speak to the issue of the value of styles. In the following, we consider each variable in turn.

Age. Age has been postulated as one of the primary socialization factors in thinking styles (Sternberg, 1988, 1997) While some studies (e.g., F. Cheung, 2002; Zhang, 2002b) did not find significant differences in thinking styles as a function of age, others indicated that older students tended to score higher on Type I thinking styles and the internal thinking style (e.g., Zhang, 1999a, 2002f, 2004a; Zhang & He, 2003). The finding that age is generally associated with Type I thinking styles is consistent with the notion that, as people get older, their thinking tends to become more complex, at least up to a certain point. There could be many possible reasons for why some studies did not reveal any significant age difference in thinking styles. One possible reason is that the participants' small age variations did not allow the detection of differences in thinking styles.

Gender. Gender is another variable that may play a role in the formation of people's thinking styles. Zhang and Sachs' (1997) study suggested that male Hong Kong university students scored higher on the global scale than did their female counterparts. This gender difference has been supported by E. Cheung's (2002) study of secondary school students in Hong Kong as well as Zhang's (2003c) study of mainland Chinese secondary school students. This finding seems to confirm the stereotypical oriental view that men are expected to focus on the bigger picture of an issue and make "important" decisions while women are expected to spend their energy on details and make "minor" decisions. For secondary school and college students, this gender difference is compatible with the phenomenon that male students tend to pay attention to the general approach of solving a problem without paying too much attention to getting every single detail correct, whereas female students tend to get involved in details without spending as much time deciding on the general approach for solving problems.

Furthermore, E. Cheung (2002) found that male university students were more legislative and liberal in their thinking styles than were females. Similarly, F. Cheung (2002; see also Wu & Zhang, 1999) found that male students scored higher on the liberal style than did female students. These results, again, suggest that thinking styles are at least partially socialized. Consider the finding that males scored higher on the legislative thinking style than did females. Traditionally, a legislative style has been more acceptable in males than in females. Men were supposed to set the rules, women to follow them. This tradition is changing, but it probably would be fair to say that many of the disadvantages women have experienced in the sciences, in business, and elsewhere have stemmed from their being labeled as stylistically inappropriate when, say, they have given rather than followed orders. We believe that even today, young girls are socialized into stylistic roles (e.g., the executive role of doing what they are told) in a way that is to their disadvantage if they later try to succeed in a variety of life pursuits.

Birth-Order. Birth-order is another variable that has been examined with thinking styles. Two studies are to be found in the literature. Unfortunately, they obtained what appear to be exactly opposite results, although there may be a cultural explanation for the difference. Among 124 American school students, Sternberg and Grigorenko (1995) found a positive relationship between being a later-born and displaying the legislative style. The authors argued that this finding is consistent with previous research evidence that first-borns tend to be more accepting of societal dictates than are later-borns. However, in his study of Hong Kong school students, Ho (1998) found a positive relationship between being an earlier-born and displaying the legislative style. However, these results may not be contradictory but rather reflect different cultural expectations. Indeed, Ho explained that this finding might be due to the fact that, in Hong Kong, older children are expected to take care of the younger ones. There are many situations in which older children are expected to handle problems independently. As a result, their creativity-relevant style (i.e., the legislative style) may have been developed out of necessity.

Although the manner in which the legislative style and birth-order are correlated with each other is directly opposite in the two studies, each finding makes sense in its own cultural context. Both support the argument that thinking styles are socialized.

Socioeconomic Status.   Socioeconomic status (SES) has long been recognized as one of the major socializing factors (e.g., Bourdieu, 1984; Collins, 1971) in schools. We, therefore, believe that students from families of different SES levels may tend to employ different thinking styles. Early in 1995, Sternberg and Grigorenko found that students from higher SES families scored higher on the legislative thinking style (a Type I style), but lower on the local, conservative, and oligarchic styles. Similarly, among Hong Kong secondary school students, Ho (1998) found that students from higher SES families scored higher on the judicial style (also a Type I style), but lower on the local, conservative, and oligarchic styles. Zhang and Postiglione's (2001) findings from Hong Kong university students are also in line with the findings from the above two studies. Students from higher SES families reported more frequent use of the legislative, judicial, and liberal thinking styles (all Type I styles) than did students from lower SES families (see also Tse, 2003). By the same token, after studying high school students in Taiwan, Yang and Lin (2004) concluded that students' SES was positively associated with the use of the judicial, hierarchical, and liberal styles (Type I styles).

The relationship between students' thinking styles and their socioeconomic backgrounds is not a matter of chance. Conceptually, a number of scholars (e.g., Astin, 1989; Perry, 1970; Piaget, 1952) have argued that cognitive development results, in part, from encountering and resolving cognitive disequilibrium. Cognitive disequilibrium is created by situations in which an individual's current way of thinking is challenged. The finding of a relationship between thinking styles and SES might be explained as follows. Students from higher SES families tend to have more exposure to different issues and situations. For example, at home, students from families of higher SES may be exposed more frequently to the discussions and evaluations of current issues around the world than are students from lower SES families. This exposure may broaden students' horizons and thus, enable students to become more analytical thinkers (as is characteristic of the judicial style). It also may enable them better to focus on the overall picture of an issue (as is characteristic of the global style). The relationship between the conservative thinking style and lower SES may be a result of the fact that students from lower SES families may not have enough intellectual challenges at home. This finding may also be explained by the notion that people from lower SES families may tend more toward authoritarianism (e.g., Adorno, Frenkel-Brunswik, Levinson, & Sanford, 1950; Christie & Jahoda, 1954; Kreml, 1977; Scarr, 1984).

School Culture. The socialization effects of culture on thinking styles have been shown at the level of school culture. Sternberg and Grigorenko (1995) did an analysis of the relationship between school ideology (an important indicator of school culture) and teachers' styles. They found that teachers tend to match the stylistic ideology of their schools. It is possible that teachers tend to gravitate toward schools that fit them ideologically. It is also possible that they tend to become like the place they are in. Either way, socialization seems to have played a role in the formation of teachers' thinking styles.

In Hong Kong, secondary schools are classified into five bands, with the top 20% of primary school graduates being admitted to Band 1 secondary schools, based on their academic achievement. Thus, students in Band 1 schools are supposedly students of highest abilities, whereas students in Band 5 schools are regarded to be students of lowest abilities. In Hong Kong, F. Cheung (2002) found that students from allegedly low-ability schools (Bands 4 and 5) were more legislative in their thinking than were students from supposedly high-ability schools (Bands 1 and 2). Cheung attributed this style difference across schools to the educational reform currently going on within the Hong Kong school system. In the past, teaching in Hong Kong classrooms was dominated by the traditional knowledge-transmission approach. Under this teaching approach, students are not encouraged to think creatively. Students accept what the teachers say, largely without question. However, the recent Hong Kong school educational reform advocates that schools cultivate creativity and problem-solving abilities. This advocacy seems to have taken more effect in schools for children with low ability levels than it has in schools with children of higher ability levels. It could be that the schools with higher ability students are already recognized as successful in Hong Kong and are not motivated to try new strategies. It may also be that the schools for students of higher ability believe that a more "executive" kind of education is needed to prepare their students for college and university entrance examinations. Students in the two different types of schools may have been affected by two different types of school cultures: one in the spirit of educational reform, and the other in trying to hold on to its traditional governance because it has worked well. According to Baker's (1968) behavior-setting theory, people comply with the forces or rules of a behavior setting. Furthermore, if people obtain satisfaction from a setting, they attempt to maintain that setting. Using Baker's theory to explain the situation of the school for children with higher ability levels, we would say that because all parties (e.g., school administers, teachers, students, and students' parents) are satisfied with students' achievement level, an important indicator for a school's success, people in the school are likely to maintain the status quo of the school.

Residential Location/Culture.   Several studies suggest that residential location affects people's thinking styles. For example, among Indian students, Verma (2001) found that rural students scored significantly higher on the hierarchical style, but lower on the oligarchic style, than did urban students. In mainland China, Wu and Zhang (1999) found that urban students were more executive than were suburban students and that students from northern China scored higher on the legislative and judicial scales than did those from southern China. In Zhang and Postiglione's (submitted) study, university students from Tibet (an autonomous region located in the remote northwest of China) scored higher on the more norm-conforming and cognitively simplistic thinking style scales (Type II styles), but lower on the creativity-generating and cognitively complex thinking style scales (Type I styles) than did students from three major cities (Beijing, Nanjing, and Shanghai) in China. In addition, compared with the students from the three cities, Tibetan students indicated a stronger preference for working with others as opposed to working independently.

One cannot help wondering how residential location affects the development of students' thinking styles. There is no simple answer to such a question. Residential location itself may not directly affect the way students think. It may be the different cultures (including educational system and religion) to which students are socialized that affect the way they think. Three recurrent themes that emerged from our interviews with Tibetan students and scholars have confirmed our survey findings and explained how students were socialized to using Type II thinking styles and the external style. These are the result of the influence of Tibetan monastery education, the impediment of poor economic conditions, and the influence of Tibetans' way of life.

Modern Tibetan education is strongly influenced by monastery education, which is typified by recitation of the Scriptures. Many Tibetan academics attended rural schools that were staffed by lamas and monks who resumed secular life as well as by other types of teachers schooled in the "old society." At school, these academics learned by reading from the scriptures and legends and by telling stories. Heavily influenced by the way they were taught, and with a lack of teaching materials due to a poor economy, these academics tended to teach their own students the same way that they were taught in the past. Therefore, Tibetan students were socialized to sit in lectures and take tests designed to assess memorization skills. Prolonged passive learning environment influences students to use Type II thinking styles.

The tendency of Tibetan students to use the external style is also a result of socialization. Tibetan students strongly believe in collective effort, which is influenced by three factors. The first has to do with students' religious background. Growing up with a religious background in Buddhism, Tibetan students consider helping one another a very good virtue. The second has to do with the reality that students need to survive their examinations. Indeed, the interviewed students stated that they needed to work together (e.g., comparing notes after class) so that they did not miss anything that the teacher said in class. The third factor relates to the Tibetan lifestyle. The majority of students were from village areas. Successful life (e.g., harvesting, farming, building a house, and so on) in the villages is heavily dependent on group efforts.

Teaching, Learning, and Work Settings. The view that styles are changeable has been empirically supported by studies of teachers teaching in different academic disciplines. In Hong Kong, Zhang and Sachs (1997) found that teachers in natural science and technological disciplines scored higher on the global thinking style than did those in social sciences and humanities. Similarly, also among Hong Kong teachers, Lam (2000) found that arts teachers were more local than were science teachers. In the United States, however, Sternberg and Grigorenko (1995) found that science teachers tended to be more local than were teachers of the humanities, whereas the latter were more liberal than were the former. The inconsistent results on the relationships between thinking styles and the academic disciplines in which teachers taught that were found between teachers in Hong Kong and teachers in the United States may be attributable to the specific cultural environments in which the teachers taught. It may also be due to the possibility that the research participants from the different studies were teaching very different subject matter, even though they were all classified as teaching within a same academic field. Categorizing teacher participants as teaching in science, social science, humanities, or even the arts might have overshadowed the relationships between particular thinking styles and each specific kind of subject matter. However, regardless of the fact that existing studies obtained contradictory findings, teachers who teach in different academic disciplines and in different teaching environments do tend to have different thinking styles. Therefore, the socialization effect of teaching environment upon thinking styles in teaching is still justifiable.

The argument that thinking styles can be socialized has also been supported by research findings obtained from other populations. Kaufman (2001) found that journalists were more executive thinkers than were creative writers, whereas creative writers scored higher on the legislative style than did journalists. Among Indian students, Verma (2001) discovered that students taking professional courses scored significantly higher on the global thinking style, whereas students taking nonprofessional courses scored significantly higher on the anarchic and oligarchic thinking styles. Tucker (1999) concluded that accounting students had a unique thinking styles profile. Finally, after studying 124 public library directors in the state of Florida, Hommerding (2003) asserted that there was an apparent influence of the library world upon the participants' thinking styles.

Extracurricular Activities. As socialization variables, students' extracurricular experiences have been examined against thinking styles. Zhang's (1999a) study of Hong Kong university students suggested that students who traveled more scored higher on the legislative, global, and liberal thinking styles—all Type I styles—than did students with less travel experience. Furthermore, students with more work experience scored higher on the judicial, liberal, and hierarchical thinking styles than did students with less or no work experience. In another study of Hong Kong university students, Zhang (2001a) found that students who had more work experience, leadership experience, and who reported a larger number of hobbies scored higher on the Type I legislative, judicial, global, hierarchical, and liberal styles.

Examination of the findings from the two studies revealed that the four student characteristics (travel experience, leadership experience, work experience, and hobbies) were invariably related to the judicial, liberal, global, legislative, and global (Type I) thinking styles. Au's (2004) study of Hong Kong secondary school students confirmed such a relationship.

A commonality shared by leadership experience, travel experience, hobbies, and work experience is the notion of becoming more experienced and more involved. All four types of experiences (work, travel, leadership opportunities, and pursuit of hobbies) tend to increase one's chances of facing more challenges. As a result, students are provided with more opportunities to solve problems. By the same token, the thinking styles that were related to these student characteristics also share a similarity. That is, these styles, by definition and by the way they are operationalized, foster creativity and require higher levels of cognitive complexity (Type I thinking styles).

Considerable research has indicated that students' extracurricular experiences may have a strong positive effect on educational outcomes, including creative thinking (e.g., Astin, 1989; Hattie, Marsh, Neill, & Richards, 1997; also see Zhang, 1999a, for details). Terenzini, Pascarella, and Blimling (1996) asserted that "students' out-of-class experiences appear to be far more influential in students' academic and intellectual development than many faculty and student affairs administrators think" (p. 157).

Therefore, we conclude with confidence that students' thinking styles are socialized. Moreover, getting involved in more extracurricular activities that provide opportunities to take up challenges is conducive for developing Type I thinking styles.

Teaching Experience.   In both Hong Kong and the United States (Sternberg & Grigorenko, 1995; Zhang & Sachs, 1997), teachers with more teaching experience scored lower on the legislative style than did less experienced teachers. This could be explained by the reality that new teachers need to keep trying different teaching strategies and adopting various teaching materials until they become comfortable with their teaching. On the contrary, experienced teachers may already believe they know what works best for them and thus may have stopped being creative in their work. Therefore, with increasing experience, teachers' thinking styles in teaching may change from being more creative to being more conservative.

Professional Experience/Training.   In studying teachers' thinking styles in teaching (i.e., teaching styles) among Hong Kong kindergarten teachers, Lee (2002) found that professionally trained teachers scored higher in the liberal, legislative, judicial, and global styles than did teachers with no professional training. By contrast, teachers with no professional training scored higher in the conservative, local, and executive styles than did teachers with professional training.

Consistent with Zhang's (1999a, 2001a; see also Au, 2004) findings among students regarding the relationships between thinking styles and extracurricular activities, Zhang and Sternberg's (2002) study suggested that duration of teachers' professional work experience outside school settings was positively related to scores on the judicial and liberal thinking styles. These results suggested that teachers who had more experiences beyond their work in school settings tended to be more interested in engaging in the evaluation of their students' tasks. Furthermore, these teachers were more likely to enjoy working in situations in which novelty and ambiguity were involved. There is a plausible explanation for this result: Teachers who had more professional experience beyond their work in school settings might have been confronted with a greater variety of situations that challenged them to think critically. On the contrary, teachers who had less professional experience outside school settings might have had fewer opportunities to deal with situations that required critical thinking. Furthermore, this result is consistent with the previous research finding that rich experiences can have positive effects on people's thinking (e.g., Astin, 1989; Batchelder & Root, 1994; Petersen, Leffert, & Graham, 1995; Zhang, 1999a).

Perceptions of Work Environments. According to Moos' (1973) social-ecological theory, the way people perceive their environment influences the way they behave in that environment. Based on this theory, we predicted that teachers' perceptions of their work environment affect their teaching behaviors, including their thinking styles in teaching. There is empirical evidence supporting this prediction.

Zhang and Sternberg (2002) found that teachers who perceived more freedom to determine the content of the subject matter they taught scored higher on the judicial, local, and conservative styles. That is, teachers who perceived their school environment as allowing for more freedom to determine the content of their teaching were more likely to be engaged in such mental activities as comparison and evaluation. There are two plausible explanations for this result. The first is that teachers who are more judicial thinkers tend to perceive more freedom to decide the content of their teaching and they therefore take a more active role in selecting the content of the courses they teach. Another possibility is that teachers who have been engaged in determining the content of own teaching become more judicial in their thinking.

Meanwhile, while carrying out tasks that involved comparisons and evaluations, the teachers tended to focus on the specific and concrete details rather than on the broad picture. This result makes sense: More often than not, teaching materials in primary and secondary schools are standardized. Therefore, when teachers were engaged in selecting the content of their teaching, they had to work on the specific details (the local thinking style) within the predetermined teaching materials. Furthermore, it may also be that teachers who perceived themselves to have more freedom to determine the content of the subject matter they taught also tended to be rule followers (the conservative thinking style). This may indicate that teachers who are conservative stay within the boundaries and feel that they have freedom of choice because they do what they are "supposed" to do, rather than being unrealistic about anticipating freedom beyond the boundary. After all, it is a matter of perception. However, these explanations are merely our post-hoc speculations. We do not have a defensible interpretation of the results at this time.

Lee's (2002) study of Hong Kong kindergarten teachers also lent support to the predicted relationship. Furthermore, she found that teachers who perceived their work environments as more positive scored higher on Type I styles and that teachers who perceived their work environments as less positive scored higher on Type II styles.

Parental Thinking Styles. The assumption of the socialization effect underlying the theory of mental self-government was also examined by testing the thinking styles of 232 children and those of their parents (Zhang, 2003c). Controlling for children's gender, results indicated that the children's thinking styles and those of their parents were correlated in a predictable way. For example, when children's gender was put under control, parents' legislative thinking style was positively related to students' use of legislative, judicial, and liberal thinking styles (partial correlation coefficients of .16, .25, and .19, respectively for the three styles), but was negatively correlated with children's use of the conservative thinking style (partial $r = -.17$). Also for instance, parental score on the judicial thinking style was positively correlated with children's score on the judicial thinking style (partial $r = .18$). By the same token, higher parental internal style was related to higher internal style among children (partial $r = .17$). These partial correlation coefficients are significant either at the .05 level or at the .01 level.

The association between children's and parents' thinking styles is consistent with previous investigations on the relationships between parents' and children's cognitive styles that were based on other theoretical frameworks (e.g., Laosa, 1980; Miller, 1994; Peake, Stehouwer, & Stehouwer, 1982). For example, after studying 43 Hispanic mothers and their children, Laosa (1980) concluded that maternal cognitive styles influenced children's cognitive styles in Hispanic families. Using Holland's (1973, 1994) model, Miller (1994) studied 40 parents and their children. Miller found that the personality types of the parents and those of their children tended to be congruent.

The relationships found between parents' thinking styles and those of children also make practical sense. A large and important part of children's socialization occurs in the family context. Within the family, parents play an important role in their children's life. Of the many parental factors that may affect children, cognitive/thinking style may be one of the most important ones, as demonstrated by research cited earlier and by the results from Zhang's study.

**Relevance of the First Line of Research
to the Controversial Issues Over Styles**

Results from the first line of investigation can be used to address at least two
of the three controversial issues over styles. The first is style malleability,
and the second, style value.

Relevance to the Issue of Style Malleability. Although none of the studies
was longitudinal and thus their research focus was not on examining the
stability (or flexibility) of thinking styles of individuals over time, results
from existing investigations of the relationships of participants' thinking
styles with personal and environmental characteristics have indicated that
people's thinking styles do change as they interact within different environments. People's thinking styles can be modified as a result of their socialization experiences. The socialization variables in different studies
have consistently revealed their function in the development of people's
thinking styles. Consequently, we conclude that thinking styles largely
represent states, not traits. People may have proclivities, however, toward
particular states. That is, some people may prefer, say, a legislative way of
seeing things; others, an executive way. But this is not to say that they
could not change states and see things in the other way if they desired to
do so.

Relevance to the Issue of Style Value. Results on the relationships of thinking styles to personal and environmental characteristics can also speak to
the issue of value of styles. As shown earlier, Type I thinking styles (characterized by creativity and cognitive complexity) are related to students' extracurricular activities, as well as to teachers' professional training and their
experience beyond teaching, all of which are normally considered positive
experiences. Furthermore, there is a tendency by which Type I thinking
styles are related to teachers' positive perceptions of their work environments. Positive perception of one's environment is one of the key characteristics normally found in an individual with superior psychological well-
being. On the contrary, Type II styles (characterized by a lack of creativity
and by cognitive simplicity) are associated with a relative lack of the above-
mentioned activities and experiences, as well as with a less positive view of
the work environment, all of which are deemed as negative attributes in
most societies. Thus, thinking styles are value-laden. Type I styles carry
more positive and adaptive values, whereas Type II styles carry more negative and less adaptive value.

The same thinking style may carry different values in different contexts.
For example, in earlier-born students, being less legislative is considered
more acceptable in the United States (e.g., Sternberg & Grigorenko, 1995).

However, in Hong Kong, earlier-born students are expected to be more legislative thinkers. In other words, being legislative may be desirable in the older sibling of one society, but undesirable in another society. That is, the legislative thinking style is value-differentiated.

The Second Line of Investigations: The Role of Thinking Styles in Student Learning and Development

The second line of research concerns investigating the relationships of thinking styles to several variables related to student learning and development, including academic achievement, self-esteem/self-rated abilities, cognitive development, psychosocial development, creative/critical thinking, students' preferred teaching styles, and personality traits. Results from this line of research speak to the issues of style value and style malleability.

Thinking Styles and Academic Achievement. Research on the relationships between thinking styles and academic achievement has been carried out at both the school level and the university level in several cultures. Findings from this line of research are diverse. Some studies suggest that except for the hierarchical style, the remaining Type I styles (i.e., legislative, liberal, judicial, and global) negatively contribute to academic achievement and that Type II styles, along with the hierarchical and internal styles, positively contribute to academic achievement. Other studies, however, find the opposite to be true. Still other studies reveal that the contributions of thinking styles to academic achievement vary as a function of culture, gender, and subject matter.

The earliest investigation into the contribution of thinking styles to academic achievement was conducted by Sternberg and Grigorenko (1993, also see Grigorenko & Sternberg, 1997) in two groups of identified gifted children participating in the Yale Summer School Program. The authors found that whereas the judicial and legislative thinking styles contributed positively to students' success in a variety of academic tasks, the executive thinking style tended to contribute negatively to students' success in these tasks.

However, in a more recent study of American university students, Zhang (2002e) found that the conservative style positively predicted students' grade point averages, whereas the global and liberal styles negatively did so. Therefore, results from this study did not support Sternberg and Grigorenko's studies. The inconsistent findings may be due to various factors, most notably, to students' different educational levels and the different types of achievement scores used in the different studies. Different schools also may value different styles. Sternberg and Grigorenko, (1995) found correlations that differed in sign between styles and academic achievement across different schools. More progressive schools valued more Type I styles, but more conservative schools valued more Type II styles.

In Hong Kong, six such studies (F. Cheung, 2002; Sun, 2000; Zhang, 2001c, 2001d, 2004a; Zhang & Sternberg, 1998) have been carried out, four in secondary school settings and two in university settings. Results from almost all studies in Hong Kong (with partial findings from Sun's [2000] and Zhang's [2001d] studies as the exceptions) suggest that, in general, thinking styles that require conformity (conservative style), respect for authority (executive style), and a sense of order (hierarchical style) are positively related to academic achievement. By contrast, thinking styles that foster creativity (legislative and liberal styles) tended to negatively contribute to academic achievement. These results support Sternberg and Grigorenko's (1995) finding that what styles correlate with academic achievement depends on local norms. Furthermore, a preference for working individually (internal style) is positively correlated with academic achievement, while a preference for working in groups (external style) is negatively associated with academic success. In a classroom that emphasizes cooperative learning, however, the opposite pattern of results might obtain. Finally, mixed findings have been obtained for the judicial style. Whereas the judicial style positively predicted achievement for secondary school students and for male university students, it negatively contributed to achievement among female university students. These disappointing results may suggest that professors have different expectations for male and female students, in particular, expecting a more assertive analytical style in men than in women.

Sun's (2000) study is partially supportive of the above general findings. He found a positive relationship between students' achievement in the Chinese language and the local and hierarchical styles among a group of students with a higher level of ability as measured by Raven's Progressive Matrices (Raven, 1998). However, within a lower ability group, a positive relationship was found between achievement in the Chinese language and the liberal thinking style.

Furthermore, one of the Hong Kong studies involved investigating the contribution of thinking styles to academic achievement among university students in mainland China (Zhang, 2001d). Results indicated that, as among many American school students, the executive thinking style negatively contributed to students' academic achievement scores.

In studying the contribution of thinking styles to academic achievement among Filipino university students, Bernardo, Zhang, and Calleung (2002) obtained results that were consistent with those obtained in the majority of Hong Kong studies and in the American university sample. That is, in general, thinking styles that require conformity, respect for authority, and a sense of order are positively correlated with academic achievement. The judicial style was positively related to academic achievement. Among university students in Spain, Cano-Garcia and Hughes (2000) also obtained similar findings to the majority of Hong Kong studies and to the Filipino study. The author concluded that higher academic achievers tended to be those who prefer to adhere to existing rules and procedures (executive style), who prefer to work individually (internal style), and who prefer not to create, formulate, and plan for problem solutions (legislative style in a negative sense).

In Israel, Nachmias and Shany (2002) examined the relationships between students' performance in virtual courses and thinking styles in eighth and ninth graders. As in the majority of studies, this study suggested that the internal style positively contributed to achievement. Meanwhile, this study also found that the liberal style contributed to better performance.

How are these findings relevant to the issues of style value and style malleability? We consider each in turn.

Value of Styles. All existing studies indicate that thinking styles significantly contribute to academic achievement. In general, the hierarchical style is valued in almost all educational systems. Furthermore, there is a general indication that the internal thinking style is conducive to good academic achievement in most studies. However, this is not to say that thinking styles are uniformly value-laden. In fact, in the context of the relationship between thinking styles and academic achievement, thinking styles are largely value-differentiated. That is, the very thinking styles (or types of thinking styles) that relate to greater academic success in one context may be associated with lesser academic success in another context. Such contexts include, but are not limited to, culture, school level, ability level, and gender. We provide one example for each case.

Whereas the executive style positively contributed to academic achievement in Hong Kong and Spain, the same style had a negative effect on student achievement in mainland China. Whereas Type I styles positively contributed to achievement and Type II styles negatively contributed to achievement among American secondary school students, the opposite was the case among American university students. Whereas the external style had a positive relationship with achievement in the Chinese language among students of lower ability levels, a negative relationship was found between the two variables among students of higher ability levels. Finally, in several studies, the judicial style was positively related to male students' achievement, but negatively related to female students' achievement. Thus, the same thinking style may carry both positive and negative values, depending on different contexts. In other words, thinking styles are value-differentiated.

It should be noted the foregoing examples are not meant to stereotype the thinking styles of any given population. In fact, the examples do not tell the whole story about the complicated relationships between thinking styles and academic achievement. The above contextual factors often interact.

Moreover, a number of issues related to research methodologies adopted in the various studies do not allow for direct comparisons of any kind. First, the research participants are from different cultures, different educational levels, different ability groups, and different academic disciplines. Second, the achievement measures used vary from specific performance tasks, to academic subject matters, to general academic performance (GPA). Third, the significant relationships found in different studies are obtained through different statistical procedures. All of these complexities dictate that thinking styles are value-differentiated in the context of their relationships to academic achievement.

Style Malleability. The findings on the relationships between thinking styles and achievement do not necessarily speak to the issue of malleability of styles because there are many factors that interact to affect student performance in different subject-matter areas, as illustrated earlier. However, at least two major findings show that thinking styles are socialized and thus are malleable. First, different thinking styles contribute positively to student achievement in the same academic subject in different learning environments (e.g., the kind of school one attends). By the same token, the same thinking style may affect student achievement in the same subject matter either positively or negatively, depending, once again, on the learning environment one is in. Students whose thinking styles fit the learning environments would be rewarded, whereas those with conflicting thinking styles would be penalized. The former students can continue to use their thinking styles to maintain their good performance, whereas the latter would have to modify their styles if they wish to improve their performance. If one does not at least try to change thinking styles to fit the learning environment, one might be less successful in that environment.

Relationships of Thinking Styles With Self-Esteem and Self-Rated Abilities. To understand the value issue of thinking styles, Zhang investigated the relationships of thinking styles to self-esteem (Zhang, 2001a; see also Zhang & Postiglione, 2001) and to self-rated abilities (Zhang, 2003c, 2004d). There are at least three reasons for anticipating a significant relationship between thinking styles and the two self-evaluation variables.

First, self-ratings are often very good indicators of actual performance on certain tasks (e.g., Shrauger & Oberg, 1981; Wells & Sweeney, 1986). According to Bandura's (1986) social cognitive theory, self-referent thought mediates between knowledge and action; the beliefs that individuals hold about their abilities as well as about the outcomes of their efforts have a powerful impact on the ways in which they behave. Thinking styles are one type of thinking behavior. Therefore, people's self-esteem and self-rated abilities should have an impact on their thinking styles.

Second, the prediction about the relationship of thinking styles with self-esteem and self-rated abilities was based on the assumption that self-esteem and self-confidence can be considered as part of personality. Thinking styles are at the interface between intelligence and personality (Sternberg, 1994). Riding and Wigley (1997) also contended that there seems to be a potential overlap between cognitive/thinking styles and personality. Meanwhile, they also pointed out that students' personalities are likely to influence their view of themselves (i.e., self-esteem). According to this logic, thinking styles should also overlap with self-esteem.

Third, the prediction drew upon previous research findings. Several scholars (e.g., Bhatnager & Rastogi, 1988; Bosacki, Innerd, & Towson, 1997; Jain, Bhatnager, & Rastogi, 1988; Shain, Farber, & Barry, 1989) have found significant relationships of self-referent variables to intellectual styles based on other theoretical frameworks (see chap. 3 for details).

Furthermore, because higher self-evaluations have been proven to be conducive for more positive outcomes such as better academic performance (e.g. Leondari, Syngollitou, & Kiosseoglou, 1998; Watkins & Gutierrez, 1990), stronger motivation for learning (e.g., Chapman, 1988; Dweck, 1986), and better peer relationships (e.g., Connor, 1994; O'Dell, Rak, Chermonte, & Hamlin, 1994), we argue that higher self-esteem and higher self-rated abilities carry positive values. Based on this argument and based on the definitions of thinking styles in Sternberg's theory, we expected that higher levels of self-esteem and self-rated abilities would be positively related to Type I thinking styles, and that lower levels of self-esteem and self-rated abilities would be positively related to Type II thinking styles.

One would be wondering if this relationship between thinking styles and self-esteem would apply in cultures that value Type II thinking styles in the schools, such as Hong Kong. Won't better school performance of the Type II's lead to higher self-esteem? Our answer: Yes, this relationship would apply to cultures in which Type II thinking styles lead to better school performance. Here is why: Students with better academic performance are not necessarily proud of themselves. Their higher achievement is usually the result of the (e.g., Hong Kong) educational system in which examination is the key. On the contrary, those students who believe that they are more creative in thinking (i.e., students with Type I thinking styles) tend to be the psychologically more healthy ones and to have higher self-esteem.

Data from two independent samples ($n1 = 794$, $n2 = 694$) of Hong Kong university students suggested that Type I thinking styles were related to higher levels of self-esteem and that Type II thinking styles were related to lower levels of self-esteem. Both studies (Zhang, 2001a; Zhang & Postiglione, 2001) took age and gender into account. Self-esteem is measured by the Self-Esteem Inventory (Adult Form, Coopersmith, 1981).

Data from three separate university student samples, one each from Hong Kong ($n = 193$), mainland China ($n = 268$), and the United States ($n = 65$), indicated that students who rated themselves as having higher levels of abilities scored higher on Type I thinking styles, but lower on Type II thinking styles, than students who rated themselves as having lower levels of abilities (see Zhang, 2004d). The types of abilities rated were analytical, creative, and practical, as defined in Sternberg's (1985, 1996) theory of successful intelligence. Results from a sample of secondary school students lent support to this finding (Zhang, 2003c).

These results make substantive sense. Students who are more self-confident (as indicated by higher levels of self-esteem and higher self-ratings of their abilities) are normally more willing to engage in creative thinking and behavior. They are more likely to do things in a norm-challenging way without being afraid of making mistakes. These creative thoughts and behaviors are also key characteristics of Type I thinkers. In contrast, students who are less self-confident will be more fearful of making mistakes. Consequently, these students will tend to follow established rules—a manifestation of Type II thinking styles.

Returning to the theme of this book, one would naturally wonder how these findings regarding the relationships of thinking styles to self-esteem and self-rated abilities address any of the three controversial issues over styles. These findings have implications for the value-laden nature of thinking styles. As mentioned earlier, higher self-evaluations are generally related to positive outcomes. Moreover, higher levels of self-esteem and higher regard for one's abilities are normally considered as desirable human traits in most cultures, whereas the opposite is generally considered undesirable. The manner in which thinking styles are correlated with the self-esteem and with self-rated abilities provides us with good reason to argue that thinking styles are value-laden. Type I thinking styles carry more adaptive value, while Type II thinking styles carry less adaptive value.

Thinking Styles and Cognitive Development. To further understand the nature of thinking styles, Zhang (2002a) investigated the relationships between thinking styles and cognitive development among Hong Kong university students. Cognitive development was measured by the Zhang Cognitive Development Inventory (ZCDI, Zhang, 1997), which was constructed based on Perry's (1970, 1981, 1999) theory of ethical and intellectual development. According to Perry, two of the critical stages of cognitive development are dualistic thinking and relativistic thinking. At the dualistic stage, students view the world dualistically using discrete, concrete, and absolute categories to understand people, knowledge, and values. Authorities have the right answers, and students are responsible for mastering these answers. These students are likely to ask: "Why do we have to learn these approaches? Why can't you teach us the right one?" At the relativistic stage, students think in relativistic terms. Different perspectives are not only acknowledged but also are seen as integral parts of a whole. They seek the big picture and can evaluate their own ideas as well as those of others.

Higher cognitive-developmental levels are generally viewed as superior to lower ones. Thus, testing thinking styles against cognitive development, a value-laden concept, would facilitate an understanding of the nature of thinking styles. Based on the characteristics of the three types of thinking styles and those of the dualistic and relativistic levels of cognitive development, it was predicted that Type I thinking styles would be related to relativistic thinking and that Type II styles would be related to dualistic thinking. Furthermore, based on Perry's notion of "retreat," it was predicted that students who are on the relativistic cognitive-developmental level would use a wider range of thinking styles than would students employing a dualistic way of thinking. Perry's theory provides three alternatives to forward progression. One alternative is retreat, in which students return to a dualistic orientation to find the security and the strength to cope with a highly challenging environment. That is, students who are at a higher level of cognitive development may, at times, think at a lower cognitive-developmental level. Therefore, it was expected that students who scored higher on the relativistic scale would report using Type I thinking styles as their primary way of dealing with tasks. Meanwhile, certain highly challenging tasks might force these students to resort to Type II and Type III thinking styles. These predictions were fully confirmed in Zhang's (2002a) study.

The relationships between thinking styles and cognitive development can speak to the issue of style value and that of style malleability. Because Type I thinking styles are related to a higher cognitive-developmental level, an attribute commonly perceived as carrying positive values, Type I styles can also be regarded as carrying positive values. By the same token, because Type II thinking styles are related to a lower cognitive-developmental level, an attribute generally perceived as carrying negative values, Type II thinking styles can also be viewed as carrying negative values.

Again, one would want to understand how we explain that schools in such cultures as Hong Kong and the Philippines seem to value Type II styles more because Type II styles tend to be associated with better academic performance. Convergent evidence (e.g., Hong Kong media, school and university mission statements, our formal and informal interviews with government officials, teachers, and students, and so forth) indicates that Hong Kong people do not value Type II styles. They value Type I styles. They want students to be creative. However, no one seems to know how, at least not at this time. This is primarily due to the reality that schools are pressured for producing students with high school grades. Therefore, there seems to be a paradox. On the one hand, schools (and universities alike) want their students to be creative. On the other hand, teaching and assessment have to be conducted in such a way that students can get good grades on the condition that they use Type II thinking styles. Thus, the association between Type II thinking styles and better academic performance is not an indicator of Type II styles being valued by Hong Kong people or people in other cultures. Instead, it seems largely to be the result of a problematic educational system.

The issue of style malleability can be addressed through the nature of cognitive development. Like many other cognitive-developmental theorists, Perry (1970, 1999) took an interactionist view. Cognitive development is the result of the interactions between people and environments. By facing challenges and resolving issues, one develops cognitively. Given the relationships found between thinking styles and cognitive development, we argue again that thinking styles can be modified on the basis of experience.

Thinking Styles and Psychosocial Development. The value-laden nature of thinking styles has also been shown through the relationships between Chinese university students' thinking styles and their sense of vocational purpose (Zhang, 2004b). Vocational purpose is one of the developmental components as defined in Chickering's (1969; also Chickering & Reisser, 1993) vector theory of psychosocial development. According to Chickering (1969), the development of vocational purpose is characterized by a higher degree of awareness about one's own unique values and interests, a greater clarity in one's vocational planning, and the recognition of the importance of a broader education as well as a deeper appreciation of knowledge and education indirectly related to one's objectives. The development of vocational purpose also involves students' development of a sense of themselves as "becoming professionals" and beginning the socialization process into their careers (Barratt & Hood, 1997).

According to Chickering, a stronger sense of vocational purpose is an indication of better development. A stronger sense of vocational purpose thus can be viewed as carrying positive value. We hypothesized that students scoring higher on Type I thinking styles would report a stronger sense of vocational purpose than those scoring higher on Type II thinking styles.

Our hypothesis was confirmed by results from several convergent statistical procedures. The findings make substantive sense. Consider the positive relationship between Type I thinking styles and vocational purpose. There are two plausible explanations of this relationship. It could be that through using Type I thinking styles (more creativity-generating and cognitively complex) in dealing with various tasks (including vocational tasks), students gain a better understanding of the pluralistic nature of the world of work. After being exposed to and after comparing various aspects of vocation-relevant issues, students achieve a better sense of vocational purpose. It could also be that students with a stronger sense of vocational purpose, knowing what their vocational goals are, would tend to use Type I thinking styles in dealing with various tasks, because using Type I thinking styles would allow them to work toward achieving their vocational goals more effectively.

Similarly, substantive sense can be made of the negative relationship between the conservative thinking style and a stronger sense of vocational purpose, as in the case of vocational competence. There are two plausible explanations to this relationship as well. On the one hand, it could be that the tendency of adhering to established rules (conservative thinking style) may have prevented the students from achieving a sense of vocational competence. These students were so rule-oriented that they tended not to think of new ways to enhance their vocational competence. As a result, they did not have much vocational competence. On the other hand, it could also be that the lack of vocational competence prevented students from being more creative in their thinking styles. Instead, these students had to seek comfort within given rules.

Regardless of which explanation is more plausible, the thinking style construct is related to the development of vocational purpose. Type I thinking styles are generally positively related to a stronger sense of vocational purpose, an attribute symbolizing better development from the perspective of psychosocial-developmental psychologists, and most likely, from the perspective of lay people in most cultural settings. Type II thinking styles are related to a weaker sense of vocational purpose, an attribute implying weaker psychosocial development. Therefore, again, thinking styles have been proven to be value-laden, with Type I styles being superior to Type II styles.

Thinking Styles and Preferred Teaching Styles. To address the value issue of thinking styles, Zhang (2004c) investigated whether or not students prefer that their teachers use some thinking styles, but not others, in teaching (i.e., teaching styles). Students' preferred teaching styles were assessed by the Preferred Thinking Styles in Teaching Inventory (PTSTI, Zhang, 2003b). Like the Thinking Styles Inventory (Revised), the PTSTI is also composed of 65 statements, with five statements each contributing to the measurement of one of the 13 thinking styles. For each statement, the participants rated themselves on a 7-point Likert scale, with 1 indicating that they *absolutely disagree that the statement describes how they prefer their teachers to teach*, and 7 denoting that they *absolutely agree that the statement describes how they prefer their teachers to teach*. Here are three sample items:

1. "It is important that teachers allow students to develop their own ways of solving problems" (legislative style);
2. "A good teacher always gives clear directions" (executive style);

3. "One of the most important things teachers do is to compare various students' progress" (judicial style).

Students' preferred thinking styles in teaching were tested against their own thinking styles in learning. Three major findings were obtained. First, Type I teaching styles (teaching styles that encourage creative thinking and complex information processing) were valued by all students, regardless of students' own thinking styles. Second, the second-most valued teaching styles are Type III styles (teaching styles that encourage either Type I or Type II thinking styles, depending on the stylistic demands of a specific task). They were favored by students with both Type II and Type III thinking styles. Third, the least valued teaching styles are Type II styles (teaching styles that encourage rule following and simple information processing). They were valued almost exclusively by students with Type II styles (except in the case of students with an oligarchic style, who also preferred Type II teaching styles, perhaps because they need the structure and priority-setting that they themselves do not provide).

This general finding indicates that thinking styles are value-differentiated, on the one hand, and value-laden on the other hand. Thinking styles are value-differentiated in that students with one type of thinking styles prefer different teaching styles than students with a different type of thinking styles. Thinking styles are value-laden because Type I teaching styles are appreciated by most students.

Thinking Styles and Personality Traits. The value-laden nature of thinking styles has also been revealed by the relationships between thinking styles and personality traits (Zhang, 2002b, 2002c; Zhang & Huang, 2001). Furnham, Jackson, and Miller (1999) found significant relationships between the Eysenck Personality Inventory (Eysenck & Eysenck, 1964) and Honey and Mumford's (1982) Learning Styles Questionnaire. Extroverts tended to be activists and introverts tended to be reflectors. Riding, Burton, Rees, and Sharratt (1995) concluded that participants' personality characteristics varied significantly as a function of Verbal-Imagery cognitive style. Verbalizers tended to be more active than imagers.

Hashway (1998) noted that many style theories are personality-based. Messick (1996) contended that style should be the construct used to build a bridge between cognition and personality in education. Sternberg (1994) argued that style is at the interface between intelligence and personality.

In testing the relationships between thinking styles and the Big Five personality traits (Costa & McCrae, 1992) in both Hong Kong and mainland Chinese university students, Zhang and her colleague (Zhang, 2002b, 2002c, Zhang & Huang, 2001) found that Type I thinking styles were positively related to scores on an openness scale, but negatively to scores on a neuroticism scale. Likewise, it was consistently found that Type II thinking styles were positively related to scores on the neuroticism scale, but negatively to scores on the openness scale. People who are high on the openness scale are characterized by such attributes as open-mindedness, an active imagination, and preference for variety. People who are high on neuroticism tend to be emotionally unstable, easily embarrassed, pessimistic, and to suffer from low self-esteem. In most cultural contexts, the attributes associated with openness to experience would be perceived as more adaptive than those associated with neuroticism.

Consider the significant relationship of openness to the legislative, judicial, and liberal thinking styles. People who are high on these styles share the same characteristics as people who score high on openness. Both types of people are open-minded, imaginative, and perceptive.

Also consider the relationship between the neuroticism scale and the executive and conservative thinking styles. As has been noted, people who are high on neuroticism tend to be emotionally unstable, easily embarrassed, pessimistic, and to suffer from low self-esteem. It is conceivable that people who experience such negative affects would be more comfortable with working in highly structured situations, being told what to do, and carrying out tasks by adhering to existing rules, all of which are also characteristics of people with executive and conservative thinking styles. Therefore, again, the way in which thinking styles and the two normally value-laden personality traits (openness and neuroticism) are associated suggests that thinking styles are value-laden. Type I thinking styles generally carry positive values, whereas Type II styles generally carry negative values.

Summary.   In this section, we have described our research, which examines the role of thinking styles in various dimensions of student learning and development. Results consistently reveal the value-laden and malleable nature of thinking styles. Of course, one could argue that findings regarding some of the dimensions of student development are based only on single studies. However, our views about the nature of thinking styles are well grounded. First, all predictions we made were based on theoretical and empirical works. Second, all findings make substantive (or practical) sense.

The Third Line of Investigation: Thinking Styles and Other Style Constructs

The third line of investigation pertains to the relationships of thinking styles to other style constructs. Results from this research suggest that thinking styles are value-laden. Furthermore, although thinking styles substantially overlap with other style constructs, they are distinguishable from such constructs. These other style constructs are Biggs' (1978, 1992) learning approaches, Trigwell and Prosser's (1996) teaching approaches, Holland's (1973, 1994) career personality types, Torrance's (1988) modes of thinking, Myers and McCaulley's (1988) personality types, and Kolb's (1976) learning style preferences.

Thinking Styles and Learning/Teaching Approaches. In four independent university student samples across Hong Kong, mainland China, and the United States, Zhang (2000a; see also Zhang & Sternberg, 2000) discovered that Type I thinking styles are related to the deep learning approach and that Type II styles are related to the surface learning approach. The first study (Zhang, 2000a) indicated that the scales in the two measures (Thinking Styles Inventory and Study Process Questionnaire) overlapped by 68.6% in a first sample and by 74.6% in a second sample, while the second study (Zhang & Sternberg, 2000) showed that the two measures overlapped by 18.52% in one sample and by 38.16% in the second sample.

Consistent with Zhang's (2000a; also Zhang & Sternberg, 2000) results among university students, Tse's (2003) findings, obtained from secondary school students, suggest that thinking styles and learning approaches overlap. Pearson's correlation coefficients ranged from .18 ($p < .05$) to .54 ($p < .01$). Except for the case of one subscale of the surface learning approach, the manner in which the thinking styles and learning approaches are correlated in Tse's study is almost identical with that in Zhang's (2000a; Zhang & Sternberg, 2000) previous studies.

Parallel to Zhang's (2000a; also Tse, 2003; Zhang & Sternberg, 2000) study of the relationships between thinking styles (in learning) and learning approaches, Zhang (2001e) investigated the relationships between thinking styles in teaching (or, "teaching styles" for short) and teaching approaches among primary and secondary school teachers. The measure of teaching styles and that of teaching approaches overlapped by 62%. Teachers who scored higher on Type I teaching styles reported a conceptual-change teaching approach (parallel to the deep learning approach), whereas teachers who scored higher on Type II teaching styles reported an information-transmission teaching approach (parallel to the surface learning approach). The manner in which the two style constructs are related has been confirmed by Lee's (2002) findings, obtained from kindergarten teachers in Hong Kong. Furthermore, the absolute values of Pearson correlation coefficients ranged from .20 ($p < .01$) to .72 ($p < .001$), with 50% of them above .51.

Thinking Styles and Career Personality Types. In two independent university student samples (one from Hong Kong and the other from mainland China), Zhang (2000b, 2001b) found that Type I thinking styles were related to the artistic-career personality type and that Type II thinking styles were related to the conventional-career personality type. One study resulted in a 44.1% overlap between the measure of thinking styles and that of career-personality types (Zhang, 2000b), and the other (Zhang, 2001b), an overlap of 61.1% between the two measures.

Thinking Styles and Modes of Thinking.   In two university student samples (one from the United States and the other from Hong Kong), Zhang (2002d, 2002f) found that Type I thinking styles were related to the holistic mode of thinking and that Type II thinking styles were related to the analytic mode of thinking. One study (Zhang, 2002d) revealed an overlap of 75.9% between the measure of thinking styles and that of modes of thinking; a second study (Zhang, 2002e) showed an overlap of 54.74% between the two measures.

Thinking Styles and Personality Types.   In studying the relationships between thinking styles and personality types as assessed by the Myers–Briggs Type Indicator (Myers & McCaulley, 1988), Sternberg (1994) found that 30 of the 128 correlations were statistically significant. Among Taiwanese senior high school students, Yang and Lin (2004) found that, in general, Type I thinking styles were related to intuitive and perceiving personality types and that Type II thinking styles were correlated with sensing and judging personality types. No clear patterns of relationship were uncovered between thinking styles and the other two personality dimensions (introverted vs. extroverted; thinking vs. feeling). After examining the thinking styles of university students, Tucker (1999) claimed that the dominant thinking styles identified among accounting students indicated a profile of individuals resembling that described by researchers who used the Myers–Briggs Type Indicator in studying accounting professionals and accounting students.

Thinking Styles and Learning Styles.   Finally, in Spain, Cano-Garcia and Hughes (2000) examined the relationships of university students' thinking styles to their learning styles as assessed by Kolb's (1976) Learning Style Inventory. The reflective observation style dimension (present in divergent and assimilative learning styles) was related to the legislative and external styles. Divergent learners are characterized by their imagination and intuition as well as the ability to see many perspectives and to generate many ideas. These characteristics are shared by people with Type I thinking styles. Assimilative learners are characterized by their distinctive abilities to engage in sound logical reasoning and theoretical model building, and to assimilate wide-ranging ideas. Again, these characteristics are shared by people with Type I thinking styles.

Relevance to the Controversial Issues Over Styles

Results obtained from the third line of investigation can speak to at least two of the three controversial issues over styles. One is that of style overlap, and the other is that of style value.

Style Overlap. The data show that thinking styles overlap substantially with intellectual styles defined in other stylistic theoretical frameworks. These results, obtained through investigations in several different cultures, have lent support to many other studies in the literature that have aimed to identify relationships among different style constructs (see chap. 3 for details). Thus, there are similarities between thinking styles and the other style constructs examined. However, by no means do these substantial overlaps and similarities give us any reason to assert that thinking styles and any of the other style constructs are identical. Each construct makes a unique contribution to the variance in the empirical data. Therefore, each theory of styles is valuable in its own way, at least to some extent.

Style Value. The third line of research has also confirmed the value-laden nature of thinking styles. Type I thinking styles are significantly related to the deep approach to learning, the conceptual-change teaching approach, the artistic-career personality type, the holistic mode of thinking, the intuitive and perceiving personality types, and the reflective observation learning style dimension, all of which are widely accepted as being desirable human attributes. Complementarily, Type II thinking styles are related to the surface approach to learning, the information-transmission teaching approach, the conventional-career personality type, the analytic mode of thinking, and the sensing and judging personality types, all of which are normally perceived as less desirable human attributes. Thus, thinking styles are value-laden, with Type I thinking styles generally superior to Type II thinking styles.

It should be noted, however, that data have not indicated any clear pattern of relationships between Type III thinking styles and the style constructs examined above. Apparently, this is due to the fact that Type III thinking styles are less stable and that the use of these styles is more contingent on the stylistic demands of particular tasks and situations. Likewise, some styles in the other style models that were tested against thinking styles are equally less stable and are also task- and situation-dependent. These include such styles as the achieving learning approach, the realistic, investigative, social, and enterprising-career personality types, the integrative mode of thinking, as well as the thinking, feeling, introverted, and extroverted personality types. These styles, along with Type III thinking styles, are more value-differentiated.

EVALUATION AND CONCLUSIONS

This chapter has presented results from three lines of investigations based on the theory of mental self-government. Each line of research reveals the nature of thinking styles as they relate to two of the three controversial issues over styles. Obviously, none of the studies was longitudinal or experimental. Furthermore, there is also a lack of qualitative studies. Nonetheless, our discussion of the nature of thinking styles is based on a rich body of literature accumulated over a period of more than a decade. This body of research indicates that thinking styles can be either value-laden or value-differentiated, but not value-free; that they are, for the most part, modifiable and hence more state-like than trait-like; and that they overlap highly with styles from other theories, while possessing their own unique characteristics.

Part IV

INTELLECTUAL STYLES:
RECONCEPTUALIZATION
AND APPLICATION

Chapter 8

A Threefold Model
of Intellectual Styles[1]

In the previous chapter, research based on the theory of mental self-government was reviewed. Apart from addressing three of the major controversial issues in the field of styles, results of this research on thinking styles indicate that much of the existing work on styles can be organized into a new integrative model—the Threefold Model of Intellectual Styles. This model is built on the three types of thinking styles identified in the process of investigating the theory of mental self-government as well as on previous findings in the styles literature. In this chapter, the presentation of the Threefold Model of Intellectual Styles is divided into five parts. The first part sets the criteria for inclusion in the Threefold Model of Intellectual Styles and the style constructs included. The second part presents the style constructs, their measurements, and empirical evidence for each of the individual models to be included in the new integrative model. The third part discusses the nature of intellectual styles. The fourth part addresses the three controversial issues within the context of the Threefold Model of Intellectual Styles. The final part concludes the chapter by discussing the contributions and validation of the new model as well as the implications of this model for educational practice and for organizational research and management.

---

[1]This chapter is based on our article "A Threefold Model of Intellectual Styles" published in *Educational Psychology Review* (Zhang & Sternberg, 2005).

CRITERIA FOR INCLUSION IN THE THREEFOLD
MODEL OF INTELLECTUAL STYLES

In selecting from the existing style models to be organized into the Three-fold Model of Intellectual Styles, three criteria were applied. First, the models selected are among those commonly considered to be influential in the styles literature. Second, the style constructs defined in the models are operationalized, and thus are empirically based. Finally, the style construct defined in a model has been tested against at least one other style construct. A survey of the existing models in the literature resulted in ten style models/constructs that satisfy all three criteria. These are

1. Sternberg's thinking styles
2. Biggs' (1978) learning approaches
3. Holland's (1973) career personality types
4. Torrance's (1988) modes of thinking
5. Myers and McCaulley's (1988) personality types based on Jung's (1923) work
6. Gregorc's (1979) mind styles
7. Kirton's (1961, 1976) adaption–innovation decision-making and problem-solving styles
8. Kagan and colleagues' (1964) reflective–impulsive styles
9. Guilford's (1950) divergent–convergent thinking
10. Witkin's (1962) field dependence/independence

STYLE CONSTRUCTS, MEASUREMENTS,
AND EMPIRICAL EVIDENCE

It is important, in reading our review, to keep in mind that whereas many theorists view people as "types," we do not. We view styles as flexible and modifiable as a function of the interaction of person, task, and situation. Hence, when we represent people as "types," we do so to preserve the meanings of the researchers, not because we believe that people are susceptible to simplistic pigeon-holing.

In this part, we describe each of the style constructs, one measurement for each construct (except for divergent–convergent thinking), and major empirical findings for each construct. It is worth noting that some of the research findings presented are, in fact, relevant to the discussion of the three major controversial issues in the styles field, although few studies are intended to serve such a function. Furthermore, because Sternberg's thinking-style construct and the research supporting it were elaborated in an ear-lier chapter, we begin the following discussion by describing Biggs' learn-ing approach construct, its measurement, and the empirical findings.

Learning Approach and the Study Process Questionnaire

According to Biggs (1978), there are three common approaches to learn-ing: surface, deep, and achieving. (See Table 8.1 for a description of each approach.) The most widely used measure of the three learning ap-proaches is the Study Process Questionnaire (SPQ, Biggs, 1987, 1992). The SPQ is a self-report test composed of 42 items on six subscales. For each item, the respondents rate themselves on a 5-point scale ranging from 1 (*low*) to 5 (*high*). The six subscales are: surface–motive, surface–strategy, deep–motive, deep–strategy, achieving–motive, and achieving–strategy.

Results from many studies show internal consistencies ranging from the mid .50s to the mid .70s for the six subscales. Both internal and external va-lidity data for the SPQ are well documented in the literature. The internal validity is assessed by examining the internal structure of the instrument. Whereas some studies support Biggs' original argument that the SPQ as-sesses three approaches to learning (surface, deep, and achieving, e.g., Bolen, Wurm, & Hall, 1994; O'Neil & Child, 1984), other studies support a two-factor (surface and deep) model (e.g., Niles, 1995; Watkins & Dahlin, 1997). The two-factor model is consistent with the model proposed by Marton (1976), who used a phenomenographic method in studying stu-dents' learning approaches. In taking a phenomenographic approach,

TABLE 8.1
Individual Styles in Nine Style Models

Style Construct	Individual Style	Key Characteristics
Learning approach	Surface	Reproduce what is taught to meet the minimum requirement
	Deep	Gain a real understanding of what is learned
	Achieving	Maximize one's academic grades
Career personality type	Realistic	Work with things
	Investigative	Engage in scientific kinds of work
	Artistic	Deal with tasks that provide opportunities to use imagination
	Social	Work in situations that provide opportunities to interact with others
	Enterprising	Work in environments in which leadership oppor-tunities are available
	Conventional	Work with data under well-structured situations

(Continued)

TABLE 8.1
(*Continued*)

Style Construct	Individual Style	Key Characteristics
Mode of thinking	Holistic	Process information in an intuitive, Gestalt-type, and synthesized manner
	Analytic	Process information in a piecemeal, analytical, and sequential manner
	Integrative	Process information in an interactive and dynamic way
Personality type	Extroversion	Enjoy action-oriented activities and group interactions
	Introversion	Enjoy reflection and individual efforts
	Sensing	Rely primarily on concrete information provided by the five senses
	Intuitive	Like to find general patterns and new ways of doing things
	Thinking	Rely primarily on impersonal and analytic reasoning in making decisions
	Feeling	Rely primarily on personal and social values in making decisions
	Judging	Prefer more structured learning environments
	Perceiving	Prefer learning situations that are more free, open, and flexible
Mind style	Abstract random	Approach learning holistically and prefer to learn in an unstructured way
	Concrete sequential	Extract information through hands-on experiences and prefer well-structured work environments
	Abstract sequential	Adopt a logical approach to learning and strong in decoding written, verbal, and image symbols
	Concrete random	Take trial-and-error, intuitive, and independent approaches to learning
Decision-making style	Innovative	Work in nontraditional ways and not concerned with the social consequences of producing less acceptable solutions
	Adaptive	Work within existing frameworks and minimize risks and conflicts
Conceptual tempo	Reflective	Tend to consider and reflect on alternative solution possibilities
	Impulsive	Tend to respond impulsively without sufficient forethought
Structure of intellect	Divergent	Deal with problems in a flexible way and tend to generate multiple solutions to a single problem
	Convergent	Deal with problems in a mechanical way and tend to see a problem and a solution as having a one-to-one relationship
Perceptual style	Field independent	Tend to see objects or details as discrete from their backgrounds
	Field dependent	Tend to be affected by the prevailing field or context

Note. From Zhang and Sternberg (2005). Reprinted with kind permission of Springer Science and Business Media.

Marton described students' learning experiences from the perspective of students, rather than looking at students' learning as an outsider.

External validity of the measure is assessed by examining the SPQ against other instruments assumed to be based on constructs similar to those measured by the SPQ. The SPQ assesses similar constructs to Entwistle's (1981) Approaches to Studying Inventory (Wilson, Smart, & Watson, 1996) and Cantwell and Moore's (1996) Strategic Flexibility Questionnaire (Cantwell & Moore, 1998). The Study Process Questionnaire was also assessed for its heuristic value in educational settings in different parts of the world. Considerable work was done to investigate the impact of student characteristics and learning context on the learning approaches that students take (e.g., Biggs, 1988; Sadler-Smith & Tsang, 1998). Meanwhile, a great deal of work also focuses on the relationships between students' learning approaches and their academic achievement (e.g., Albaili, 1997; Biggs, 1988; Zhang, 2000a).

As has been detailed in the chapter on the theory of mental self-government and corresponding research, putting Biggs' notion of learning approaches within the context of the styles literature, Zhang and Sternberg (2000; also Tse, 2003; Zhang, 2000a) examined the associations between learning approaches and thinking styles in Sternberg's (1988, 1997) theory of mental self-government. In all three studies, significant overlap was found between thinking styles and learning approaches. Students who reported a deep approach to learning scored higher on Type I thinking styles; students who reported a surface approach to learning scored higher on Type II thinking styles. Furthermore, as noted earlier, learning approaches are malleable and they are not value-free.

Career Personality Type and the Self-Directed Search

According to Holland (1973), people are characterized by six personality types corresponding to six occupational environments: realistic, investigative, artistic, social, enterprising, and conventional (see also Table 8.1). The Self-Directed Search (SDS, Holland, 1985, 1994) is the most popular inventory used to assess the six career personality types. The SDS is a self-administered and self-scored inventory in which the respondents indicate their likes and dislikes of the activities and occupations in the six types of environments and rate their competencies in each of the six areas.

The SDS has been widely used in studies carried out in both Western and non-Western cultures (e.g., Bickham, Miller, O'Neal, & Clanton, 1998; Brand, Van-Noorwyk, & Hanekom, 1994; Glidden & Greenwood, 1997). Apart from being used as a career-counseling tool, the SDS has also been examined against people's individual differences in other traits, such as competencies, values, and intellectual styles. For example, Alvi and his colleagues conducted a series of three studies (Alvi, Khan, Hussain, & Baig, 1988; Khan & Alvi, 1986; Khan, Alvi, & Kwong, 1985) on the relationships between Holland's career personality types as assessed by the SDS and Witkin et al.'s field dependence/independence construct as assessed by the Group Embedded Figures Test (GEFT, Witkin, Oltman, Raskin, & Karp, 1971) among Canadian and Pakistani secondary and university students. The authors found, among both the Canadian and Pakistani samples, that students with two- or three-letter codes consisting of R (realistic), I (investigative), and A (artistic) in any order, obtained higher GEFT scores than did those with two- or three-letter codes composed of S (social), E (enterprising), and C (conventional).

In examining the relationships of thinking styles with career personality types, Zhang (1999b) designed the Short-Version Self-Directed Search (SVSDS), which aims at overcoming the gender bias for which the SDS is often criticized and at maintaining participants' attention when responding to the questionnaire. The SVSDS is a self-report questionnaire containing 24 items, with each set of 4 items contributing to the assessment of one of the six career personality types.

Reliability and validity data of the SVSDS are recorded in two of Zhang's studies (Zhang, 2000b, 2001b). Cronbach's alpha coefficients for the six scales ranged from the mid .50s to the mid .80s, with the majority in the high .70s. Internal validity of the inventory was assessed by factor analysis. Both sets of data yielded a two-factor solution, with each factor containing high loadings from precisely the same scales. One factor is dominated by high loadings from the realistic, investigative, and conventional scales; the other is dominated by high loadings from the artistic, social, and enterprising scales. Each of the two factors consists of three career personality scales that are adjacent to one another, which is supportive of Holland's notion of "consistency" of the SDS scales. External validity of the inventory was assessed by testing its scales against the thinking styles in the Thinking Styles Inventory (Sternberg & Wagner, 1992) among Hong Kong Chinese and mainland-Chinese university students. Similar correlations between scales in the two measures were obtained in the two studies. The artistic career personality type was negatively correlated with Type II thinking styles, whereas the conventional career personality type was positively correlated with Type II thinking styles. Furthermore, the social and enterprising types were positively associated with the external thinking style, but negatively with the internal thinking style.

In cross-examining the findings from Alvi et al.'s studies of the relationships between career personality types and field dependent/independent styles and those from Zhang's studies of the relationships between career personality types and thinking styles, we noticed that the artistic type carries more adaptive value than does the conventional type. Whereas the artistic type is highly associated with the field-independent style and Type I thinking styles (both having been empirically shown to be related to human attributes that carry more adaptive value), the conventional type is strongly related to the field-dependent style and Type II thinking styles (both having been empirically shown to be related to human attributes that carry less adaptive value).

Finally, the issue of style malleability has been clearly addressed. This argument has both conceptual and empirical support. Conceptually, almost anyone who has taken the SDS test would remember how dramatically different the occupational codes are for each of the occupations in his or her "occupational daydreams" list. That is, the great majority of people change their career interests (career personality types) as they grow up and as they interact with their environments. Undoubtedly, an individual's great change of career interests stops at a certain age (Holland, Powell, & Fritzsche, 1994). However, this attainment of career maturity does not mean that people's career interests cease to change with age (Holland et al., 1994). Also, conceptually, each occupation has its own characteristic profile. Of course, one could argue that people of similar career interests tend to gravitate toward the same occupation. However, it is also highly possible that people are socialized to become even more similar in their career interests after they enter the same occupation.

Empirically, people's career personality types vary as a function of several demographic characteristics. For example, men tend to score higher on the realistic and investigative scales, whereas women tend to score higher on the conventional and social scales (e.g., Henry, Bardo, Mouw, & Bryson, 1987; Holland et al., 1994; Price, 2003). Based on Holland's study of the normative samples (of high school students, college students, and adults), Holland et al. (1994) concluded that education and social status are related to people's SDS profiles in similar ways. Usually, higher scores on the realistic scale are related to lower levels of education and social status. On the other hand, higher scores on the investigative scale are often associated with higher levels of education and social status.

Mode of Thinking and the Style of Learning and Thinking

Mode of thinking has been traditionally known as brain dominance or hemispheric specificity. Research from the past 20 years suggests that the two hemispheres are more dynamic than static and that they are more interactive than was once believed. Thus, the terms *brain dominance* and *hemispheric specificity* have been gradually replaced by the terms *hemispheric style* and *hemispheric thinking style* (e.g., Albaili, 1993, 1996; Hassan & Abed, 1999). More recently, Zhang (2002a, 2002b) cast the term brain dominance in yet another light—that of mode of thinking. The three modes of thinking are analytic (originally left-brain dominance), holistic (originally right-brained dominance), and integrative (originally whole-brained) (see also Table 8.1).

The Style of Learning and Thinking (SOLAT, Torrance, McCarthy, & Kolesinski, 1988) is designed to measure alleged brain dominance. It is a self-report inventory comprising 28 items (each containing two statements), with each item allowing the respondents to choose one of the two statements or both. One of the statements is supposedly characterized by left-brained dominance, the other by right-brained dominance. Choosing both statements results in scoring on the whole-brained dominance scale.

Reliability and validity statistics for the SOLAT (Youth Form) are reported in the SOLAT Administrator's Manual (Torrance, 1988). Cronbach's alpha is .77 for the analytic scale and .74 for the holistic scale. No reliability data are reported for the integrative scale. In her study of Hong Kong university students, Zhang (2002a) reported Cronbach's alphas of .75 for the analytic scale, .70 for the holistic scale, and .85 for the integrative scale. Similarly, her study of U.S. university students (Zhang, 2002b) resulted in the following reliability data: .75 for the analytic scale, .73 for the holistic scale, and .83 for the integrative scale.

Not much can be found in the literature regarding the SOLAT's validity (Youth Form). However, as Torrance (1988) pointed out, evidence for its validity rests primarily on evidence accumulated for a few older versions of the SOLAT (for details, see Torrance, 1988). In general, although creative problem solving and creative thinking require both analytic and holistic modes of thinking, the essence of creative behavior calls for a holistic mode of thinking. Among the existing studies of brain dominance, several major findings emerge. First, male research participants are more right-brain dominant than are their female counterparts (e.g., Albaili, 1993; Helfeldt, 1983; Tan-Willman, 1981). Second, traditional schooling favors so-called left-brain dominant students while often ignoring or even penalizing so-called right-brain dominant students (e.g., Bracken, Ledford, & McCallum, 1979; Torrance, Reigel, Reynolds, & Ball, 1976; Yellin, 1983). Third, creativity is highly associated with the use of the holistic mode of thinking (e.g., Harnad, 1972; Kim & Michael, 1995; Krueger, 1976; Okabayashi & Torrance, 1984; Tan-Willman, 1981; Torrance & Reynolds, 1978). Finally, brain dominance or mode of thinking can be developed (e.g., Bever & Chiarrello, 1974; Gazzaniga, 1971; Reynolds & Torrance, 1978) and each is socialized (e.g., Gadzella & Kneipp, 1990; Kinsbourne, 1982; Petty & Haltman, 1991).

Placing the mode of thinking (brain dominance) within the context of intellectual styles, Zhang (2002a, 2002b) investigated the correlations between the modes of thinking as assessed by Torrance et al.'s (1988) Style of Learning and Thinking and thinking styles as measured by the Thinking Styles Inventory (Sternberg & Wagner, 1992). In both studies, the holistic mode of thinking was associated with Type I thinking styles, and the analytic mode of thinking was associated with Type II thinking styles.

Personality Type and the Myers–Briggs Type Indicator

Jung (1923) proposed that people attend selectively to elements in a learning environment, seeking out learning environments compatible with their alleged type, and avoiding or leaving incompatible environments. They also prefer to use certain learning tools and to avoid others. Furthermore, according to Jung, these preferences lie along three dimensions: extroversion–introversion, sensing–intuitive, and thinking–feeling. Myers and McCaulley (1988) extended Jung's work by adding a further dimension—judging–perceiving. (See Table 8.1 for a brief description of each individual personality type.)

The Myers–Briggs Type Indicator (Myers & McCaulley, 1988) is a forced-choice personality type inventory assessing the four aforementioned dimensions of preferences. Split-half reliability estimates for the four scales (each representing a dimension of personality types) range from .80 to .87 (Myers, 1962; Myers & McCaulley, 1988; Stricker & Ross, 1963). Test–retest reliability estimates range from .48 (which is marginal) to .73 (Levy, Murphy, & Carlson, 1972; Myers & McCaulley, 1988; Stricker & Ross, 1962). The scales distinguish among groups of people and correlate with other inventories as expected by type theory (e.g., Carlson, 1985; McCaulley, 1981). Furthermore, the MBTI scales do not correlate with measures of unrelated constructs (see McCaulley, 1990).

The MBTI has been widely used in both academic and nonacademic settings. Significant correlations can be found between styles derived from the MBTI and mastery of a second language (Ehrman, 1994), creative performance on the job (Jacobson, 1993), and many other activities (cf. Hahn-Rollins & Mongeon, 1988). Furthermore, as has been discussed in the chapter on styles research and applications in nonacademic settings, the sensing and judging types tend to be adaptors and the intuitive and perceiving types tend to be innovators (Carne & Kirton, 1982; Jacobson, 1993). Meanwhile, the sensing and judging types tend to score higher on the Concrete Sequential scale on the Gregorc Style Delineator, and the intuitive and perceiving types tend to score higher on the Concrete Random scale in the Gregorc Style Delineator (e.g., Bokoros, Goldstein, & Sweeney, 1992; Drummond & Stoddard, 1992; Harasym, Leong, Juschka, Lucier, & Lorscheider, 1996; Stuber, 1997). In addition, research also indicates that the intuitive and perceiving types of people tend to be field independent and that the sensing and judging types of people tend to be field dependent (e.g., Carey, Fleming, & Roberts, 1989; Holsworth, 1985). Collectively, this research on testing the MBTI indicates that the personality type construct overlaps with other style constructs. Moreover, this research reveals that the intuitive and perceiving types tend to carry more adaptive value than do the sensing and judging types.

Research does not provide a clear indication of how the thinking–feeling and introversion–extraversion dimensions relate to scales in the other style inventories. For instance, the relationship between Kirton's adaption–innovation and the extraversion–introversion and thinking–feeling dimensions is unclear (Jacobson, 1993; also see Myers, 1962). Similarly, there are inconsistent findings regarding the relationships of field dependence/ independence with the extraversion–introversion and thinking–feeling dimensions (Thomas, 1983; also see Evans, 1967; Feather, 1967). Therefore, these two dimensions are largely value-differentiated.

Personality types are malleable. Research indicates that people become clearer about their personality preferences as they grow older (e.g., Myers & McCaulley, 1985; see also Cummings, 1995). There is a general trend that women are more extraverted than are men (e.g., Abbott & McCaulley, 1984; Simon, 1979; Szymanski, 1977). Gender differences in the thinking–feeling dimension were acknowledged on the establishment of the MBTI, which are manifested by the need for separate norms for males and females. Males tend to score higher on the thinking scale, whereas females tend to score higher on the feeling scale (see also McCrae & Costa, 1989). The effect of gender on personality types has also been shown to interact with birth order. For instance, Stansbury and Coll's (1998) research suggested that whereas first-born female university students scored the highest on the judging scale, the reverse was true for male students. In turn, birth order interacted with socioeconomic status in influencing personality types. Stansbury and Coll (1998) found that within the lowest family-income group, first-born students were significantly more introverted than were middle-born and last-born students. Within higher family income groups, however, first-born students were significantly more extraverted than were later-born students.

The malleability of personality types is also evidenced in the phenomenon that people in the same occupation (or academic major) tend to have similar personality types. For example, artists are more intuitive (as opposed to sensing) than is the general population (e.g., Gridley, 2004; see also Nickel, 1995). Among a sample of Polish university students, Tobacyk and Cieslicka (2000) found that the type distribution of English-language students was almost the opposite to that of marketing/management students. Compared with the marketing/management group, the English-language group had greater proportions of introversion than extraversion, intuition than sensing, thinking than feeling, and of perceiving than judging (see also Boreham & Watts, 1998). Further information on the correspondence between occupations and personality types can be found in Appendix D of the MBTI Manual (Myers & McCaulley, 1985, pp. 244–292).

Again, one could argue that people of similar personality types tend to be drawn into the same occupation or academic field. Once again, it is equally likely that after one enters a particular occupation, one's personality styles are further shaped by the occupational/learning environment. In some cases, occupational/learning environment may modify one's personality styles to a great extent.

Mind Style and the Gregorc Style Delineator

Gregorc (1979, 1984, 1985) suggested that individuals' tendency to use mediation channels or mind styles (often referred to in other theories as "learning styles") could be understood in terms of two basic dimensions: use of space and use of time. Space refers to perceptual categories for acquiring and expressing information. It is divided into concrete (or physical) and abstract (or metaphorical) space. Time is divided into two different ways of ordering facts and events: sequential (i.e., in a step-by-step or branchlike manner) and random ordering (i.e., in a web-like or spiral manner). These two poles of the two dimensions form four styles that are referred to by Gregorc as mind styles: abstract random, concrete sequential, abstract sequential, and concrete random (see also Table 8.1).

The Gregorc Style Delineator (GSD, Gregorc, 1982) is a self-report inventory composed of 40 words organized into 10 columns, each consisting of four words. The respondents are required to rank the four words relative to their preference for receiving and processing information. The technical manual for the inventory (Gregorc, 1984) reported alpha coefficients ranging from .89 to .93, whereas Joniak and Isaksen's study (1988) resulted in scale alpha coefficients ranging from .23 to .66. Also in his 1984 work, Gregorc reported good construct validity as assessed through factor analysis. Submitting the items of the GSD to a factor analysis, Joniak and Isaksen (1988) obtained several orthogonal factors. Employing confirmatory factor analysis, O'Brien (1990) examined the construct validity of the GSD, but found only minimal validity.

Consider additional evidence regarding Gregorc's theory. First, Gregorc's styles are related to students' academic achievement scores. In general, students' academic achievement does not vary as a function of their learning styles (e.g., Harasym, Leong, Juschka, Lucier, & Lorscheider, 1996; O'Brien & Wilkinson, 1992). Similarly, although some studies suggest that students' learning styles make a difference in their instructional preferences (e.g., Ross, 2000; Seidel & England, 1999), others do not reveal a relationship between learning styles and instructional preferences (e.g., Elsberry, 1995; Perchaluk-Kemppainen, 1997). Still other studies show that Gregorc's styles are related to teaching behaviors (e.g., Stuber, 1997) and to job satisfaction (e.g., Willis, 1995).

As mentioned in the previous section, the mind-style construct overlaps with other style constructs. For example, individuals who prefer the concrete sequential learning style tend to be sensing and judging types of people, whereas individuals who prefer the concrete random learning style tend to be intuitive and perceiving types of people (Bokoros, Goldstein, & Sweeney, 1992; Drummond & Stoddard, 1992; Harasym, Leong, Juschka, Lucier, & Lorscheider, 1996; Stuber, 1997). Further, Joniak and Isaksen (1988) concluded that Gregorc's sequential types tend to be adaptors and that the random types tend to be innovators. Across the two sets of empirical findings, it appears that the concrete random style is superior to the concrete sequential style.

The malleability of mind styles has been evidenced in some empirical work. For example, in studying a group of undergraduate athletic training students and a group of program directors, Gould (2003) discovered that female participants tended to employ multiple styles in reaching course outcomes. Meanwhile, compared with students, educators (program directors) were more likely to prefer mind styles that are concrete and structured.

Not surprisingly, people in the same occupation (or academic field) tend to have similar mind styles. In investigating styles of university students, Seidel and England (1999) found that 86% of science majors scored high in the sequential direction and that 85% of humanities majors scored high in the random direction (see also Drysdale, Ross, & Schulz, 2001). Willis (1995) found the concrete–sequential style dominant among computer programmers (see also Van Voorhees, Wolf, Gruppen, & Stross, 1988). O'Brien (1991) found distinctive differences in mind styles based on gender, academic discipline, and levels of academic achievement. Males tended to score higher on the AS (abstract-sequential) and CR (concrete-random) scales, whereas females tended to score higher on the AR (abstract-random) scale. Students majoring in Early Childhood or Elementary Education and in Rehabilitation and Special Education tended to score lower on the AS (abstract-sequential) scale than did students from other academic disciplines (e.g., Adult Education, Vocational Teacher Education, and Arts and Science). Students reporting grade point averages less than or equal to 1.0 scored significantly lower on the AS (abstract-sequential) scales than did the remaining students.

Decision Making and Problem Solving Styles and the Kirton Adaption–Innovation Inventory

Kirton (1976) designed the Kirton Adaption–Innovation Inventory (KAII), a measure of "style of decision making, problem-solving, and by implication, creativity" (Kirton, 1988, p. 65). Consisting of three scales (Originality, Efficiency, and Group Rule Conformity), the KAII is a 32-item self-report test in which respondents indicate the difficulty (or ease) involved in maintaining a certain image consistently for a relatively long time (e.g., as manifested in an individual's tendency for continuing to pursue a creative idea). Scores indicate whether the respondents tend to be innovators or adaptors (see also Table 8.1). Cronbach's alpha coefficients range from the high .70s to the low .90s. Test–retest reliability coefficients normally fall in the mid .80s. The internal structure of the inventory was assessed through factor analysis. External validity of the inventory was examined by testing the KAII against measures of creativity. Results suggest the independence of Kirton's decision-making style from creativity (e.g., Clapp, 1993; Joniak & Isaksen, 1988; Kirton, 1994; Taylor, 1994).

In the chapter on styles research in nonacademic settings, we have discussed extensively existing research based on the Kirton Adaption–Innovation Inventory. Therefore, in this chapter, we will not elaborate further on this research. Suffice it to say that decision-making styles are malleable; they overlap significantly with other style constructs, and the innovative style reveals more positive value than does the adaptive style.

Reflectivity–Impulsivity and the Matching Familiar Figures Test

The reflectivity–impulsivity style construct, also referred to as conceptual tempo, was originally introduced by Kagan and his colleagues (Kagan, Rosman, Day, Albert, & Philips, 1964). Reflectivity is the tendency to consider and reflect on alternative solution possibilities. Impulsivity is the tendency to respond impulsively without sufficient forethought (Block, Block, & Harrington, 1974; Kagan & Messer, 1975). This construct is often measured by the Matching Familiar Figures Test (MFFT, Kagan et al., 1964), in which an individual is instructed to select from several alternatives the one that exactly matches a standard picture. The examiner measures the number of errors and the time to complete the test. The median point of each measure is viewed as a proper score for categorizing individuals. People with faster times and relatively more errors are called impulsive, whereas those with longer times and fewer errors are called reflective. Different forms of the MFFT are available for preschoolers, school children, and adults.

Reliability and validity studies for the MFFT demonstrate only fair reliability for the test. For example, Messer (1976) obtained internal consistency coefficients of .76 for response time and .50 for errors. Messer also found test–retest coefficients of .56 and .78, respectively, for errors and response time. Subsequent research (e.g., Becker, Bender, & Morrison, 1978; Cairns, 1977) also suggests that the MFFT's reliability, especially for the error score, is less than satisfactory. Consequently, efforts were made to revise the instrument. Among these efforts, Cairns and Cammock's (1978) and Zelniker and Jeffrey's (1976) stand out. Research indicates that the reliability of the MFFT has been improved (e.g., Buela-Casal, Carretero-Dios, De-los-Santos-Roig, & Bermudez, 2003; Kirchner-Nebot & Amador-Campos, 1998). For example, Cairns and Cammock (1978) reported split-half correlations of .91 for latency and .89 for errors; Kirchner and Amador-Campos (1998) reported internal consistency of .94 for latencies and .77 for errors.

Many studies have investigated the relationship between the reflectivity–impulsivity construct and the construct of field dependence/independence (e.g., Ausburn, 1979; Banta, 1970; Campbell & Douglas, 1972; Keogh & Donlon, 1972; Logan, 1983; Massari, 1975; Neimark, 1975; Schleifer & Douglas, 1973). The studies confirmed a significant relationship between the two constructs. In general, people who are high on the reflective style are more field independent than are those high on the impulsive style. The overlap between the two constructs may be due to the common process involved in the measures assessing reflectivity–impulsivity and field dependence/independence (Messer, 1976).

Reflectivity can be developed (e.g., Brown & Lawson, 1975; Epstein, Hallahan, & Kauffman, 1975; Huey-You, 1985; see also reviewed studies in Jonassen & Grabowski, 1993 and in Messer, 1976). For example, forced delay of response resulted in a marked improvement in the performance of impulsive children (e.g., Albert, 1969; Brown & Lawson, 1975). Another example is that of modeling. Students became more reflective after observing reflective adult models and after being taught by more reflective teachers (e.g., Denney, 1972; Yando & Kagan, 1968).

A related issue to the malleability/modifiability of conceptual tempo is that of whether it is value-laden or value-free. All training programs have been aimed at cultivating research participants' reflectivity, rather than impulsivity (see studies on malleability). The reason is that reflectivity is superior to impulsivity in almost all adaptive situations. These include, but are not limited to, situations requiring problem-solving skills, cognitive complexity, particular personality traits, social behaviors, and moral development. For example, Messer (1976) and Jonassen and Grabowski (1993) showed that reflectives consistently outperform impulsives on a variety of conceptual, perceptual, and perceptuomotor problem-solving tasks that involve response uncertainty (Kagan, 1966a; Messer, 1976). Reflectives also do better in reading, writing, and memory tasks, as well as on a wide range of achievement tests (e.g., Becker, Bender, & Morrison, 1978; Gullo, 1988; Joffe, 1987; Logan, 1983). Regarding personality traits and social behaviors, Messer (1976) reviewed studies dealing with the relationships of the reflectivity–impulsivity style with such variables as anxiety over error, attentiveness, aggressiveness, locus of control, moral behavior, and delay of gratification. For example, Thomas (1971) found that impulsive boys display more aggressive behaviors than do reflective ones. Taking all this existing research evidence into account, it is only fair to conclude that reflectivity–impulsivity is value-laden, with reflectivity a more desirable style than impulsivity.

Divergent–Convergent Thinking and Its Measurement

The concept of divergent–convergent thinking (see also Table 8.1) was introduced by Guilford (1950, 1967) when he proposed his model of the "structure of intellect." No single universally accepted test is associated with the assessment of the divergent–convergent dimension. Instead, the tendency toward divergent–convergent thinking usually is inferred from one's performance on various tests. Furthermore, the construct is also assessed by tests (typically open-ended questions) that require respondents to generate multiple answers (Riding & Cheema, 1991).

Research evidence relevant to the issue of style malleability is still scanty, although in practice, people are challenged to think, in most cases, more divergently, and in some cases, more convergently. Either way, the point is that we modify the way we use our abilities as we interact with our environments, academic or nonacademic. Alpaugh and Birren (1977) found that older research participants were as intelligent as younger ones. However, the former performed less well on Guilford's tests of divergent thinking. Zhang (1985) concluded that students in higher grades tended to score higher in divergent thinking. Olive (1972a) found that female adolescents were superior to their male counterparts on 5 of the 7 divergent-thinking subtests they administered.

Like many other style constructs, the divergent–convergent construct was also tested against constructs from the styles literature. For example, Gelade (1995) tested the relationship between Guilford and Guilford's Consequences and Alternate Uses tests and the Kirton Adaption–Innovation Inventory. Although the adaptors and the innovators produced roughly the same number of common responses, the innovators produced a larger number of uncommon responses. Using two styles (the convergent and divergent learning styles) from Kolb's (1976) Learning Style Inventory (LSI), Donoghue (1995) examined the relationships of the divergent–convergent construct with scales from the Myers–Briggs Type Indicator. The author discovered a significant relationship between the LSI divergent/convergent styles and the combinations of intuition–perceiving and sensing–judging types. Jonassen (1980) found that field independence was the best predictor of students' performance on divergent tasks in an introductory instructional media course (see also Bloomberg, 1971; Noppe & Gallagher, 1977).

Finally, the issue of whether or not the divergent–convergent construct carries any value orientation has also been addressed in the literature, both conceptually and empirically. Conceptually, for example, Dirkes (1977) discussed the importance of cultivating divergent thinking among students. One could argue that there are courses on such topics as logic, mathematics, and physics that teach convergent thinking. However, these are rare cases. The majority of learning activities aim at promoting students' divergent thinking. For decades, many educational systems from all over the world set developing students' divergent thinking as a major institutional goal. Empirically, the manner in which convergent–divergent thinking styles related to other style constructs (e.g., divergent thinking with innovative and field-independent styles; convergent thinking with adaptive and field-dependent styles) shows that the divergent style is superior to the convergent style. Moreover, the relationship between divergent–convergent thinking and other variables support the value-laden nature of the two styles. For instance, Taft (1971) found that undergraduate students who scored high on divergent-thinking tests of originality were more competent, stable, and resourceful. Divergent thinkers tend to have better academic achievement than do convergent ones (e.g., Bennett, 1973; Eastwood, 1965; Feldhusen, Treffinger, Van-Mondfrans, & Ferris, 1971; Olive, 1972b).

Field Dependence/Independence and the Group Embedded Figures Test

Field dependence/independence is also referred to as psychological differentiation (Witkin, Dyk, Faterson, Goodenough, & Karp, 1962). It is the extent to which people are dependent vs. independent of the organization of the surrounding perceptual field (see also Table 8.1).

Several instruments have been developed to assess the field dependence/independence (FDI) construct, including the widely used Group Embedded Figures Test (GEFT, Witkin, Oltman, Raskin, & Karp, 1971). The GEFT is a group-administered and timed paper-and-pencil performance test adapted from the individually administered Embedded Figures Test. The test takers are presented with 8 simple figures and 25 complex figures. One of the 8 simple figures is embedded within each of the 25 complex figures. The test-takers' task is to locate and trace, within the context of the complex figures, as many of the simple figures as possible within three timed sections (of 2, 5, and 5 minutes). The score on the GEFT is the number of items correctly traced. The higher one's score, the more field independent one is; the lower one's score, the more field dependent one is.

Good reliability data on the GEFT have been obtained in various forms, including test–retest, parallel forms, split-half, and scale internal consistencies (e.g., Lewin, 1983; Melancon & Thompson, 1989; Murphy, Casey, Day, & Young, 1997; Panek, Funk, & Nelson, 1980; Snyder, 1998). However, although supported by most of the studies (e.g., Lewin, 1983; Melancon & Thompson, 1989; Murphy, Casey, Day, & Young, 1997), the validity of the inventory occasionally has been challenged (e.g., Cakan, 2003; Panek, Funk, & Nelson, 1980).

The field dependence/independence (FDI) construct is probably the most extensively researched style construct, although it is often criticized for not being a style construct, but rather a perceptual ability (e.g., Dubois & Cohen, 1970; Jones, 1997b; Richardson & Turner, 2000; Satterly, 1976; Spotts & Mackler, 1967; Stuart, 1967; Weisz, O'Neill, & O'Neill, 1975). Empirical evidence for the FDI construct has been discussed extensively elsewhere in this book (including other parts of this chapter). It has been established that field dependence/independence are value-laden, with field independence generally carrying more positive value than field dependence (see also Kogan, 1989; Messick, 1994, 1996). The FDI construct significantly overlaps with other style constructs. Finally, the styles can be modified. In the following, we only further address the issue of style malleability by introducing the training of field independence.

Since the late 1960s and early 1970s, various training programs aimed at enhancing people's field independence have been designed and carried out. These training programs, including training in depth perception (e.g., Mshelia & Lapidus, 1990), meditation (e.g., Linden, 1973), and hunting ecology (e.g., MacArthur, 1973) indicate that field independence can be developed (see also Collins, 1994; Pysh, 1970). For example, in their study of 167 Nigerian fourth graders, Mshelia and Lapidus (1990) conducted a training program as part of their experimental study. The aim of the program was to raise children's performance level on depth-perception tasks (tasks that require the field independence). Having had their initial levels of field dependence/independence determined by their scores on the Group Embedded Figures Test, the children were ranked and assigned to four groups. Two groups received Depth Picture Perception training with Mshelia's Sets A and B items. During the Depth Picture Perception training, each child individually observed for 6 minutes a sixth-grade student model (either male or female) previously trained on the Mshelia pictures. Immediately after that, each child spent 6 minutes with an experimenter for a posttest. A third group received training with the GEFT odd items. Children in this group observed the same trainers completing the GEFT odd items. The fourth group was a control group that received no training. Posttest results indicated that children who received training on depth picture perception tasks performed better on an alternative form of a parallel task and on the GEFT. Furthermore, children who received training on the

GEFT scored higher on field independence than did children in the control group.

Summary

To summarize, this review of the nine individual models (along with the theory of mental self-government introduced in chapter 7) and of the empirical findings supporting these models provided in this and previous chapters suggests the following with regard to the three controversial issues over styles. First, styles are not value-free. Second, styles are malleable and they can be developed. Third, any one of the style constructs reviewed is significantly related to at least one of the other nine style constructs. Furthermore, there are three characteristics of the manner in which these styles are related to one another. First, those styles carrying "positive values" (see earlier discussion, e.g., field independent, reflective, legislative, artistic, perceiving, deep, and so forth) are positively correlated with one another and are related to human attributes that are commonly perceived as positive. Second, styles that carry "negative values" (also see earlier discussion, e.g., field dependent, impulsive, executive, conventional, judging, surface, and so forth) are positively related to one another and are associated with human attributes that are usually perceived as negative. Finally, in the style models that address more than just bipolar intellectual styles, some styles (e.g., internal, introverted, thinking, feeling, achieving, and so forth) do not indicate consistent relationship patterns with style constructs that have only bipolar styles. Table 8.2 lists major studies revealing significant relationships among intellectual styles.

THE NATURE OF INTELLECTUAL STYLES

People's intellectual styles can be classified into three types based on individual differences in people's preferences for each of the underlying concepts (i.e., structured vs. free of structure, cognitive simplicity vs. cognitive complexity, conformity vs. nonconformity, authority vs. autonomy, and group vs. individual). They correspond to the three types of thinking styles discovered through research on Sternberg's theory of mental self-government. In other words, the three types of thinking styles are the groundwork for the three types of intellectual styles discussed in this chapter. (Obviously, thinking styles are now put within the framework of intellectual styles, as are the other style constructs.)

Type I intellectual styles normally fall on the right end of each of the first four continua of preference: low degrees of structure, cognitive complexity, nonconformity, and autonomy. That is, Type I intellectual styles denote pref-

TABLE 8.2
Selected Studies Supporting Significant Relationships Among Intellectual Styles

Style Construct	a	b	c	d	e	f	g	h	i	j
[a]Learning approach		Zhang, 2004								Zhang, 2000a
[b]Career personality type									Alvi et al., 1988; Khan & Alvi, 1986	Zhang, 2000b
[c]Mode of thinking										Zhang, 2002a
[d]Personality type					Bokoros et al., 1992; Drummond & Stoddard, 1992	Carne & Kirton, 1982; Jacobson, 1993			Carey et al., 1989; Holsworth, 1985	Sternberg, 1994; Tucker, 1999
[e]Mind style				Harasym et al., 1996; Stuber, 1997		Joniak & Isaksen, 1988				Sternberg, 1994
[f]Decision-making style				Fleenor & Taylor, 1994; Goldsmith, 1986					Robertson et al., 1987	

(Continued)

TABLE 8.2
(Continued)

Style Construct	a	b	c	d	e	f	g	h	i	j
[g]Conceptual tempo									Banta, 1970; Campbell & Douglas, 1972; Keogh & Donlon, 1972	
[h]Structure of intellect						Donoghue, 1995			Bloomberg, 1971; Jonassen, 1980	
[i]Perceptual style		Khan et al., 1985					Massari, 1975; Messer, 1976; Neimark, 1975; Schleifer & Douglas, 1973	Noppe & Gallagher, 1977		
[j]Thinking style	Zhang & Sternberg, 2000	Zhang, 2001b	Zhang, 2002b							

Note. Theoretical foundations: [a]Biggs' theory of student learning, [b]Holland's theory of career personality types, [c]Torrance's construct of brain dominance, [d]Jung's theory of personality types, [e]Gregorc's model of mind styles, [f]Kirton's model of decision-making styles, [g]Kagan's model of reflectivity–impulsivity conceptual tempo, [h]Guilford's model of structure of intellect, [i]Witkin's construct of field dependence/independence, [j]Sternberg's theory of mental self-government. From Zhang and Sternberg (2005). Reprinted with kind permission of Springer Science and Business Media.

erences for tasks that have low degrees of structure, that require individuals to process information in a more complex way, and that allow originality and high levels of freedom to do things in one's own way. Based on both the descriptions of specific styles in the 10 models illustrated earlier and the existing research findings generated by these models, the following styles are classified as Type I intellectual styles: the deep-learning approach, the artistic career personality type, the holistic mode of thinking, the intuitive and perceiving personality types, the concrete random mind style, the innovative decision-making style, the reflective conceptual tempo, divergent thinking, and the field independent perceptual style, as well as the Type I thinking styles of legislative, judicial, global, hierarchical, and liberal.

Type II intellectual styles normally fall on the left end of each of the first four continua of preference: structure, cognitive simplicity, conformity, and authority. That is, Type II intellectual styles suggest preferences for tasks that are structured, that allow individuals to process information in a more simplistic way, and that require conformity to traditional ways of doing things and high levels of respect for authority. Similarly, based on the descriptions of the individual styles in the 10 models reviewed and on the existing research findings, the following styles are categorized as Type II intellectual styles: the surface-learning approach, the conventional career personality type, the analytic mode of thinking, the sensing and judging personality types, the concrete sequential mind style, the adaption decision-making style, the impulsive conceptual tempo, convergent thinking, the field dependent perceptual style, as well as the Type II thinking styles of executive, local, monarchic, and conservative.

Finally, Type III intellectual styles fall neither into Type I nor Type II groups. Instead, they manifest the characteristics of both Type I and Type II intellectual styles, depending on the stylistic demands of a specific task and on an individual's level of interest in the task. Again, based on the nature of the particular styles in the 10 models and on existing research findings relevant to these style constructs, the following styles are categorized as Type III intellectual styles: the achieving learning approach, the realistic, investigative, social, and enterprising career personality types, the integrative mode of thinking, the thinking, feeling, introversion, and extraversion personality types, the abstract random and abstract sequential mind styles, and the Type III thinking styles of oligarchic, anarchic, internal, and external.

Although it is included as one of the five pairs of concepts underlying intellectual styles, the preference dimension of group vs. individual was not mentioned in the discussion of either Type I or Type II intellectual styles. It is in the context of Type III intellectual styles that people's group vs. individual preference plays a major role. Type III intellectual styles are dominated by styles that suggest sociological preferences, including the social and enterprising career personality types, the introverted and extraverted personality types, and the internal and external thinking styles. The styles that denote sociological preferences and the remaining Type III styles share a common characteristic: They may be employed as either Type I or Type II styles, depending, as mentioned earlier, on the stylistic demands of a specific task and on the individual's feelings about the task. For example, an individual with the social career personality type may perform a task in a creative way and invest a great deal of complex thinking in an attempt to do a good job if the task requires the individual to do so and if the individual is interested in the specific task at hand. In this case, the social career personality type manifests the characteristics of Type I intellectual styles. The same person may also perform the task in an established way, however, without putting too much thought into what he or she is doing if the task does not require much creativity or deep thinking and if the individual is not terribly interested in the task at hand. Under such circumstances, the social career personality type shows the features of Type II intellectual styles.

Table 8.3 presents details on each of the three types of styles. It includes the original name for each of the intellectual style constructs and the labels for each of the individual styles within each theoretical model. The footnote specifies the theoretical foundation for each style construct.

THE THREE CONTROVERSIAL ISSUES AND THE THREEFOLD MODEL OF INTELLECTUAL STYLES

The Threefold Model of Intellectual Styles implies a stand on each of the three main controversial issues mentioned earlier regarding styles: trait vs. state, value-laden vs. value-free, and different style constructs vs. similar constructs with different style labels. These three issues were discussed in previous chapters and in the review of the nine style models and empirical findings supporting these models in the present chapter. We now discuss these issues within the context of the Threefold Model of Intellectual Styles.

Style Malleability

Regarding the issue of styles as traits or states, investigations focusing on thinking styles indicate, as elaborated in the previous chapter, that thinking styles represent states because they can be socialized and modified. By the same token, other intellectual styles from other style models also can be socialized and modified, as discussed earlier. This argument is supported by the fact that many training programs are aimed at modifying people's intellectual styles. This effort to modify people's intellectual styles has made some of the once strong believers in the notion of styles as traits change their theoretical positions over time. For example, in the early stage of

TABLE 8.3
Intellectual Styles

	Style Type	Type I	Type II	Type III
	aLearning approach	Deep	Surface	Achieving
	bCareer personality type	Artistic	Conventional	Realistic, Investigative, Social, Enterprising
	cMode of thinking	Holistic	Analytic	Integrative
	dPersonality type	Intuitive, Perceiving	Sensing, Judging	Thinking, Feeling, Introversion, Extraversion
Style Construct	eMind style	Concrete random	Concrete sequential	Abstract random, Abstract sequential
	fDecision-making style	Innovation	Adaptation	
	gConceptual tempo	Reflectivity	Impulsivity	
	hStructure of intellect	Divergent thinking	Convergent thinking	
	iPerceptual style	Field independent	Field dependent	
	jThinking style	Legislative, Judicial, Global, Hierarchical	Executive, Local, Monarchic, Conservative	Oligarchic, Anarchic, Internal, External

Note. Theoretical foundations: aBiggs' theory of student learning, bHolland's theory of career personality types, cTorrance's construct of brain dominance, dJung's theory of personality types, eGregorc's model of mind styles, fKirton's model of decision-making styles, gKagan's model of reflectivity–impulsivity conceptual tempo, hGuilford's model of structure of intellect, iWitkin's construct of field dependence/independence, jSternberg's theory of mental self-government. From Zhang and Sternberg (2005). Reprinted with kind permission of Springer Science and Business Media.

studying Witkin's concept of field dependence/independence, the Witkin group advanced the idea that field dependence/independence represents a highly stable and pervasive construct with deep roots in personality and possibly even in biology. However, in his 1977 Heinz Werner Lectures delivered at Clark University, Witkin discussed an ongoing training program aimed at enhancing restructuring skills. States can be changed, whereas traits are much more stable. Some scholars suggest that traits are built-in characteristics that are hard to change. Because our research (e.g., Zhang, 1999a, 2001a; Zhang & Sachs, 1997; Zhang & Sternberg, 2002) and that of other scholars (e.g., Collins, 1994; Huey-You, 1985; Linden, 1973; Mshelia & Lapidus, 1990) indicates that the majority of styles are trainable (and/or socialized), we argue that the styles in the Threefold Model of Intellectual Styles represent states.

However, status as states does not mean that intellectual styles constantly change. They can normally be rather stable, except when there is a demand for change of styles by specific situations. Therefore, to be more precise, we posit that intellectual styles largely represent relatively stable states. Furthermore, Type I and Type II styles are relatively more stable than are Type III styles, because Type III styles are more contingent on the nature of a task and on one's feelings about the task.

Style Value

Regarding the value issue of styles, research on thinking styles has led to our position that thinking styles, especially Type I and Type II styles, are value-laden, rather than value-free. Likewise, it can be easily argued that all the other intellectual styles (especially Type I and Type II) discussed are also value-laden (see earlier review of each of the individual style models). For example, Kogan (1989) used convincing examples to support the argument that styles have never been value-free. He pointed out, with regard to Witkin's notion of field dependence/independence, that training studies have tried to make individuals more field independent rather than field dependent. He further noted that similar considerations hold even more strongly in the case of reflectivity–impulsivity as a style construct. All training efforts have been directed at the enhancement of the reflective style. Positive characteristics associated with an impulsive style have yet to be demonstrated. Indeed, much research concludes that, in general, reflectivity is associated with better academic and cognitive performances of various kinds (see Messer, 1976 for a comprehensive review; also Stahl, Erickson, & Rayman, 1986; Zelniker & Oppenheimer, 1973).

Yet, it should be noted that some scholars have also proposed the concept of value differentiation based on the contention that styles are typically bipolar and that each pole of a style dimension has different adaptive implications. That is, in the context of styles, an individual can be both good and poor at tasks, depending on the nature of the task (e.g., Messick, 1994; Riding, 1997). For example, whereas field dependence can be viewed as a deficiency attributable to the absence of those skills associated with field independence, it can, at the same time, be perceived as a valuable asset because field dependence is also associated with a set of well-developed interpersonal and social skills (e.g., Miller, 1987). However, we argue that such an example cannot be taken completely at face value. Whereas it is true that one can find something positive to say about any intellectual style, the majority of intellectual styles, especially Type I and Type II styles, are heavily value directional. In the Threefold Model of Intellectual Styles, Type I intellectual styles are predominantly positive, whereas Type II intellectual styles are predominantly negative. The word "predominantly" is used to qualify our position on the value domain to allow for any style's occasional manifestation of the characteristics of the styles that are of the opposite type, assuming that Type I and Type II styles are each other's opposites. That is, Type I styles may occasionally exhibit the characteristics of Type II styles and vice versa. Thus, the concept of value differentiation may occasionally apply to Type I and Type II intellectual styles. Meanwhile, this concept of value differentiation applies to Type III intellectual styles to a much greater extent. That is, Type III intellectual styles are more value differentiated. As discussed earlier, Type III styles can be carried out either with the characteristics of Type I intellectual styles or with those of Type II styles. In other words, Type III styles have both "positive" and "negative" adaptive values, which fact satisfies the condition of their being value differentiated. Therefore, the Threefold Model of Intellectual Styles implies that Type I and Type II intellectual styles are predominantly value-laden, whereas Type III styles are value differentiated. However, intellectual styles cannot be value-free.

Style Overlap

As for the third major controversial issue, that of style constructs being distinct constructs versus being similar constructs with different style labels, research on thinking styles, as discussed in the previous chapter, demonstrates that style constructs overlap to varying degrees. By the same token, numerous empirical studies based on other style models also indicate that different degrees of overlap exist among different style constructs. The style construct underlying any one of the 10 style models included in this newly proposed model of intellectual styles has been empirically shown to be correlated with at least one of the other style constructs. Therefore, on the issue of styles being distinct constructs versus styles being similar constructs with different style labels, the Threefold Model of Intellectual Styles does not take either position. Instead, based on empirical research findings, we contend that those constructs with different style labels overlap to varying degrees. These overlaps indicate that style constructs are neither completely different constructs nor similar constructs with different style labels. Instead, these style constructs share certain degrees of similarities, with each possessing its own uniqueness.

CONCLUSIONS

In this chapter, a new integrative style model has been proposed: the Threefold Model of Intellectual Styles. Inevitably, three major questions arise relevant to this model. First, "What contributions has this model made?" Second, "What should a research agenda look like in order for the model to be validated?" Third, "What implications does this model have for educational practice and organizational management?" The remainder of this chapter addresses these three questions.

Contributions

Five major contributions of this model are worth mentioning. First, this model is the first integrative style model that explicitly takes a stand on each of the three major controversial issues regarding styles. Second, other models tend to mention one kind of styles, but not others. Specifically, whereas both Miller (1987) and Riding and Cheema (1991) referred to their integrative models as models of *cognitive styles*, Curry (1983) referred to her model as one of *learning styles*. In our new model, we choose to use *intellectual styles* as the umbrella term for all existing style labels, including cognitive and learning styles. Third, compared with the existing integrative models of styles, this model is the most general because it is capable of accommodating individual models with any number of style dimensions, regardless of the approach (personality, cognition, or activity) that an individual model takes. Fourth, the model has built a bridge between intellectual styles and other aspects of human learning and development. Finally, this model takes an open-system approach. Any individual model that meets the three criteria specified earlier can become part of the Threefold Model of Intellectual Styles.

Research Agenda

The Threefold Model of Intellectual Styles is not only a heuristic device, but also a summary of empirical relationships. What is perhaps lacking in the previous integrative models (except for Riding and Cheema's model) is adequate empirical evidence. We discuss a possible research agenda and make testable predictions from the model.

To test the validity of this model, a number of research procedures need to be implemented so that the following three questions can be answered, each relating to one of the three controversial issues addressed in the Threefold Model of Intellectual Styles. First, assuming that different style constructs are related (this assumption is made based on the research evidence presented throughout this book), how are they related? Second, are styles more dynamic or more static? Third, are styles relatively more value-laden or more value-differentiated?

One of the research procedures that can be used to answer the first question is a quantitative study in which all participants respond to all inventories discussed above that are relevant to the 10 individual style models. Analysis of this set of data can be focused on the manner in which the style scales from the 10 inventories are related to one another, identified by a simple exploratory factor analysis or a canonical correlation procedure. We predict that the style scales from all 10 inventories will load on three factors, with each factor dominated by styles of the same type (i.e., Type I, Type II, and Type III), respectively. Furthermore, we predict the following correlations: Individual styles within each type will be positively related to one another; Type I styles will be negatively correlated with Type II styles; and Type III styles will be moderately positively related to Type I and Type II styles.

To answer the question about the malleability of intellectual styles, one can design and conduct programs that aim at developing particular intellectual styles. We predict that all styles will be modifiable, but to varying degrees, depending on the nature of each style construct. We predict that the success of changing Type I styles into Type II styles (suppose some training programs attempt to develop Type II styles), or vice versa, will take more effort and a relatively longer period of time to achieve; whereas the cultivation of Type III styles will be relatively easier. In other words, as we argued earlier, Type I and Type II styles are relatively more stable than Type III styles.

The question on the value issue of styles can be answered from two different angles. The first is to collect information about the nature of the existing training programs. We predict that almost all training programs will attempt to develop Type I intellectual styles. The second is to investigate the relationship between any of the intellectual style constructs and variables that are cognitive, affective, physiological, psychological, or sociological in nature. We have three predictions, the first two of which are relevant to variables that are cognitive, affective, physiological, and psychological in nature, and the third related to variables that are sociological in nature. First, Type I intellectual styles will be positively related to any variable that denotes a positive value (e.g., higher levels of cognitive development, higher self-esteem, openness to experience, more motivation for achieving success, and higher physical-energy levels). Second, Type II styles will be positively related to any variable that denotes a negative value (e.g., lower levels of cognitive development, lower self-esteem, neuroticism, more motivation for avoiding failure, and lower physical-energy level). Third, Type III styles and sociological variables will be related. However, the ways in which they are associated with each other are more adaptive. In other words, as previously discussed, Type I and Type II intellectual styles are predominantly value-laden and more stable, whereas Type III styles are value-differentiated and more dynamic.

Implications for Educational Practice

For educational practice, the present model has three major implications. First, the model suggests that educators can make use of the interrelationships among the intellectual styles to limit testing time. For example, when time is limited, an educational practitioner could use one or two inventories to identify students' intellectual styles, rather than administering a whole range of inventories. Then, given the interrelationships among the intellectual styles, one could predict with reasonable confidence scores on particular styles that are not tested.

Second, the Threefold Model of Intellectual Styles can help address one of the major concerns often expressed by teachers to whom the notion of styles is new. Scholars who do research on styles and who promote style awareness among teachers are often asked: "So, you are telling us that there are many different styles and that our teaching should take styles into account. Then the problem is: How could our teaching accommodate so many different styles?" The present model would answer this question by stating that, in general, teachers need only to address the three broad types of intellectual styles by attending to the five basic dimensions of preferences underlying intellectual styles: high degrees of structure vs. low degrees of structure, cognitive simplicity vs. cognitive complexity, conformity vs. nonconformity, authority vs. autonomy, and group vs. individual. Furthermore, we believe that good teaching treats the two polar terms of each dimension as the two ends of a continuum and provides a balanced amount of challenge and support along each dimension.

Finally, the Threefold Model of Intellectual Styles provides a practical framework to educational practitioners in their endeavors in fostering students' development in multiple dimensions: cognitive, affective, physiological, psychological, and sociological. Educational programs can be designed more systematically so that not only are students' intellectual styles taken into account but also their characteristics in other aspects such as the five dimensions of preferences.

Implications for Organizational Research and Management

Like for educational practice, the new integrative model of intellectual styles also has three principal implications for organizational research and development. First, in the past, style research on organizations tended to be limited to the use of MBTI and KAII (Kirton Adaptation–Innovation Inventory). The new integrative model suggests that the remaining individual style constructs in the integrative model can also be used to assess styles of people in nonacademic organizations. Even if several of the inventories (e.g., Biggs's Study Process Questionnaire and Torrance's Style of Learning and Thinking) were originally designed for assessing styles of students, they can be easily adapted for use with nonacademic populations. Such an endeavor would mean that organizational researchers are to have greater access to research tools.

Second, the Threefold Model of Intellectual Styles may have practical value for designing leadership training programs for managers of all levels. The model designates that the three types of intellectual styles can be developed. Organizational leaders of all levels should understand that the work environments that they create for their supervisees can help to cultivate, broadly speaking, three types of cognitive climates, each dominated by one type of intellectual styles. To create these cognitive climates, leaders should take into account the five basic dimensions of preferences underlying intellectual styles. Again, the key to good management is to strike a balance on each of the five continua.

Finally, the new model also makes available a practical framework to organizational leaders in designing and implementing staff development programs. Given that intellectual styles are characterized by their multiple facets (cognitive, affective, physiological, psychological, and sociological), organizational leaders can cultivate the desired type of intellectual styles by designing and implementing staff development programs that take into consideration both the five dimensions of preferences and the five characteristics of intellectual styles.

Chapter 9

Conclusions and Future Directions

In this book, we have described some of the major works, both empirical and theoretical, in the field of intellectual styles. We have also proposed a new integrative model of intellectual styles. One obvious question arises with respect to the new model: Why should one even care about another theoretical model of styles? To answer that question, this chapter will be presented in four parts. The first part summarizes major empirical evidence supporting the notion of intellectual styles and draws conclusions about the nature of intellectual styles. The second part illustrates the implications of the new integrative model for future research directions. The third part discusses the model's practical implications for different aspects of our life, at both the individual and the societal levels. Finally, we close with a caveat about the future of the new model.

MAJOR FINDINGS AND CONCLUSIONS

The bulk of this book presents research evidence that intellectual styles do exist and that they matter in many aspects of human performance and behaviors. These performances and behaviors include, but are not limited to, our learning, teaching, work, career, conduct, and social behaviors, learning and job performance, cognitive and psychosocial development, and psychological well-being. It has also been demonstrated that people's intellectual styles are associated with both personal characteristics (age, gender, birth order, ability, personality, and socioeconomic status) and environmental characteristics (educational background, parental intellectual style,

176

residential location, national culture, professional and nonprofessional experience, academic discipline, school and organizational culture, occupational group, work position, job function, and actual and perceived learning and work environments). Moreover, these personal and environmental characteristics serve as moderators in the relationships of intellectual styles to our performance and behaviors.

Collectively, these findings inform us about the nature of intellectual styles. Our view of the nature of intellectual styles has been elucidated on the basis of our positions on three controversial issues: style malleability, style overlap, and style value. We conclude, first, that intellectual styles are malleable. Second, existing style labels overlap significantly, although each has its own unique features. Finally, intellectual styles are largely value-laden and can sometimes be value-differentiated; however, they are not value-free.

But the question remains: Why do we need the threefold model of intellectual styles? As noted in the previous chapter, the threefold model of intellectual styles is not only a heuristic device, but also a summary of empirical relationships: It is a natural product of existing work in the field. Put differently, the model was there; it just needed to be discovered. As for its accomplishments, the model speaks to the three longstanding controversial issues regarding styles. It also establishes a common theoretical framework and a common language for the study of styles. Thus, the threefold model of intellectual styles can serve as a useful guide for future research. Moreover, the new model also makes it more meaningful for us to talk about the applied and practical implications of intellectual styles. In the following section, we discuss the possible areas of our lives in which the notion of intellectual styles could be used.

GENERAL IMPLICATIONS: VARIETY IN INTELLECTUAL STYLES SHOULD BE PRAISED, NOT CONDEMNED

Educational Settings

Student Self-Esteem and Learning Motivation. An understanding of intellectual styles may enhance students' self-esteem and increase their learning motivation. Low academic achievers sometimes attribute their poor performance to their low abilities or their belief that something is "wrong" with them. By understanding that other factors (including not only their own intellectual styles, but also their teachers' intellectual styles) play an important role in their learning performance, students may start developing adaptive attributions to their successes and failures. They may explain that the environment in which they learn may not be suitable for their learning styles. Consequently, instead of feeling badly about themselves, they may start exploring ways of either adapting to or shaping their learning environments. That is, they may modify their own learning styles to improve their learning and performance; or they may better communicate with teachers, who in turn can make the learning environment more accommodating to the students' learning styles.

Diversifying Instructional and Assessment Methods. Teachers could allow students to use different intellectual styles by diversifying their instructional methods and assessment schemes. When students are taught and assessed in different ways, they have opportunities to demonstrate their strengths and correct for their weaknesses. For instance, students who tend to think more creatively (Type I intellectual styles) may prefer working on a project, whereas students who are adept at using their memories (Type II intellectual styles) may find a multiple-choice test more attractive. Students who appear mediocre on one type of assessment may excel on another. Effective teachers diversify their instruction and assessment so that students, no matter what their intellectual styles are, have the opportunity to study and grow intellectually in a learning environment that is both accommodating (i.e., students are able to use their preferred intellectual styles) and challenging (i.e., students are provided with the opportunities to develop other styles).

A Change in Teachers' Attitudes. In general, like students, teachers without knowledge of intellectual styles also tend to believe that students' poor academic performance is mainly due to their low abilities. Moreover, they may be inclined to attribute poor performance to laziness. With some knowledge of the role of intellectual styles in academic achievement, teachers may also consider other factors that affect student learning and performance, which may lead them to adjust their expectations of students. Teachers may become more aware that their own intellectual styles likely play a role in their expectations of students. They may realize that they hold an unconscious bias against students with intellectual styles that are discrepant from their own. This awareness may enable teachers to reformulate and better communicate their expectations to students.

Enhancing Interpersonal Relationships. Recognition of different intellectual styles can also foster the development of interpersonal relationships. For instance, because they know students have different styles of learning, teachers may facilitate cooperative learning. Cooperative learning provides students with opportunities to interact with their peers, opportunities whereby they demonstrate their strengths and at the same time learn from others about more effective ways of dealing with problems. By working together, students not only learn intellectual skills from one other, but also how to communicate their ideas more effectively and how to tolerate different people, ideas, and values.

Administrators' Considerations. There are many ways in which university/school administrators can apply their knowledge of intellectual styles to their work. We discuss two. First, administrators must learn that teachers and staff vary in their intellectual styles and thereby create a work environment that allows for the use of different intellectual styles. Administrators may allow sufficient autonomy to teachers and staff so that they work at their own pace and in their own preferred ways. A second, and perhaps a more serious, implication of styles knowledge relates to the staffing issue at the university level. In many higher educational institutions around the world, teaching evaluations (completed by students) are used as one of the major performance indicators of academic staff members. Yet, much research has indicated that teaching effectiveness is multifaceted (e.g., French, 1974; Herrmann, 1996; Phillips, 1999). Many factors, including intellectual styles, affect the way students rate their teachers' teaching (e.g., Abrami, Leventhal, Perry, & Breen, 1976; Hale, 1980; Phillips, 1999). Thus, teaching evaluations can be fairly subjective. It is, therefore, important that administrators be aware of the potential bias inherited in teaching evaluations arising from students' unique intellectual styles. Although the possible effects of intellectual styles on teaching evaluations should always be kept in mind, it becomes even more critical when an employment decision is involved. Thus, if a teacher gets consistent low student ratings over several courses, it may not be merely a matter of effects of intellectual styles.

Business Settings

Human Resource Management. Human resource management personnel may benefit in at least two ways from applying the knowledge of intellectual styles. First, they may take intellectual styles into account in the selection of people for jobs. Second, after the selection procedure is complete, they may view available personnel as a total human-resources portfolio with diverse intellectual styles, and thus delegate tasks more sensibly. Agor (1991), after studying thinking styles in business organizations, concluded that "In the final analysis, what most helps an organization avoid errors and gain advantages from two perspectives, is the systematic integration of intuitive and traditional management skills and styles" (p. 13).

Collaborative Work and Conflict Resolution. Ordinary workforce leaders and organizational leaders alike could benefit from the knowledge of intellectual styles. Such knowledge can raise people's awareness of their own styles as well as the styles of their colleagues (or supervisors and supervisees). Such awareness could be instrumental to the effectiveness of organizational behavior in general, and to conflict resolution and group cohesiveness in particular.

Training and Development Programs. Providers of management training and development programs may want to understand the relationship between intellectual styles and work environments. With this knowledge, program designers could create training and development programs that are congruent with the intellectual styles of the trained personnel.

Social Settings

Recognizing and allowing for diverse intellectual styles should have at least two significant implications. The first relates to a challenge we all face—globalization. The second pertains to several social values that are held by most people around the globe.

Facing the Challenges of Globalization. One of the newest and most successful buzzwords of the past few years has been "globalization." The world is progressively more connected through technology, trade, and population movements. Globalization has been examined in several academic fields, including anthropology, education, economics, and history (see, e.g., Suárez-Orozco & Qin-Hillard, 2004). What does globalization have to do with intellectual styles? As a result of globalization, we live in a world in which we deal with people from increasingly diverse cultures and backgrounds. Teachers are teaching more international students and students are interacting with more international classmates. People in organizational settings often find themselves working with people beyond those from their immediate work settings. Business managers deal with more and more international business travelers. Doctors are seeing more medical tourists (i.e., patients who go to foreign countries for medical treatment). Many of us find ourselves dealing with people we've never met and perhaps will never meet. To successfully meet the challenges of globalization, we should foster awareness that people have different intellectual styles. Such awareness would facilitate communication among people of different backgrounds, particularly different cultural backgrounds.

Diversity of Intellectual Styles and Social Values. Recognizing and allowing for different intellectual styles promotes autonomy, choice, democracy, diversity, pluralism, and tolerance. These social values play an increasingly important role in the effective operation of social groups at different levels, including family, community, organizational, and national. For any social group to thrive, and indeed, even to survive, effective communication is paramount. To communicate effectively, members of a society must realize that people use their abilities differently and prefer different ways of carrying out tasks (i.e., different intellectual styles), among other things. One can respect the various social values mentioned before in different ways. For example, people in leadership positions can allow their followers to find a niche by exercising democratic values, giving their followers a sense of autonomy and choice, and taking into account the diverse views of people who work for and with them. Consider the process of rule making: Rules and regulations are to be followed by people. For any rule/regulation to be carried out successfully, it should be based on wide consultation of people with different ways of thinking. If people are involved in the establishment of an organizational rule, they feel more responsible for abiding by it. A rule that is autocratically dictated by one person or a small group of people in leadership positions tends to be met with resistance. Therefore, an effective leader (teacher, business executive, or anyone in power) consults widely before finalizing any rules and regulations.

Members of a society can allow for different intellectual styles by being accepting and tolerant of a wide variety of differences: age, gender, race, culture, religious belief, opinion, socioeconomic status, and value. The recipe for success for different social groups could vary. However, one of the common ingredients is likely to be the collaboration among people of different intellectual styles.

SPECIFIC IMPLICATIONS: CULTIVATING TYPE I INTELLECTUAL STYLES

At a more specific level, the threefold model of intellectual styles signifies that Type I intellectual styles should be nurtured. We propose several strategies that may be applied to both the academic and nonacademic settings.

Serve As a Role Model for Creative Thinking

Intellectual styles are socialized, and thus can be taught and learned. There are, of course, many channels for promoting creative intellectual styles, one of which is role modeling. We believe that if one has the opportunity to watch and emulate a role model who demonstrates the use of Type I intellectual styles, one can develop his or her own creativity-generating styles, at least in theory. In academic settings, the way teachers teach has a direct impact on how students learn. For example, if a teacher mostly lectures about the content of the textbook, students are more likely to confine themselves to learning the contents of the textbooks as well. However, if a teacher draws from different resources, uses a wide variety of teaching methods, and provokes creative thoughts, students tend to be inspired to go beyond the textbooks and initiate other means of learning.

The same can be said about the nonacademic world. Imagine the intellectual styles of supervisees who see their supervisors maintain the status quo. Chances are these supervisees use intellectual styles that are basically conservative in outlook, local in orientation, and based on following directions closely within a structure that is provided by their supervisors. In contrast, supervisees who often witness their supervisors embarking on new efforts in response to the rapid changes of the world tend to use styles that are associated with a more progressive outlook, a more global orientation, and creating rather than following directions.

Allow Mistakes

No one wants to risk thinking creatively (at least on the same issue, or within the same work environment) after having been knocked down for a "mistake" while testing out a new idea. In schools and business organizations alike, people must be given chances to make mistakes. Creative ideas that lead to successful products are typically the result of experimenting by trial and error over a relatively long period of time. One cannot nurture Type I intellectual styles without tolerating mistakes and encouraging sensible risk taking.

Reward Creative Ideas and Products

It is not enough to tell someone that we value creativity-generating intellectual styles. We need to show that we really do by rewarding creative thinking. For example, when a teacher grades papers, not only should knowledge and analytical skills count, but also creative ideas. In a business setting, employees' performance should not only be judged by how well they can execute tasks, but also how often they come up with innovative ideas or products that better the organization.

Enriching Experience

Type I intellectual styles can be fostered by enriching people's experiences beyond their professional life (e.g., Astin, 1989; Hattie, Marsh, Neill, & Richards, 1997; Zhang & Sternberg, 2002). Underlying these experiences are opportunities to be confronted with conflicts that people seldom face in the professional sphere. Such conflicts present different types of challenges for individuals. There is strong evidence that effective thinking (creative thinking being one kind) can be facilitated by working through problem-solving procedures and that inadequate experience may interfere with effective thinking (e.g., Batchelder & Root, 1994; Gordon, 1990; Petersen, Leffert, & Graham, 1995). Such evidence suggests that teachers, business leaders, or any individuals in power should create environments in which their subordinates have opportunities to broaden their horizons by participating in various activities and taking on different roles.

The successful implementation of the strategies proposed earlier for cultivating Type I intellectual styles requires strong leadership. Such leaders favor creating a humanistic learning climate (Beane, Lipka, & Ludewig, 1980) in school settings and adopt the assumptions of Theory Y (Mc-Gregor, 1960) in work settings. Both the humanistic approach and Theory Y are characterized by their strong belief in human beings' capacity for change and for voluntarily taking responsibility. Only when they have a sense of ownership and when they perceive autonomy do people initiate creative thinking (see Amabile, 1988).

Be True to Our Values

Although there is a general indication that Type I intellectual styles are valued in some places, and although one of the major goals of education is to produce the leaders of tomorrow (who are characterized by Type I styles, see Sternberg & Zhang, in press), much of our current practice promotes Type II styles and constrains Type I styles. For example, in the educational institutions of many countries, more progressive organizations tend to favor and give higher grades to students with Type I styles, whereas more conservative organizations tend to favor and give higher grades to students with Type II intellectual styles (Bernardo, Zhang, & Calleung, 2002; Cano-Garcia & Hughes, 2000; Sternberg, 1997, Sternberg & Grigorenko, 1995). The former is far outnumbered by the latter. In business settings and indeed in society at large, too often, creative thinking is stifled.

What's going on? Haven't we espoused throughout this book that Type I styles are more valued than Type II styles? Yes! In theory, people value Type I styles. However, not everyone can personalize what he or she values (Chickering & Reisser, 1993); that is, some people are not able to affirm their values and act on them. There are obvious reasons for such a disconnect. In the education arena, many teachers are obliged to deal with an exam-oriented educational system. A critical measure of an educational institution's success is how many students pass high-stakes exams. No one can afford to risk not preparing students for these exams, because passing or excelling at them is still the primary ticket for a decent future for students around the world. Unfortunately, when schools increasingly emphasize tests that deemphasize or even penalize creative thinking, such as fill-in-the-blank or multiple-choice tests, they are implicitly valuing Type II over Type

I intellectual styles. The former kind may not lead to transformational, charismatic, or WICS-based (Wisdom, Intelligence, Creativity, Synthesized) leadership (Sternberg, 2003a, 2003b). These styles, carried to the extreme, could encourage blind conformity rather than creative flexibility. By disguising these facts under the banner of "academic rigor" or adherence to the "three Rs" (reading, writing, and arithmetic), they may penalize societies by facilitating the passage of Type II thinkers into positions of leadership via higher grades and education in elite schools, and hindering or even blocking the advancement of Type I thinkers. This is not the way to promote optimal leadership in organizations of any kind.

In business settings and in society at large, creativity-generating intellectual styles are often not appreciated even when they should be. For example, even in an organization such as a research center, where the essential mission of the organization is to create new knowledge, some leaders may not give their employees enough room for creative thinking. These leaders can tolerate creative thoughts only to a certain extent and only with respect to certain domains and issues. However, they do not want their authority challenged. This phenomenon of suppressing creative thinking for fear of losing one's power can be detected in almost every human relationship in which there is a power imbalance between two parties—parent–child, teacher–student, doctor–nurse, officer–soldier . . . the list could go on and on.

Unfortunately, all of those fears and pretensions are severe impediments to the advancement of society. We need to be honest with ourselves. If we truly value creative thinking, we should make available environments that nurture creative thinking. We need the courage to allow creative thinking. In the short run, we may lose a few battles. However, in the long run, we will win the war to educate the leaders of tomorrow and improve the human race.

A FINAL CAVEAT: THE FUTURE
OF THE THREEFOLD MODEL

No one believes that conclusions based on the current literature on intellectual styles will remain unchanged, even a few years from now. We cannot predict what the changes will be. We can predict, however, that, as dictated by natural law, our threefold model of styles eventually will become dated. It is through scholars' persistent research and theorization that the field of intellectual styles progresses.

References

Abbott, E. F., & McCaulley, M. H. (1983). *High school students in Florida Future Scientist Program* (1974–1982). Unpublished raw data.

Abrami, P. C., Leventhal, L., Perry, R. P., & Breen, L. J. (1976). Course evaluation: How? *Journal of Educational Psychology, 68*(3), 300–304.

Adams, D. G. (2001). Cognitive styles in hearing impaired students. *Educational Psychology, 21*(3), 351–364.

Adderley, K. B. V. (1987). The effects of student cognitive style, teacher cognitive style, and instructional method on the achievement of baccalaureate nursing students. *Dissertation Abstracts International, 47*(8-A), 2949.

Adorno, T. W., Frenkel-Brunswick, E. F., Levinson, D. J., & Sanford, R. N. (1950). *The authoritarian personality*. New York: Harper & Row.

Agor, W. H. (1991). How intuition can be used to enhance creativity in organizations. *The Journal of Creative Behavior, 25*(1), 11–19.

Ahmad, S., & Varghese, A. R. (1991). Learning styles of Indian managers: Some explorations. *Journal of the Indian Academy of Applied Psychology, 17*(1–2), 55–59.

Albaili, M. A. (1993). Inferred hemispheric thinking style, gender, and academic major among United Arab Emirates college students. *Perceptual and Motor Skills, 76*, 971–977.

Albaili, M. A. (1996). Inferred hemispheric style and problem-solving performance. *Perceptual and Motor Skills, 83*, 427–434.

Albaili, M. A. (1997). Differences among low-, average-, and high-achieving college students on learning and study strategies. *Educational Psychology, 17*(1 & 2), 171–177.

Albert, J. (1969). *Modification of the impulsive conceptual style*. Unpublished doctoral dissertation, University of Illinois.

Allinson, C. W., & Hayes, J. (1996). The Cognitive Style Index: A measure of intuition-analysis for organizational research. *Journal of Management Studies, 33*(1), 119–135.

Allinson, C. W., & Hayes, J. (1997). *Cross-national differences in cognitive style: Implications for management*. Discussion paper distributed at the Second Annual ELSIN conference, Birmingham.

Allinson, C. W., Armstrong, S. J., & Hayes, J. (2001). The effects of cognitive style on leader–member exchange: A study of manager–subordinate dyads. *Journal of Occupational and Organizational Psychology, 74*, 201–220.

Allinson, C. W., Hayes, J., & Davis, A. (1994). Matching the cognitive styles of management students and teachers: A preliminary study. *Perceptual and Motor Skills, 79*(3), 1256–1258.

Allport, G. W. (1937). *Structure et développement de la personnalité*. Neuchâtel: Delachaux-Niestlé.

Alpaugh, P. K., & Birren, J. E. (1977). Variables affecting creative contributions across the adult life span. *Human Development, 20*(4), 240–248.

Alvi, S. A., Khan, S. B., Hussain, M. A., & Baig, T. (1988). Relationship between Holland's typology and cognitive styles. *International Journal of Psychology, 23*, 449–459.

Amabile, T. M. (1988). A model of creativity and innovation in organizations. *Research in Organizational Behavior, 10*, 123–167.

Anastasi, A. (1988). *Psychological testing*. New York: Macmillan.

Armstrong, S. J. (1999). *Cognitive style and dyadic interaction: A study of supervisors and subordinates engaged in working relationships*. Unpublished doctoral thesis, University of Leeds, UK.

Armstrong, S. J. (2000). The influence of individual cognitive style on performance in management education. *Educational Psychology, 20*(3), 323–339.

Astin, A. W. (1989). Student involvement: A developmental theory for higher education. In G. D. Kuh, J. B. Bean, D. Hossler, & F. K. Stage (Eds.), *ASHE reader on college students* (pp. 226–236). Needham Heights, MA: Ginn Press.

Atkinson, G., Murrell, P. H., & Winters, M. R. (1990). Career personality types and learning styles. *Psychological Reports, 66*(1), 160–162.

Au, E. (2004). *Thinking styles and performance in different assessment formats among Hong Kong secondary school students*. Unpublished manuscript. The University of Hong Kong.

Ausburn, L. J. (1979). *Impact of learning styles on Air Force technical training: Relationships among cognitive style factors and perceptual types* (Report) AFHRL-TR-78-91(1). Oklahoma.

Avallone, A. J. (1997). Cognitive styles of successful expatriates. *Dissertation Abstracts International, 58*(8-A), 1805.

Avery, A. E. (1986). An assessment of the relationship between teacher teaching style/student learning style and the academic achievement of twelfth grade students. *Dissertation Abstracts International, 46*(12A), 3541.

Bagley, C., & Mallick, K. (1998). Field independence, cultural context and academic achievement: A commentary. *British Journal of Educational Psychology, 68*, 581–587.

Baillargeon, R., Pascual-Leone, J., & Roncadin, C. (1998). Mental-attentional capacity: Does cognitive style make a difference? *Journal of Experimental Child Psychology, 70*(3), 143–166.

Baker, R. G. (1968). *Ecological psychology: Concepts and methods for studying the environment of human behavior*. Stanford, CA: Stanford University Press.

Bandura, A. (1986). *Social foundations of thought and action: A social cognitive theory*. Englewood Cliffs, NJ: Prentice-Hall.

Banks, G. N. (1978). An examination of the relationships among the teacher's learning style, principal's learning style, and the degree of teacher's satisfaction with the principal's job performance. *Dissertation Abstracts International, 38*(11-A), 6419.

Banta, T. J. (1970). Tests for the evaluation of early childhood education: The Cincinnati Autonomy Test Battery (CATB). In J. Hellmuth (Ed.), *Cognitive studies, Vol. 1* (pp. 424–490). New York: Brunner-Mazel.

Bargar, R. R., & Hoover, R. L. (1984). Psychological type and the matching of cognitive styles. *Theory Into Practice, 23*(1), 56–63.

Barratt, W. R., & Hood, A. B. (1997). Assessing development of purpose. In A. B. Hood (Ed.), *The Iowa student development inventories (2nd ed.)* (pp. 78–92). Iowa City, IA: HITECH Press.

Barrie, S. M. (2002). Using cognitive style to study decision making: Hospital CEOS evaluate strategies to reduce hospital length of stay. *Dissertation Abstracts International, 63*(4-B), 2081.

Bartlett, F. C. (1932). *Remembering: A study in experimental and social psychology.* Cambridge, England: Cambridge University Press.

Batchelder, T. H., & Root, S. (1994). Effects of an undergraduate program to integrate academic learning and service: Cognitive, prosocial cognitive, and identity outcomes. Special Issue: School-Based Community Service. *Journal of Adolescence, 17*(4), 341–355.

Beane, A., Lipka, R. P., & Ludewig, J. W. (1980). Synthesis of research on self concept. *Educational Leadership, 38,* 84–89.

Beck, M. L. (1992). Learners' strategies in foreign-language acquisition: Studies on the acquisition of the German declension system. *Studies in Second Language Acquisition, 14*(2), 239–240.

Becker, L. D., Bender, N. N., & Morrison, G. (1978). Measuring impulsivity–reflection: A critical review. *Journal of Learning Disabilities, 11*(10), 626–632.

Bennett, S. N. (1973). Divergent thinking abilities: A validation study. *British Journal of Educational Psychology, 43*(1), 1–7.

Berg, I. A. (1967). *Response set in personality assessment.* Chicago: Aldine.

Bernardo, A. B., Zhang, L. F., & Callueng, C. M. (2002). Thinking styles and academic achievement among Filipino students. *Journal of Genetic Psychology, 163*(2), 149–163.

Berry, J. W. (1976). *Human ecology and cognitive style: Comparative studies in cultural and psychological adaptation.* New York: Wiley.

Bever, T. G., & Chiarello, R. S. (1974). Cerebral dominance in musicians and non-musicians. *Science, 186,* 537–539.

Beyler, J., & Schmeck, R. R. (1992). Assessment of individual differences in preferences for holistic–analytic strategies: Evaluation of some commonly available instruments. *Educational and Psychological Measurement, 52*(3), 709–719.

Bhatnager, P., & Rastogi, M. (1986). Cognitive style and basic ideal disparity in males and females. *Indian Journal of Current Psychological Research, 1,* 36–40.

Bickham, P. J., Miller, M. J., O'Neal, H., & Clanton, R. (1998). Comparison of error rates on the 1990 and 1994 revised self-directed search. *Perceptual and Motor Skills, 86*(3, Pt 2), 1168–1170.

Bieri, J., & Messerley, S. (1957). Differences in perceptual and cognitive behavior as a function of experience type. *Journal of Consulting Psychology, 21,* 217–221.

Biggs, J. B. (1978). Individual and group differences in study processes. *British Journal of Educational Psychology, 48,* 266–279.

Biggs, J. B. (1979). Individual differences in study processes and the quality of learning outcomes. *Higher Education, 8,* 381–394.

Biggs, J. B. (1987). *Student approaches to learning and studying.* Hawthorn, Australia: Australian Council for Educational Research.

Biggs, J. B. (1988). Assessing student approaches to learning. *Australian Psychologist, 23*(2), 197–206.

Biggs, J. B. (1992). *Why and how do Hong Kong students learn? Using the Learning and Study Process Questionnaires,* Education Paper No. 14, Faculty of Education, The University of Hong Kong.

Biggs, J. B. (2001). Enhancing learning: A matter of style or approach? In R. J. Sternberg & L. F. Zhang (Eds.), *Perspectives on thinking, learning, and cognitive styles* (pp. 73–102). Mahwah, NJ: Lawrence Erlbaum Associates.

Blanch, P. E. D. (2001). Teaching styles of faculty and learning styles of their students: Congruent versus incongruent teaching styles with regards to academic disciplines and gender. *Dissertation Abstracts International, 61*(10-A), 3869.

Block, C. F. (1981). The relationship between teacher–student cognitive style distance and academic achievement. *Dissertation Abstracts International, 42*(4-A), 1388.

Block, J., Block, J. H., & Harrington, D. M. (1974). Some misgivings about the Matching Familiar Figures Test as a measure of reflection–impulsivity. *Developmental Psychology, 11,* 611–632.

Bloomberg, M. (1971). Creativity as related to field independence and mobility. *Journal of Genetic Psychology, 118,* 3–12.

Bokoros, M. A., Goldstein, M. B., & Sweeney, M. M. (1992). Common factors in five measures of cognitive styles. *Current Psychology Research and Reviews, 11*(2), 99–109.

Bolen, L. M., Wurm, T. R., & Hall, C. W. (1994). Factorial structure of the Study Process Questionnaire. *Psychological Reports, 75*(3), 1235–1241.

Boreham, B. W., & Watts, J. D. (1998). Personality type in undergraduate education and physics students. *Journal of Psychological Type, 44,* 31–56.

Borg, M. G., & Riding, R. J. (1993). Teacher stress and cognitive style. *British Journal of Educational Psychology, 63*(2), 271–286.

Bosacki, S., Innerd, W., & Towson, S. (1997). Field independence–dependence and self-esteem in preadolescents: Does gender make a difference? *Journal of Youth and Adolescence, 26*(6), 691–703.

Bourdieu, P. (1984). *Distinction.* Cambridge, MA: Harvard University Press.

Bracken, B. A., Ledford, T. L., & McCallum, R. S. (1979). Effects of cerebral dominance on college-level achievement. *Perceptual and Motor Skills, 49,* 445–446.

Bradley, C. (1985). The relationship between students' information processing styles and LOGO programming. *Journal of Educational Computing Research, 1,* 427–433.

Brand, H. J., Van-Noorwyk, J. S., & Hanekom, J. D. (1994). Administering the Self-Directed Search on a group of Black adolescents. *South African Journal of Psychology, 24*(2), 47–52.

Brooks, L., Simutis, Z., & O'Neil, H. (1985). The role of individual differences in learning strategies research. In R. Dillon (Ed.), *Individual differences in cognition* (Vol. 2, pp. 219–251). Orlando, FL: Academic Press.

Brophy, J., & Good, T. (1970). Teachers' communication of differential expectations for children's classroom performance. *Journal of Educational Psychology, 61*(5), 365–374.

Brown, G., & Lawson, T. W. (1975). Sex differences in the stability of reflectivity/impulsivity in infant school pupils. *Educational Studies, 1*(2), 99–104.

Buela-Casal, G., Carretero-Dios, H., De-los-Santos-Roig, M., & Bermudez, M. P. (2003). Psychometric properties of a Spanish adaptation of the Matching Familiar Figures Test (MFFT-20). *European Journal of Psychological Assessment, 19*(2), 151–159.

Burns, T., & Stalker, R. M. (1961). *The management of innovation.* London: Tavistock.

Busato, V. V., Prins, F. J., Elshout, J. J., & Hamaker, C. (1999). The relation between learning styles, the Big Five personality traits and achievement motivation in higher education. *Personality and Individual Differences, 26*(1), 129–140.

Cafferty, E. I. (1981). An analysis of student performance based upon the degree of match between the educational cognitive style of the teacher and the educational cognitive style of the students. *Dissertation Abstracts International, 41*(7-A), 2908.

Cairns, E. (1977). The reliability of the Matching Familiar Figures Test. *British Journal of Educational Psychology, 47*(2), 197–198.

Cairns, E., & Cammock, T. (1978). Development of a more reliable version of the Matching Familiar Figures Test. *Developmental Psychology, 14*(5), 555–560.

Cakan, M. (2003). Psychometric data on the Group Embedded Figures Test for Turkish undergraduate students. *Perceptual and Motor Skills, 96*(3), 993–1004.

Campbell, B. J. (1991). Planning for a student learning style. *Journal of Education for Business, 66*(6), 356–360.

Campbell, S. B., & Douglas, V. I. (1972). Cognitive styles and responses to the threat of frustration. *Canadian Journal of Behavioral Science, 4*(1), 30–42.

Canfield, A. (1988). *Manual for Learning Styles Inventory.* Los Angeles: Western Psychological Services.

Canfield, A. A. (1976). *Learning Styles Inventory.* Ann Arbor, MI: Humanics Media.

Canfield, A. A. (1980). *Learning styles inventory manual.* Ann Arbor, MI: Humanics Media.

Canfield, A. A., & Canfield, J. S. (1976). *Instructional Styles Inventory.* Ann Arbor, MI: Humanics Media.

Cano-Garcia, F., & Hughes, E. H. (2000). Learning and thinking styles: An analysis of their relationship and influence on academic achievement. *Educational Psychology, 20*(4), 413–430.

Cantwell, R. H., & Moore, P. J. (1996). The development of measures of individual differences in self-regulatory control and their relationship to academic performance. *Contemporary Educational Psychology, 21*, 500–517.

Cantwell, R. H., & Moore, P. J. (1998). Relationships among control beliefs, approaches to learning, and the academic performance of final-year nurses. *The Alberta Journal of Educational Research, 44*(1), 98–102.

Carey, J. C., Fleming, S. D., & Roberts, D. Y. (1989). The Myers-Briggs Type Indicator as a measure of aspects of cognitive style. *Measurement and Evaluation in Counseling and Development, 22*, 94–99.

Carlson, J. G. (1985). Recent assessments of the Myers-Briggs Type Indicator. *Journal of Personality Assessment, 49*, 356–365.

Carlyn, M. (1976). The relationship between Myers-Briggs personality types and teaching preferences of prospective teachers. *Dissertation Abstracts International, Section A: Humanities and Social Sciences, 37*(A), 3494.

Carne, G. C., & Kirton, M. J. (1982). Styles of creativity: Test-score correlations between Kirton Adaption–Innovation Inventory and Myers-Briggs Type Indicator. *Psychological Reports, 50*, 31–36.

Cattell, R. B. (1973). *Personality and mood by questionnaire.* San Francisco: Jossey-Bass.

Cattell, R. B., Cattell, A. K., & Cattell, H. E. (1978). *16 Personality Factor Questionnaire.* Champaign, IL: Institute for Personality and Ability Testing, Inc.

Caverni, J. P., & Drozda-Senkowska, E. (1984). L'agregation des criteres de notation: influence du mode d'explicitation dans ses rapports avec le style cognitif de l'expert [Aggregating marking criteria: The influence of experts' cognitive style on the way they correct essays]. *Travail Humain, 47*(2), 97–111.

Chang, C. (1988). Matching teaching styles and learning styles and verification of students' learning adaptation model. *Bulletin of Educational Psychology*, 113–172.

Chapman, J. (1988). Learning disabled children's self-concepts. *Review of Educational Research, 58*, 347–371.

Cheney, P. (1980). Cognitive style and student programming ability: An investigation. *AEDS Journal, 13*, 285–291.

Cheung, E. (2002). *Students' thinking styles, learning approaches, and instructional preferences: Their relationships with academic achievement in different disciplines.* Unpublished manuscript. The University of Hong Kong.

Cheung, F. (2002). *Thinking styles and achievement in mathematics and language learning.* Unpublished manuscript. The University of Hong Kong.

Chickering, A. (1969). *Education and identity.* San Francisco: Jossey-Bass.

Chickering, A., & Reisser, L. (1993). *Education and identity* (2nd ed.). San Francisco: Jossey-Bass.

Christie, R., & Jahoda, M. (1954). *Studies in the scope and method of "The authoritarian personality."* Chicago: The Free Press.

Clapp, R. G. (1993). The stability of cognitive style in adults and some implications: A longitudinal study of the Kirton Adaption–Innovation Inventory. *Psychological Reports, 73*(3), 1235–1245.

Clapp, R. G., & De Ciantis, S. M. (1989). Adaptors and innovators in large organizations: Does cognitive style characterize actual behavior of employees at work? An exploratory study. *Psychological Reports, 65*, 503–513.

Clarke, R. M. (1986). Students' approaches to studying in an innovative medical school: A cross-sectional study. *British Journal of Educational Psychology, 56*, 309–321.

Clements, D. (1986). Effects of LOGO and CAI environments on cognition and creativity. *Journal of Educational Psychology, 78*, 309–318.

Coates, S. (1972). *Preschool embedded figures test.* Palo Alto, CA: Consulting Psychologists Press.

Coates, S., Lord, M., & Jakabovics, E. (1975). Field dependence independence, social–nonsocial play and sex differences. *Perceptual and Motor Skills, 40*, 195–202.

Cochran, K. F., & Davis, J. (1987). Individual differences in inference processes. *Journal of Research in Personality, 21*(2), 197–210.

Cohen, R. A. (1967). *Primary group structure, conceptual styles and school achievement.* Unpublished doctoral dissertation. University of Pittsburgh.

Coles, C. R. (1985). Differences between conventional and problem-based curricula in their students approaches to studying. *Medical Education, 19*, 308–309.

Collins, J. N. (1994). Some fundamental questions about scientific thinking. *Research in Science and Technological Education, 12*(2), 161–173.

Collins, P. (1971). Functional and conflict theories of educational stratification. *American Sociological Review, 36*, 1002–1019.

Compagnone, P. (1980). The relationship of student achievement in high school chemistry to matched student–teacher cognitive style. *Dissertation Abstracts International, 41*(2-A), 616.

Conner, D., Kinicki, A. J., & Keats, B. W. (1994). Integrating organizational and individual information processing perspectives on choice. *Organizational Science, 5*(3), 294–308.

Connor, M. J. (1994). Peer relations and peer pressure. *Educational Psychology in Practice, 9*(4), 207–215.

Cook, M. (1993). *Levels of personality.* London: Cassell.

Cooper, S. E., & Miller, J. A. (1991). MBTI learning style & teaching style discongruencies. *Educational and Psychological Measurement, 51*(3), 699–706.

Coopersmith, S. (1981). *Self-esteem inventories.* Palo Alto, CA: Consulting Psychologists Press, Inc.

Copenhaver, R. (1979). *The consistency of student learning styles as students move from English to mathematics.* Unpublished doctoral dissertation, Indiana University.

Costa, P. T., Jr., & McCrae, R. R. (1985). *The NEO Personality Inventory.* Odessa, FL: Psychological Assessment Resources.

Costa, P. T., Jr., & McCrae, R. R. (1992). *The NEO-PI-R: Professional manual.* Odessa, FL: Psychological Assessment Resources.

Crandall, V. J., & Sinkeldam, C. (1964). Children's dependent and achievement behaviors in social situations and their perceptual field dependence. *Journal of Personality, 32*, 1–22.

Crookes, F. W. (1977). An investigation of the interaction of educational cognitive style, teaching style, and instructional area for selected community college instructors. *Dissertation Abstracts International, 37*(12A, Pt 1), 7504.

Cummings, W. H. (1995). Age group differences and estimated frequencies of the Myers-Briggs Type Indicator. *Measurement and Evaluation in Counseling and Development, 28*(2), 69–77.

Cupkie, L. F. (1980). The effects of similarity of instructor preferred teaching style and student preferred learning style on student achievement in selected courses in a metropolitan community college. *Dissertation Abstracts International, 41*(3-A), 988.

Curry, L. (1983). *An organization of learning styles theory and constructs.* ERIC Document 235, 185.

Curry, L. (1987). *Integrating concepts of cognitive or learning style: A review with attention to psychometric standards.* Ottawa, Ontario, Canada: Canadian College of Health Service Executives.

Curry, L. (1991). Patterns of learning style across selected medical specialties. *Educational Psychology, 11*(3–4), 247–278.

Cutright, P. S. (1990). Predicting adaption–innovation styles: Selected demographic characteristics and the Kirton inventory. *Perceptual and Motor Skills, 70,* 173–174.

Dai, D. Y., & Feldhusen, J. F. (1999). A validation of the thinking styles inventory: Implications for gifted education. *Roeper Review, 21*(4), 302–307.

Davenport, J. A. (1986). Learning style and its relationship to gender and age among Elderhostel participants. *Educational Gerontology, 12*(3), 205–217.

Davey, B. (1990). Field dependence/independence and reading comprehension questions: Task and reader interactions. *Contemporary Educational Psychology, 15*(3), 241–250.

Davies, S. M., Rutledge, C. M., & Davies, T. C. (1997). The impact of student learning styles on interviewing skills and academic performance. *Teaching and Learning in Medicine, 9*(2), 131–135.

Davis, J. K. (1991). Educational implications of field dependence–independence. In S. Wapner & J. Demick (Eds.), *Field dependence–independence: Cognitive styles across the life span* (pp. 149–176). Hillsdale, NJ: Lawrence Erlbaum Associates.

Deng, Z., Li, D., & Zhang, Q. (2000). Cognitive styles, scholastic attainments with the Cattell's 16PF: A correlative approach. *Psychological Science China, 23*(2), 234–235.

Denney, D. R. (1972). Modeling effects upon conceptual style and cognitive tempo. *Child Development, 43,* 105–119.

Denton, D. (1974). *Existentialism and phenomenology in education.* New York: Teachers College.

Devore, R. N. (1984). The relationship of cognitive style, cognitive level, and achievement in science to the development of positive attitudes toward science and science teaching. *Dissertation Abstracts International, 45*(2-A), 482.

Dewan, S. (1982). *Personality characteristics of entrepreneurs.* Unpublished doctoral thesis, Institute of Technology, Delhi.

Dirkes, M. A. (1977). Learning through creative thinking. *Gifted Child Quarterly, 21*(4), 526–537.

DiStefano, J. J. (1969). Interpersonal perceptions of field independent and field dependent teachers and students. *Dissertation Abstracts International, Section A: Humanities and Social Sciences, 31*(A), 463–464.

Donoghue, M. L. (1995). Problem solving effectiveness: The relationship of divergent and convergent thinking. *Dissertation Abstracts International (Section A): Humanities and Social Sciences, 55*(10A), 3073.

Drummond, R. J., & Stoddard, A. H. (1992). Learning style and personality type. *Perceptual and Motor Skills, 75*(1), 99–104.

Drysdale, M. T. B., Ross, J. L., & Schulz, R. A. (2001). Cognitive learning students and academic performance in 19 first-year university courses: Successful students versus students at risk. *Journal of Education for Students Placed at Risk, 6*(3), 271–289.

Dubois, T. E., & Cohen, W. (1970). Relationship between measures of psychological differentiation and intellectual ability. *Perceptual and Motor Skills, 31,* 411–416.

Dulin, K. L. (1993). A study of the relationship between middle school-aged students' tendency toward field-independence or field-dependence and their preference toward learning in a cooperative or a traditional classroom. *Dissertation Abstracts International, 54*(4A), 1215.

Dunn, R., Dunn, K., & Price, G. E. (1975, 1979, 1981, 1985). *Learning styles inventory.* Lawrence, KS: Price Systems.

Dunn, R., Dunn, K., & Price, G. E. (1986). *Productivity environmental preference survey.* Lawrence, KS: Price Systems.

Dunn, R., Gemake, J., Jalali, F., Zenhausern, R., Quinn, P., & Spriridakis, J. (1990). Cross-cultural differences in the learning styles of fourth-, fifth-, and sixth-grade students of Afro, Chinese, Greek, and Mexican heritage. *Journal of Multicultural Counseling and Development, 18*(2), 68–93.

Dunn, R., & Griggs, S. A. (1990). Research on the learning style characteristics of selected ra-cial and ethnic groups. *Journal of Reading, Writing, and Learning Disabilities International,* 6(3), 261–280.

Dweck, O. S. (1986). Motivational processes affecting learning. *American Psychologist, 41,* 1040–1048.

Dyk, R. B., & Witkin, H. A. (1965). Family experiences related to the development of differen-tiation in children. *Child Development, 30,* 21–55.

Eastwood, G. R. (1965). Divergent thinking and academic success. *Ontario Journal of Educa-tional Research, 7*(3), 241–254.

Elder, R. L. (1989). Relationships between adaption–innovation, experienced control, and state–trait anxiety. *Psychological Reports, 65,* 47–54

Elsberry, J. B. (1995). A comparison of selected variables of instructional choice and achieve-ment between group lecture method and facilitated self-paced method in college health science physics. *Dissertation Abstracts International (Section A): Humanities and Social Sciences,* 55(7A), 1790.

Elshout, J. J., & Akkerman, A. E. (1975). *Vijf persoonlijkheids–faktoren test 5 PFT.* Nijmegen: Berhout Nijmegen.

Entwistle, N. (1981). *Styles of teaching and learning: An integrated outline of educational psychology for students, teachers, and lecturers.* New York: Wiley.

Entwistle, N. (1988). Motivation and learning strategies. *Educational and Child Psychology, 59,* 326–339.

Entwistle, N., McCune, V., & Walker, P. (2001). Conceptions, styles, and approaches within higher education: Analytical abstractions and everyday experience. In R. J. Sternberg & L. F. Zhang (Eds.), *Perspectives on thinking, learning, and cognitive style* (pp. 103–136). Mahwah, NJ: Lawrence Erlbaum Associates.

Entwistle, N., & Ramsden, P. (1983). *Understanding student learning.* London: Croom Helm.

Entwistle, N. J., & Tait, H. (1994). *The Revised Approaches to Studying Inventory.* University of Ed-inburgh, Center for Research into Learning and Instruction.

Epstein, M. H., Hallahan, D. P., & Kauffman, J. M. (1975). Implications of the reflec-tivity–impulsivity dimension for special education. *Journal of Special Education, 9*(1), 11–25.

Ettlie, J. E., & O'Keefe, R. D. (1982). Innovative attitudes, values, and intentions in organiza-tions. *Journal of Management Studies, 19,* 163–182.

Evans, F. J. (1967). Field dependence and Maudsley Personality Inventory. *Perceptual and Motor Skills, 24,* 526.

Eysenck, H. J. (1978). The development of personality and its relation to learning. In S. Murray-Smith (Ed.), *Melbourne studies in education* (pp. 134–181). Melbourne, Australia: Melbourne University Press.

Eysenck, H. J., & Eysenck, S. B. G. (1964). *Manual of the Eysenck Personality Inventory.* London: Hodder and Stoughton.

Eysenck, H. J., & Eysenck, S. B. G. (1975a). *The Eysenck Personality Questionnaire.* London: Hodder and Stoughton.

Eysenck, H. J., & Eysenck, S. B. G. (1975b). *Manual of the Eysenck Personality Questionnaire.* San Diego: EdITS Publishers.

Feather, N. T. (1967). Some personality correlates of external control. *Australian Journal of Psy-chology, 19,* 253–260.

Feij, J. A. (1976). Field independence, impulsiveness, high school training, and academic achievement. *Journal of Educational Psychology, 68*(6), 793–799.

Feldhusen, J. F., Treffinger, D. J., Van-Mondfrans, A. P., & Ferris, D. R. (1971). The relation-ship between academic grades and divergent thinking scores derived from four different methods of testing. *Journal of Experimental Education, 40*(1), 35–40.

Fleenor, J. W., & Taylor, S. (1994). Construct validity of three self-report measures of creativity. *Educational and Psychological Measurement, 54*(2), 464–470.

Foley, I. F. (1999). Teacher learning style preferences, student learning style preferences, and student reading achievement. *Dissertation Abstracts International, 60*(4-A), 0995.

Ford, N. (1995). Levels and types of mediation in instructional systems: An individual differences approach. *International Journal of Human-Computer Studies, 43,* 241–259.

Ford, N., & Chen, S. Y. (2000). Individual differences, hypermedia navigation and learning: An empirical study. *Journal of Educational Multimedia and Hypermedia, 9*(4), 281–311.

Fourqurean, J. M., Meisgeier, C., Swank, P. (1990). The link between learning style and Jungian psychological type: A finding of bipolar preference dimensions. *Journal of Experimental Education, 58*(3), 225–237.

Foxall, G. R. (1986a). Managers in transition: An empirical test of Kirton's adaption–innovation theory and its implications for the mid-career MBA. *Technovation, 4,* 219–232.

Foxall, G. R. (1986b). Managerial orientations of adaptors and innovators. *Journal of Managerial Psychology, 1,* 24–27.

Foxall, G. R. (1990). An empirical analysis of mid-career managers' adaptive–innovative cognitive styles and task orientations in three countries. *Psychological Reports, 66,* 1115–1124.

Foxall, G. R., & Hackett, P. M. W. (1992). Cognitive style and extent of computer use in organizations: Relevance of sufficiency of originality, efficiency and rule-conformity. *Perceptual and Motor Skills, 74,* 491–497.

Foxall, G. R., & Payne, A. F. (1989). Adaptors and innovators in organizations: A cross-cultural study of the cognitive styles of managerial functions and subfunctions. *Human Relations, 42*(7), 639–649.

Foxall, G. R., Payne, A. F., & Walters, D. A. (1992). Adaptive–innovative cognitive styles of Australian managers. *Australian Psychologist, 27*(2), 118–122.

Frank, B. M. (1983). Flexibility of information processing and the memory of field-independent and field-dependent learners. *Journal of Research in Personality, 17*(1), 89–96.

Frank, B. M., & Keene, D. (1993). The effect of learners' field independence, cognitive strategy instruction, and inherent word-list organization on free-recall memory and strategy use. *Journal of Experimental Education, 62*(1), 14–25.

Freedman, R. D., & Stumpf, S. A. (1980). Learning style theory: Less than meets the eye. *Academy of Management Review, 5*(3), 445–447.

French, J. W., Ekstron, R., & Price, L. (1963). *Kit of reference tests for cognitive factors.* Princeton, NJ: Educational Testing Service.

French, L. G. (1974). Predictability of students' evaluations of college teachers from component ratings. *Journal of Educational Psychology, 66*(3), 373–385.

Friedman, C. P., & Stritter, F. T. (1976). An empirical inventory comparing instructional preferences of medical and other professional students. *Research in Medical Education Processing.* 15th Annual conference. November, San Francisco, pp. 85–90.

Fritz, R. L. (1981). The role of field-dependence and field-independence in secondary school students' re-enrollments in vocational education and their attitudes towards teachers and programs. *Dissertation Abstracts International, 42*(4A), 1607.

Furnham, A. (1992). Personality and learning style: A study of three instruments. *Personality and Individual Differences, 13*(4), 429–438.

Furnham, A. (1995). The relationship of personality and intelligence to cognitive learning style and achievement. In D. Saklofske & M. Zeidner (Ed.), *International handbook of personality and intelligence* (pp. 397–413). New York: Plenum.

Furnham, A. (1996a). The big five versus the big four: The relationship between the Myers-Briggs type indicator (MBTI) and NEO-PI five factor model of personality. *Personality and Individual Differences, 21*(2), 303–307.

Furnham, A. (1996b). The FIRO-B, the learning style questionnaire and the five-factor model. *Journal of Social Behavior and Personality, 11*(2), 285–299.

Furnham, A., Jackson, C. J., & Miller, T. (1999). Personality, learning style and work performance. *Personality and Individual Differences, 27,* 1113–1122.

Gadzella, B. M. (1999). Differences among cognitive-processing styles groups on personality traits. *Journal of Instructional Psychology, 26*(3), 161–166.

Gadzella, B. M., & Kneipp, L. B. (1990). Differences in comprehension processes as a function of hemisphericity. *Perceptual and Motor Skills, 70,* 783–786.

Galton, F. (1883). *Inquiries into human faculty and its development.* London: MacMillan.

Gardner, R. W., & Schoen, R. A. (1962). Differentiation and abstraction in concept formation. *Psychological Monographs, 76.*

Gazzaniga, M. S. (1971). Changing hemisphere dominance by changing reward probability in split-brain monkeys. *Experimental Neurology, 33,* 412–419.

Gelade, G. (1995). Creative style and divergent production. *Journal of Creative Behavior, 29*(1), 36–53.

Getreu, M. R. (1997). Structural interrelationships between vocational interests and personality traits in those who are male sex-typed, female sex-typed, and androgynous. *Dissertation Abstracts International (Section B): The Sciences & Engineering, 58*(3B), 1577.

Gibbs, G., Habeshaw, S., & Habeshaw, T. (1988). *53 interesting ways to appraise your teaching.* Bristol: Technical and Educational Services.

Ginter, E. J., Brown, S., Scalise, J., & Ripley, W. (1989). Perceptual learning styles: Their link to academic performance, sex, age, and academic standing. *Perceptual and Motor Skills, 68*(3, Pt 2), 1091–1094.

Giunta, S. F. (1984). Administrative considerations concerning learning style, its relationship to teaching style, and the influence of instructor/student congruence on high schoolers' achievement and educators' perceived stress. *Dissertation Abstracts International, 45*(1A), 32.

Glidden, R. C., & Greenwood, A. K. (1997). A validation study of the Spanish Self-Directed Search using back-translation procedures. *Journal of Career Assessment, 5*(1), 105–113.

Goldsmith, R. E. (1984). Personality characteristics associated with adaption–innovation. *Journal of Psychology, 117,* 159–165.

Goldsmith, R. E. (1985). The factorial composition of the Kirton Adaption–Innovation Inventory. *Educational and Psychological Measurement, 45,* 245–250.

Goldsmith, R. E. (1986). Personality and adaptive–innovative problem solving. *Journal of Social Behavior and Personality, 1*(1), 95–106.

Goldsmith, R. E., McNeilly, K. M., & Russ, F. A. (1989). Similarity of sales representatives' and supervisors' problem-solving styles and the satisfaction–performance relationship. *Psychological Reports, 64,* 827–832.

Goldstein, K. M., & Blackman, S. (1981). Cognitive styles. In F. Fransella (Ed.), *Personality: Theory, measurement and research* (pp. 119–143). London: Methuen.

Goode, P. E., Goddard, P. H., & Pascual-Leone, J. (2002). Event-related potentials index cognitive style differences during a serial-order recall task. *International Journal of Psychophysiology, 43*(2), 123–140.

Gordon, D. E. (1990). Formal operational thinking: The role of cognitive-developmental processes in adolescent decision-making about pregnancy and contraception. *American Journal of Orthopsychiatry, 60*(3), 346–356.

Gough, H. G. (1975). *California Psychological Inventory.* Palo Alto, CA: Consulting Psychologists Press.

Gough, H. G. (1987). *California Psychological Inventory administrator's guide.* Palo Alto, CA: Consulting Psychologists Press.

Gould, T. E. (2003). A correlational analysis of undergraduate athletic training students' and faculty educators' mind styles and preferences of teaching methods. *Dissertation Abstracts International (Section A): Humanities and Social Sciences, 64*(5A), 1511.

Greenberg, L. W., Goldberg, R. M., Foley, R. P. (1996). Learning preference and personality type: Their association in pediatric residents. *Medical Education, 30,* 307–311.

Gregorc, A. F. (1979). Learning/teaching styles: Potent forces behind them. *Educational Leadership, 36,* 234–236.

Gregorc, A. F. (1982). *Gregorc Style Delineator.* Maynard, MA: Gabriel Systems.

Gregorc, A. F. (1984). *Gregorc style delineator: Development technical and administration manual.* Maynard, MA: Gabriel Systems.

Gregorc, A. F. (1985). *Inside styles: Beyond the basics.* Maynard, MA: Gabriel Systems.

Gridley, M. C. (2004). Myers Briggs personality types of art collectors. *Psychological Reports, 94*(2), 736–738.

Grigorenko, E. L., & Sternberg, R. J. (1993a). *Set of Thinking Styles Tasks for Students.* Unpublished test, Yale University.

Grigorenko, E. L., & Sternberg, R. J. (1993b). *Students' Thinking Styles Evaluated by Teachers.* Unpublished test, Yale University.

Grigorenko, E. L., & Sternberg, R. J. (1993c). *Thinking Styles in Teaching Inventory.* Unpublished test, Yale University.

Grigorenko, E. L., & Sternberg, R. J. (1995). Thinking styles. In D. Saklofske & M. Zeidner (Eds.), *International handbook of personality and intelligence* (pp. 205–229). New York: Plenum.

Grigorenko, E. L., & Sternberg, R. J. (1997). Styles of thinking, abilities, and academic performance. *Exceptional Children, 63*(3), 295–312.

Grout, C. M. (1991). An assessment of the relationship between teacher teaching style and student learning style with relation to academic achievement and absenteeism of seniors in a rural high school in north central Massachusetts. *Dissertation Abstracts International, 51*(8-A), 2619.

Gryskiewicz, N. D., & Tullar, W. L. (1995). The relationship between personality type and creativity style among managers. *Journal of Psychological Type, 32,* 30–35

Gryskiewicz, S. S. (1982). *The Kirton Adaption–Innovation Inventory in creative leadership development.* Proceedings of the British Psychological Society. Brighton: University of Sussex.

Gryskiewicz, S. S., Hills, D. W., Holt, K., & Hills, K. (1986). *Understanding managerial creativity: The Kirton Adaption–Innovation Inventory and other assessment measures.* Greensboro, NC: Centre for Creativity and Leadership.

Gryskiewicz, S. S., Hills, D. W., Holt, K., & Hills, K. (1987). *Understanding managerial creativity: The Kirton Adaption–Innovation Inventory and other assessment measures* (Technical Report, Center for Creativity and Leadership). Greensboro, NC.

Guilford, J. P. (1950). Creativity research: Past, present and future. *American Psychologist, 5,* 444–454.

Guilford, J. P. (1959). *Personality.* New York: McGraw-Hill.

Guilford, J. P. (1967). *The nature of human intelligence.* New York: McGraw-Hill.

Gullo, D. (1988). An investigation of cognitive tempo and its effects on evaluating kindergarten children's academic and social competencies. *Early Child Development and Care, 34,* 201–215.

Gurley, M. P. (1984). Characteristics of motivation, field independence, personality type, learning style, and teaching preference of the adult learner as compared with traditional-age college students. *Dissertation Abstracts International, Section A: Humanities and Social Sciences, 45A,* 1268.

Hageman, P. T. (1990). An investigation of the relationship between cognitive styles, selected dimensions of organizational climate, and job satisfaction of registered professional staff nurses. *Dissertation Abstracts International, 51*(7), 3323-B.

Hahn-Rollins, D., & Mongeon, J. E. (1988). Increasing the acceptance of the MBTI in organizations. *Journal of Psychological Type, 15,* 13–19.

Haldeman, J. (1979). Individual teacher–student interaction when matched and mismatched on cognitive style and the effect upon student self concept. *Dissertation Abstracts International, 39*(8-A), 4822.

Hale, N. S. (1980). A study of differences in student perception of male and female faculty members' teaching effectiveness as measured by student evaluation of classroom teaching. *Dissertation Abstracts International (Section A): Humanities and Social Sciences, 40*(8A), 4382.

Hambrick, D. C., Davison, S. C., Snell, S. A., & Snow, C. C. (1998). When groups consist of multiple nationalities: Toward a new understanding of the implications. *Organization Studies, 19*(2), 181–205.

Hansen, H. R. (1981). Instructors' cognitive style or psychological type and the teaching of freshman composition. *Dissertation Abstracts International, 41*(8-A), 3444.

Harasym, P. H., Leong, E. J., Juschka, B. B., Lucier, G. E., & Lorscheider, F. L. (1996). Relationship between Myers-Briggs Type Indicator and Gregorc Style Delineator. *Perceptual and Motor Skills, 82,* 1203–1210.

Hardy, S. B. (1997). A study to determine the effect employee learning style has on job satisfaction for middle managers in the banking industry. *Dissertation Abstracts International, 57*(7-A), 2855.

Harnad, S. (1972). Creativity, lateral saccades, and the nondominant hemisphere. *Perceptual and Motor Skills, 34,* 653–654.

Harrison, A. F., & Bramson, R. M. (1977). *INQ administration and interpretation manual.* Berkeley, CA: Bramson, Parlette, Harrison, & Associates.

Harrison, T. D. (1997). Non-traditional teachers: Personal learning styles and teaching styles. *Dissertation Abstracts International, 58*(5-A), 1663.

Hartlage, L. C. (1970). Sex-linked inheritance of spatial ability. *Perceptual and Motor Skills, 31,* 610.

Hashway, R. M. (1998). *Developmental cognitive styles: A primer to the literature including an introduction to the theory of developmentalism.* Bethesda, MD: Austin & Winfield.

Hassan, M. M., & Abed, A. S. (1999). Differences in spatial visualization as a function of scores on hemisphericity of mathematics teachers. *Perceptual and Motor Skills, 88,* 387–390.

Hattie, J., Marsh, H. W., Neill, J. T., & Richards, G. E. (1997). Adventure education and outward bound: Out-of-class experiences that make a lasting difference. *Review of Educational Research, 67*(1), 43–87.

Hayes, J., & Allinson, C. W. (1994). Cognitive style and its relevance for management practice. *British Journal of Management, 5,* 53–71.

Hayes, J., & Allinson, C. W. (1998). Cognitive style and the theory and practice of individual and collective learning in organizations. *Human Relations, 51*(7), 847–871.

Hayward, G., & Everett, C. (1983). Adaptors and innovators: Data from the Kirton Adaptor–Innovator Inventory in a local authority setting. *Journal of Occupational Psychology, 56,* 339–342.

Helfeldt, J. P. (1983). Sex-linked characteristics of brain functioning: Why Jimmy reads differently. *Reading World* (March), 190–196.

Henry, P., Bardo, H. R., Mouw, J. T., & Bryson, S. (1987). Medicine as a career choice and Holland's theory: Do race and sex make a difference? *Journal of Multicultural Counseling and Development, 15*(4), 161–170.

Henson, K. T., & Borthwick, P. (1984). Matching styles: A historical look. *Theory Into Practice, 23*(1), 3–9.

Herrmann, N. (1996). Supervisor evaluation: From theory to implementation. *Academic Psychiatry, 20*(4), 205–211.

Hickcox, L. K. (1995). Learning styles: A survey of adult learning style inventory models. In R. R. Sims & S. J. Sims (Eds.), *The importance of learning styles: Understanding the implications for learning, course design, and education* (pp. 25–47). Westport, CT: Greenwood Press.

Hill, J. E. (1976). *The educational sciences.* Bloomfield Hills, MI: Oakland Community College Press.

Hill, J., Alker, A., Houghton, P., & Kennington, C. (1998, June). *Learning styles of Central and Eastern European and former Soviet managers: An interim report.* Paper presented at the Third Annual ELSIN Conference, Sutherland, UK.

Hill, J., Puurula, A., Sitko-Lutek, A., & Rakowska, A. (2000). Cognitive style and socialization: An exploration of learned sources of style in Finland, Poland and the UK. *Educational Psychology, 20*(3), 285–305.

Hilliard, R. I. (1995). How do medical students learn: Medical student learning styles and factors that affect these learning styles. *Teaching and Learning in Medicine*, 7(4), 201–210.

Ho, H. K. (1998). *Assessing thinking styles in the theory of mental self-government: A mini validity study in a Hong Kong secondary school.* Unpublished manuscript. The University of Hong Kong.

Hofstede, G. (1991). *Cultures and organizations: Software of the mind.* New York: McGraw-Hill.

Holland, J. L. (1973). *Making vocational choices: A theory of careers.* Englewood Cliffs, NJ: Prentice-Hall.

Holland, J. L. (1985). *Making vocational choices: A theory of vocational personalities and work environments* (2nd ed.). Englewood Cliffs, NJ: Prentice-Hall.

Holland, J. L. (1994). *Self-directed search.* Odessa, FL: Psychological Assessment Resources.

Holland, J. L., Powell, A. B., & Fritzsche, B. A. (1994). *Self-Directed Search—Technical manual.* Odessa, FL: Psychological Assessment Resources.

Holland, P. (1985). Banking in the eighties: Adaption or innovation? *Service Industries Journal, 5*, 515–525.

Holland, P. A. (1987). Adaptors and innovators: Application of the Kirton Adaption–Innovation Inventory to bank employees. *Psychological Reports, 60*, 263–270.

Holland, P. A., Bowskill, I., & Bailey, A. (1991). Adaptors and innovators: Selection versus induction. *Psychological Reports, 68*, 1283–1290.

Holsworth, T. E. (1985). Perceptual style correlates for the MBTI. *Journal of Psychological Type, 10*, 32–35.

Holzman, P. S., & Klein, G. S. (1954). Cognitive-system principles of leveling and sharping: Individual differences in visual time-error assimilation effects. *Journal of Psychology, 37*, 105–122.

Hommerding, L. (2003). Thinking style preferences among the public library directors of Florida. *Dissertation Abstracts International (Section B): The Sciences & Engineering, 63*(11B), 5545.

Honey, P., & Mumford, A. (1982). *The manual of learning styles.* Maidenhead, Berkshire, UK: Honey Press.

Honey, P., & Mumford, A. (1986). *The manual of learning styles* (2nd ed.). Maidenhead, Berkshire, UK: Honey Press.

Honey, P., & Mumford, A. (1992). *The manual of learning styles* (3rd ed.). Maidenhead, Berkshire, UK: Honey Press.

Hossaini, H. R. (1981). *Leadership effectiveness and cognitive style among Iranian and Indian middle managers.* Unpublished doctoral dissertation, Institute of Technology, Delhi.

Huey-You, P. A. (1985). A comparison of two cognitive behavior modification strategies designed to increase reflective test response of mildly language-impaired first graders. *Dissertation Abstracts International (Section A): Humanities and Social Sciences, 46*, 2996.

Ingham, J. (1989). *An experimental investigation of the relationships among learning style perceptual strength, instructional strategies, training achievement and attitudes of corporate employees.* Unpublished doctoral dissertation, St. John's University, New York.

Jackson, C., & Lawty-Jones, M. (1996). Explaining the overlap between personality and learning style. *Personality and Individual Differences, 20*(3), 293–300.

Jacobson, C. M. (1993). Cognitive styles of creativity: Relations of scores on the Kirton Adaption–Innovation Inventory and the Myers-Briggs Type Indicator among managers in USA. *Psychological Reports, 72*, 1131–1138.

Jain, N., Bhatnager, P., & Rastogi, M. (1988). Effect of age, sex and cognitive style on self consistency. *Indian Journal of Current Psychological Research, 3*, 34–38.

Jakabovics, E. H. (1974). Field dependence and social behavior in preschool children (Doctoral dissertation, City University of New York). *Dissertation Abstracts International, 34*, 6211B–6212B. (University Microfilms No. 74-13,443).

James, C. D. R. (1973). *A cognitive style approach to teacher–pupil interaction and the academic performance of Black children.* Unpublished master's thesis. Rutgers University.

James, W. (1890). *The principles of psychology* (Vol. 2). London: MacMillan.

Joffe, R. T. (1987). Reflection–impulsivity and field independence as factors in reading achievement of children with reading difficulties. *Dissertation Abstracts International (Section A): Humanities and Social Sciences, 48,* 867.

Johnson, J., & Kane, K. (1992). Developmental and task factors in LOGO programming. *Journal of Educational Computing Research, 8*(2), 229–253.

Jolly, P. E. (1981). Student achievement in biology in terms of cognitive styles of students and teachers. *Dissertation Abstracts International, 41*(8-A), 3403–3404.

Jonassen, D. H. (1980, April). *Cognitive style predictors of performance.* Paper presented at the annual meeting of the Association for Educational Communications and technology, Denver. (ERIC Document Reproduction service No. ED 194 072).

Jonassen, D. H. (1981, April). *Personality and cognitive style: Predictors of teaching style preferences.* Paper presented at the annual meeting of the Association for Educational Communications and Technology, Philadelphia. (ERIC Document No. ED 207 500)

Jonassen, D. H., & Grabowski, B. L. (1993). *Handbook of individual differences: Learning and instruction.* Hillsdale, NJ: Lawrence Erlbaum Associates.

Jones, A. E. (1997a). Reflection–impulsivity and wholist–analytic: Two fledglings? Or is R–I a cuckoo? *Educational Psychology, 17*(1 & 2), 65–77.

Jones, A. E. (1997b). *Field dependence revisited: An evaluation of issues for education and psychology.* Unpublished doctoral dissertation, University of Lancaster, England.

Jones, C. F. N. (2001). Are learning styles subject-area sensitive? *Dissertation Abstracts International Section A: Humanities and Social Sciences, 61*(9-A), 3453.

Jones, V. C. (1982). Cognitive style and the problem of low school achievement among urban Black low SES students: Grades 2, 4, and 6. *Dissertation Abstracts International, 42*(7-A), 3074–3075.

Jong, P. J. D., Merckelbach, H., & Nijman, H. (1995). Hemisphere preference, anxiety, and covariation bias. *Personality and Individual Differences, 18*(3), 363–371.

Joniak, A. J., & Isaken, S. G. (1988). The Gregorc Style Delineator: Internal consistency and its relationship to Kirton's adaptive–innovative distinction. *Educational and Psychological Measurement, 48*(4), 1043–1049.

Jorde, P. (1984). *Change and innovation in early childhood education: The relationship between selected personal characteristics of administrators and willingness to adopt computer technology.* Unpublished doctoral dissertation, Stanford University.

Jung, C. (1923). *Psychological types.* New York: Harcourt Brace.

Kagan, D. M. (1989). Inquiry mode, occupational stress, and preferred leadership style among American elementary school teachers. *Journal of Social Psychology, 129*(3), 297–305.

Kagan, D. M., & Smith, K. E. (1988). Beliefs and behaviors of kindergarten teachers. *Educational Research, 30*(1), 26–35.

Kagan, J. (1965a). Individual differences in the resolution of response uncertainty. *Journal of Personality and Social Psychology, 2,* 154–160.

Kagan, J. (1965b). Information processing in the child. In P. M. Mussen, J. J. Conger, & J. Kagan (Eds.), *Readings in child development and personality* (pp. 313–326). New York: Harper & Row.

Kagan, J. (1965c). *Matching familiar figures test.* Cambridge, MA: Author, Harvard University.

Kagan, J. (1966a). Developmental studies in reflection and analysis. In A. H. Kidd & J. L. Rivoire (Eds.), *Perceptual development in children* (pp. 487–522). New York: International University Press.

Kagan, J. (1966b). Reflection–impulsivity: The generality and dynamics of conceptual tempo. *Journal of Abnormal Psychology, 71,* 17–24.

Kagan, J. (1976). Commentary on reflective and impulsive children: strategies of information processing underlying differences in problem solving. *Monographs of the Society for Research in Child Development, 41,* No. 5 (Serial No. 168), pp. 48–52.

Kagan, J., & Kogan, N. (1970). Individual variation in cognitive processes. In P. A. Mussen (Ed.), *Carmichael's manual of child psychology* (Vol. 1, pp. 1273–1365). New York: Wiley.

Kagan, J., & Messer, S. B. (1975). A reply to "Some misgiving about the Matching Familiar Figures Test as a measure of reflection–impulsivity." *Developmental Psychology, 11,* 244–248.

Kagan, J., & Moss, H. A. (1963). Psychological significance of styles of conceptualization. In J. E. Wright & J. Kagan (Eds.), *Basic cognitive processes in children.* Monograph of The Society for Research in Child Development, *28*(2), 73–112.

Kagan, J., Rosman, B. L., Day, D., Albert, J., & Philips, W. (1964). Information processing in the child: Significance of analytic and reflective attitudes. *Psychological Monographs, 78*(1, Whole No. 578).

Kagan, D. M., & Smith, K. E. (1988). Beliefs and behaviors of kindergarten teachers. *Educational Research, 30*(1), 26–35.

Kalsbeek, D. H. (1989). Linking learning style theory with retention research: The TRAILS Project. *Association for Institutional Research, 32,* 1–7.

Kanske, C. A. (1999). The learning styles of pilots currently qualified in United States Air Force aircraft. *Dissertation Abstracts International, 60*(2-A), 0334.

Kaufman, J. C. (2001). Thinking styles in creative writers and journalists. *Dissertation Abstracts International (Section B): The Sciences and Engineering, 62*(3B), 1069.

Keefe, J. W., & Monk, J. S. (1989). *Learning style profile.* Reston, VA: National Association of Secondary School Principals.

Keller, R. T., & Holland, W. E. (1978a). A cross-validation study of the Kirton Adaption–Innovation Inventory in three research and development organizations. *Applied Psychological Measurement, 2*(4), 563–570.

Keller, R. T., & Holland, W. E. (1978b). Individual characteristics of innovativeness and communication in research and development organizations. *Journal of Applied Psychology, 63*(6), 759–762.

Keogh, B. K., & Donlon, G. (1972). Field dependence, impulsivity and learning disabilities. *Journal of Learning Disabilities, 5,* 331–336.

Khan, S. B., & Alvi, S. A. (1986). *A study of validation and structure of Holland's theory of careers.* Toronto, Canada: Ontario Institute for Studies in Education.

Khan, S. B., Alvi, S. A, & Kwong, S. L. (1985). *Field-dependence and field-independence cognitive styles of intermediate and high school students in relation to differences in age/grade, gender, and academic and vocational orientations.* Toronto, Canada: The Ontario Institute for Studies in Education.

Khaneja, D. (1982). *Relationship of the adaption–innovation continuum to achievement orientation in entrepreneurs and non-entrepreneurs.* Unpublished doctoral dissertation, Institute of Technology, Delhi.

Kim, J., & Michael, W. B. (1995). The relationship of creativity measures to school achievement and preferred learning and thinking style in a sample of Korean high school students. *Educational and Psychological Measurement, 55*(1), 60–74.

Kim, K. (1993). The relationship between teaching style and personality characteristic of group piano teacher. *Dissertation Abstracts International, 53*(12-A), 4244–4245.

Kim, M. H. (1996). Cognitive style (Witkin): A comparative study of Korean and Korean-American christians. *Dissertation Abstracts International Section A: Humanities and Social Sciences, 57*(5-A), 1945.

Kinsbourne, M. (1982). Hemispheric specialization and the growth of human understanding. *American Psychologist, 37,* 411–420.

Kirby, J. R., & Pedwell, D. (1991). Students approaches to summarization. *Educational Psychology, 11*(3/4), 297–307.

Kirchner-Nebot, T., & Amador-Campos, J. A. (1998). Internal consistency of scores on Matching Familiar Figures Test-20 and correlation of scores with age. *Perceptual and Motor Skills, 86*(3), 803–807.

Kirton, M. J. (1961). *Management initiative.* London: Acton Society Trust.

Kirton, M. J. (1976). Adaptors and innovators: A description and measure. *Journal of Applied Psychology, 61,* 622–629.

Kirton, M. J. (1978a). Adaptors and innovators in culture clash. *Current Anthropology, 19,* 611–612.

Kirton, M. J. (1978b). Have adaptors and innovators equal levels of creativity? *Psychological Reports, 42,* 695–698.

Kirton, M. J. (1980). Adaptors and innovators in organizations. *Human Relations, 33,* 213–224.

Kirton, M. J. (1988). Adaptors and innovators: Problem solvers in organizations. In K. Gronhaug & G. Kaufman (Eds.), *Innovation: A cross-disciplinary perspective.* Oslo, Norway: Norwegian University Press.

Kirton, M. J. (Ed.). (1989). *Adaptors and innovators: Styles of creativity and problem solving.* New York: Routledge.

Kirton, M. J. (1993). Personal communication of unpublished data. Occupational Research Center, Hatfield, UK.

Kirton, M. J. (1994). *Adaptors and innovators* (2nd ed.). London: Routledge.

Kirton, M. J., & De Ciantis, S. M. (1986). Cognitive style and personality: The Kirton Adaption–Innovation and Cattell's Sixteen Personality Factor Inventories. *Personality and Individual Differences, 7*(2), 141–146

Kirton, M. J., & Kubes, M. (1992). *KAI Manual—Slovak Language Supplement.* Bratislava, Slovakia: Maxman.

Kirton, M. J., & McCarthy, R. M. (1988). Cognitive climate and organizations. *Journal of Occupational Psychology, 61,* 175–184.

Kirton, M. J., & Pender, S. R. (1982). The adaption–innovation continuum, occupational type and course selection. *Psychological Reports, 51,* 883–886.

Kogan, N. (1971). Educational implications of cognitive styles. In G. Lesser (Ed.), *Psychology and educational practice* (pp. 242–292). Glenview, IL: Scott, Foresman.

Kogan, N. (1980). A style of life, a life of style—Review of cognitive styles in personal and cultural adaptation. *Contemporary Psychology, 25,* 595–598.

Kogan, N. (1989). A stylistic perspective on metaphor and aesthetic sensitivity in children. In T. Globerson & T. Zelniker (Eds.), *Cognitive style and cognitive development* (Human Development, Vol. 3, pp. 192–213). Norwood, NJ: Ablex.

Kolb, D. A. (1976). *The learning style inventory: Technical manual.* Boston, MA: McBer.

Konopka, M. A. (1999). The Myers-Briggs Type Indicator as a predictor of the learning styles of middle- and upper-level civilian managers of the United States Army. *Dissertation Abstracts International, 59*(10-A), 3735.

Koppelman, K. L. (1980). An ethnographic investigation of teacher behavior as a function of cognitive style. *Dissertation Abstracts International, 40*(7-A), 3743–3744.

Kreml, W. P. (1977). *The anti-authoritarian personality.* New York: Pergamon Press.

Krueger, T. H. (1976). *Visual imagery in problem solving and scientific creativity.* Derby, CT: Seal Press.

Kubes, M. (1989). The Kirton Adaption–Innovation Inventory in Czechoslovakia. In *Proceedings of International Conference on Psychological Problems of Creative Scientific Work.* Bratislava, Slovakia: Slovak Academy of Sciences, pp. 151–167.

Kubes, M. (1992). Cognitive style and interpersonal behavior: The Kirton Adaption–Innovation and Schutz's FIRO-B inventories. *Journal of Human Behavior, 29,* 33–38.

Kwan, D. (2002). *Thinking styles, learning approaches, and academic achievement.* Unpublished manuscript. The University of Hong Kong.

Lam, P. Y. (2000). *The usefulness of thinking styles in reflecting how individuals think and explaining school performance.* Unpublished manuscript. The University of Hong Kong.

Lange, C. M. (1973). A study of the effects on learning of matching the cognitive styles of students and instructors in nursing education. *Dissertation Abstracts International, 33*(9-A), 4742–4743.

Laosa, L. M. (1980). Maternal teaching strategies and cognitive styles in Chicano families. *Journal of Educational Psychology, 72*(1), 45–54.

Lawrence, M. V. M. (1997). Secondary school teachers and learning style preferences: Action or watching in the classroom. *Educational Psychology, 17*(1–2), 157–170.

Lee, K. L. (2002). *Thinking styles and approaches in teaching among Hong Kong kindergarten teachers.* Unpublished manuscript. The University of Hong Kong.

Leondari, A., Syngollitou, E., & Kiosseoglou, G. (1998). Academic achievement, motivation and future selves. *Educational Studies, 24*(2), 153–163.

Leventhal, G., & Sisco, H. (1996). Correlations among field dependence/independence, locus of control and self-monitoring. *Perceptual and Motor Skills, 83*, 604–606.

Levy, N., Murphy, C., & Carlson, R. (1972). Personality types among Negro college students. *Educational and Psychological Measurement, 32*, 641–653.

Lewin, Z. G. (1983). A study about the validity of the Group Embedded Figures Test. *Arquivos Brasileiros de Psicologia, 35*(2), 11–35

Lewis, B. N. (1976). Avoidance of aptitude–treatment trivialities. In S. Messick (Ed.), *Individuality in learning* (pp. 35–72). San Francisco: Jossey-Bass.

Linden, W. (1973). Practicing of meditation by school children and their levels of field dependence-independence, test anxiety, and reading achievement. *Journal of Consulting and Clinical Psychology, 41*(1), 139–143.

Lindsay, P. (1985). Counseling to resolve a clash of cognitive styles. *Technovation, 3*, 57–67.

Liu, M., & Reed, W. M. (1994). The relationship between the learning strategies and learning styles in a hypermedia environment. *Computers in Human Behavior, 10*(4), 419–434.

Logan, J. W. (1983). Cognitive style and reading. *Reading Teacher, 36*(7), 704–707.

Lowe, E. A., & Taylor, W. G. K. (1986). The management of research in the life sciences: The characteristics of researchers. *R & D Management, 16*, 45–61.

MacArthur, R. (1973). Some ability patterns: Central Eskimos and Nsenga Africans. *International Journal of Psychology, 8*(4), 239–247.

MacNeil, R. D. (1980). The relationship of cognitive style and instructional style to the learning performance of undergraduate students. *Journal of Educational Research, 73*, 354–359.

Mahlios, M. C. (1981). Instructional design and cognitive styles of teachers in elementary schools. *Perceptual and Motor Skills, 52*(2), 335–338.

Makkar, M., Malhotra, D., & Jerath, J. M. (1999). Perceptual strategies in short-term memory. *Studia-Psychologica, 41*(3), 231–237.

Malinsky, M. A. (2001). Matched learning styles of teacher and student: A study of its relationship to achievement and self-esteem. *Dissertation Abstracts International, Section A: Humanities and Social Sciences, 62*(3-A), 901.

Mansfield, E. A. (1998). Working memory development in adolescence: A neo-Piagetian investigation. *Dissertation Abstracts International (Section A): Humanities and Social Sciences, 58*(8A), 3001.

Martinsen, O. (1994). *Cognitive style and insight.* Unpublished doctoral dissertation, Faculty of Psychology, University of Bergen, Norway.

Marton, F. (1976). What does it take to learn? Some implications on an alternative view of learning. In N. J. Entwistle (Ed.), *Strategies for research and development in higher education* (pp. 200–222). Amsterdam: Swets & Zeitlinger.

Massari, D. J. (1975). The relation of reflection–impulsivity to field-dependence-independence and internal–external control in children. *Journal of Genetic Psychology, 126*, 61–67.

Matson, J. L. (1980). Acquisition of social skills by mentally retarded adult training assistants. *Journal of Mental Deficiency Research, 24*(2), 129–135.

McCarthy, R. (1993). *The relationship between work pressure, cognitive style, sex role attitudes and coping behavior in women managers and secretaries.* Unpublished doctoral dissertation, University of Hertfordshire, UK.

McCaulley, M. H. (1981). Jung's theory of psychological types and the Myers-Briggs Type Indicator. In P. McReynolds (Ed.), *Advances in personality assessment* (Vol. 5, pp. 294–352). San Francisco: Jossey-Bass.

McCaulley, M. H. (1990). The Myers-Briggs Type Indicator in counseling. In C. E. Watkins, Jr., & V. L. Campbell (Eds.), *Testing in counseling practice* (pp. 91–134). Hillsdale, NJ: Lawrence Erlbaum Associates.

McCaulley, M. H., & Natter, F. L. (1974). *Psychological (Myers-Briggs) type differences in education.* Gainesville, FL: Center for Applications of Psychological Type.

McCrae, R. R., & Costa, P. T., Jr. (1989). Reinterpreting the Myers-Briggs Type Indicator from the perspective of the five-factor model of personality. *Journal of Personality, 57*(1), 17–40.

McDermott, P. A. (1984). Comparative functions of preschool learning style and IQ in predicting future academic performance. *Contemporary Educational Psychology, 9*(1), 38–47.

McGregor, D. (1960). *The human side of enterprise.* New York: McGraw-Hill.

McKay, E. (2000). Measurement of cognitive performance in computer programming concept acquisition: Interactive effects of visual metaphors and the cognitive style construct. *Journal of Applied Measurement, 1*(3), 257–291.

McKenna, F. P. (1983). Field dependence and personality: A re-examination. *Social Behavior and Personality, 11*, 51–55.

Mehdi, B. (1974). Creativity, intelligence and achievement: Some findings of recent research. *Indian Educational Review, 9*(1), 1–10.

Mehdikhani, N. (1983). The relative effects of teacher teaching style, teacher learning style, and student learning style upon student academic achievement. *Dissertation Abstracts International, 44*(2-A), 374.

Meisgeier, C., & Murphy, E. A. (1987). *The Murphy-Meisgeier Type Indicator for Children.* Palo Alto, CA: Consulting Psychologists Press.

Melancon, J. G., & Thompson, B. (1989). Measurement characteristics of the Finding Embedded Figures Test. *Psychology in the Schools, 26*(1), 69–78.

Melear, C. T. (1989). *Cognitive processes in the Curry learning style framework as measured by the learning style profile and the Myers-Briggs type indicator among non-majors in college biology.* Unpublished doctoral dissertation, Ohio State University.

Melear, C. T., & Alcock, M. W. (1999). Learning styles and personality types of African American children: Implications for science education. *Journal of Psychological Type, 48*, 22–33.

Mesquita, B., & Frijda, N. (1992). Cultural variations in emotions: A review. *Psychological Bulletin, 112*, 179–204.

Messer, S. B. (1976). Reflection–impulsivity: A review. *Psychological Bulletin, 83*(6), 1026–1052.

Messick, S. (1984). The nature of cognitive styles: Problems and promise in educational practice. *Educational Psychologist, 19*, 59–74.

Messick, S. (1994). The matter of style: Manifestations of personality in cognition, learning, and teaching. *Educational Psychologist, 29*, 121–136.

Messick, S. (1996). Bridging cognition and personality in education: the role of style in performance and development. *European Journal of Personality, 10*, 353–376.

Miller, A. (1987). Cognitive styles: An integrated model. *Educational Psychology, 7*(4), 251–268.

Miller, C. D., Finley, J., & McKinley, D. L. (1990). Learning approaches and motives: Male and female differences and implications for learning assistance programs. *Journal of College Student Development, 31*(2), 147–154.

Miller, M. J. (1994). Congruence between parents' and children's three-letter Holland Codes. *Psychological Reports, 74*, 1387–390.

Moore, C. A. (1973). Styles of teacher behavior under simulated teaching conditions. *Dissertation Abstracts International, Section A: Humanities and Social Sciences, 34*(A), 3149–3150.

Moos, R. (1973). Conceptualization of human environment. *American Psychologist, 28,* 652–665.

Morgan, H. (1997). *Cognitive styles and classroom learning.* Westport, CT: Praeger.

Mshelia, A. Y., & Lapidus, L. B. (1990). Depth picture perception in relation to cognitive style and training in non-Western children. *Journal of Cross-cultural Psychology, 21*(4), 414–433.

Murphy, H. J., Casey, B., Day, D. A., & Young, J. D. (1997). Scores on the Group Embedded Figures Test by undergraduates in information management. *Perceptual and Motor Skills, 84*(3), 1135–1138.

Murray, M. J. (1979). Matching preferred cognitive mode with teaching methodology in learning a novel motor skill. *Research Quarterly, 50,* 80–87.

Myers, I. B. (1962). *The Myers-Briggs Type Indicator: Manual.* Palo Alto, CA: Consulting Psychologists Press.

Myers, I. B., & McCaulley, M. H. (1985). *Manual: A guide to the development and use of the Myers-Briggs Type Indicator.* Palo Alto, CA: Consulting Psychologists Press.

Myers, I. B., & McCaulley, M. H. (1988). *Manual: A guide to the development and use of the Myers-Briggs Type Indicator.* Palo Alto, CA: Consulting Psychologists Press.

Nachmias, R., & Shany, N. (2002). Learning in virtual courses and its relationship to thinking styles. *Journal of Educational Computing Research, 27*(3), 315–329.

Neimark, E. D. (1975). Longitudinal development of formal operations thought. *Genetic Psychology Monographs, 91,* 171–225.

Nickel, S. B. (1995). A determination and comparison of the personality type profiles of Oklahoma Cooperative Extension Service field staff as measured by the Myers-Briggs Type Indictor. *Dissertation Abstracts International (Section A): Humanities and Social Sciences, 56*(4A), 1218.

Niles, F. S. (1995). Cultural differences in learning motivation and learning strategies: A comparison of overseas and Australian students at an Australian university. *International Journal of Intercultural Relations, 19*(3), 369–385.

Noppe, L. D., & Gallagher, J. M. (1977). A cognitive style approach to creative thought. *Journal of Personality Assessment, 41,* 85–90.

Nunn, G. D. (1995). Effects of a learning styles and strategies intervention upon at-risk middle school students' achievement and locus of control. *Journal of Instructional Psychology, 22*(1), 34–39.

O' Brien, T. P. (1990). Construct validation of the Gregorc Style Delineator: An application of LISREL 7. *Educational and Psychological Measurement, 50*(3), 631–636.

O' Brien, T. P. (1991). Relationships among selected characteristics of college students and cognitive style preferences. *College Student Journal, 25*(1), 492–500.

O'Brien, T. P., & Wilkinson, N. C. (1992). Cognitive styles and performance on the National Council of State Boards of Nursing Licensure Examination. *College Student Journal, 26*(2), 156–161.

O'Dell, F. L., Rak, C. F., Chermonte, J. P., & Hamlin, A. (1994). The boost club: A program for at-risk third- and fourth-grade students. *The Journal for Specialists in Group Work, 19*(4), 227–231.

Ogunyemi, E. L. (1973). Cognitive styles and student science achievement in Nigeria. *Journal of Experimental Education, 42*(1), 59–63.

Okabayashi, H., & Torrance, E. P. (1984). Role of style of learning and thinking and self directed learning readiness in the achievement of gifted students. *Journal of Learning Disabilities, 17*(2), 104–107.

Olive, H. (1972a). A note on sex differences in adolescents' divergent thinking. *Journal of Psychology, 82*(1), 39–42.

Olive, H. (1972b). The relationship of divergent thinking to intelligence, social class, and achievement in high school students. *Journal of Genetic Psychology, 121*(2), 179–186.

O'Neil, M. J., & Child, D. (1984). Biggs' SPQ: A British study of its internal structure. *British Journal of Educational Psychology, 54,* 228–234.

O'Neill, W. J. (1990). Relationship of match/mismatch of student–teacher learning styles, stress, and academic achievement. *Dissertation Abstracts International, 50*(10-A), 3166.

Osipow, S. H. (1969). Cognitive styles and educational–vocational preferences and selections. *Journal of Counseling Psychology, 16,* 534–546.

Pacini, R., & Epstein, S. (1999). The relation of rational and experiential information processing styles to personality, basic beliefs, and the ratio–bias phenomenon. *Journal of Personality and Social Psychology, 76*(6), 972–987.

Packer, J., & Bain, J. D. (1978). Cognitive style and teacher–student compatibility. *Journal of Educational Psychology, 70*(5), 864–871.

Panek, P. E., Funk, L. G., & Nelson, P. K. (1980). Reliability and validity of the Group Embedded Figures Test across the life span. *Perceptual and Motor Skills, 50*(3), 1171–1174.

Paradise, L. V., & Block, C. (1984). The relationship of teacher–student cognitive style to academic achievement. *Journal of Research and Development in Education, 17*(4), 57–61.

Parisi, J. C. (1980). An investigation into the relationship between the field dependent-independent cognitive styles of teachers and students and student ratings of college teachers. *Dissertation Abstracts International, 41*(2-A), 520–521.

Pask, G. (1972). A fresh look at cognition and the individual. *International Journal of Man–Machine Studies, 4,* 211–216.

Pask, G., & Scott, B. C. E. (1972). Learning strategies and individual competence. *International Journal of Man-Machine Studies, 4,* 217–253.

Pavlovich, N. S. (1971). Cognitive types of teachers and pupils in relation to classroom interaction. *Dissertation Abstracts International, 32*(2-A), 797.

Peake, T. H., Stehouwer, S. R., & Stehouwer, N. D. (1982). Schematic portrayal: Parents' cognitive styles and children's developmental health. *Journal of Psychology and Theology, 10*(1), 47–54.

Penn, B. K. (1991). Correlations among learning styles, clinical specialties, and personality types of U.S. Army nurses. *Dissertation Abstracts International, 53*(2), 393-A.

Perchaluk-Kemppainen, M. M. (1997). Learning styles and their link to preferences and participation for medical business managers. *Dissertation Abstracts International (Section A): Humanities and Social Sciences, 57*(9A), 3781.

Perry, W. G. (1970). *Forms of intellectual and ethical development in the college years: A scheme* (2nd ed.). New York: Holt, Rinehart and Winston.

Perry, W. G. (1981). Cognitive and ethical growth: The making of meaning. In A. Chickering (Ed.), *The modern American college* (pp. 76–116). San Francisco: Jossey-Bass.

Perry, W. G. (1999). *Forms of intellectual and ethical development in the college years: A scheme* (3rd ed.). San Francisco: Jossey-Bass.

Petersen, A. C., Leffert, N., & Graham, B. L. (1995). Adolescent development and the emergence of sexuality. *Suicide and Life Threatening Behavior, 25,* 4–17.

Peterson, E. R., Deary, I. J., & Austin, E. J. (2003). The reliability of Riding's cognitive style analysis test. *Personality and Individual Differences, 34,* 881–891.

Pettigrew, A. C., & King, M. O. (1997). Adaptors and innovators: A description of staff nurses. *Psychological Reports, 81,* 16–18.

Pettigrew, F. E., Bayless, M. A., Zakrajsek, D. B., & Goc-Karp, G. (1985). Compatibility of students' learning and teaching styles on their ratings of college teaching. *Perceptual and Motor Skills, 61,* 1215–1220.

Petty, G., & Haltman, E. (1991). Learning style and brain hemisphericity of technical institute students. *Journal of Studies in Technical Careers, 13,* 79–91.

Phillips, S. B. (1999). Student evaluation of faculty instruction: Inflated results and student feedback. *Dissertation Abstracts International (Section A): Humanities and Social Sciences, 60*(5A), 1478.

Piaget, J. (1952). *The origins of intelligence in children.* New York: International Universities Press.

Piers, V. (1984). *Piers-Harris Children's Self Concept Scale, revised manual.* Los Angeles, CA: Western Psychological Services

Plovnick, M. (1974). *Individual learning styles and the process of career choice in medical students.* Unpublished doctoral dissertation, Sloan School of Management, Massachusetts Institute of Technology.

Powell, G. N., & Butterfield, D. A. (1978). The case for subsystem climate in organizations. *Academy of Management Review, 3,* 151–157.

Pozzi, F. T. (1979). *A study of student and teacher cognitive styles.* Unpublished doctoral dissertation, Miami Univer.

Prato Previde, G. (1984). Adaptors and innovators: The results of the Italian standardization of the KAI (Kirton Adaptation-Innovation Inventory)/Adattatori ed Innovatori i risultati della standardizzazione italiana del KAI (Kirton Adaptation-Innovation Inventory). *Ricerche di Psicologia, 8*(4), 81–134.

Prato Previde, G. (1991). Italian adaptors and innovators: Is cognitive style underlying culture? *Personality and Individual Differences, 12,* 1–10.

Price, A. L. (2003). Values of engineering majors: A step beyond Holland's model. *Dissertation Abstracts International, (Section A): Humanities and Social Sciences, 63*(7A), 2459.

Prosser, M., & Trigwell, K. (1997). Relations between perceptions of the teaching environment and approaches to teaching. *British Journal of Educational Psychology, 67,* 25–35.

Pysh, F. (1970). The relationship of field-dependence-independence to performance on Piagetian-type tasks incorporating the Euclidean coordinate system. *Western Psychologist, 1*(4), 137–143.

Quinn, J. M. (1988). Cognitive style, personality, and classroom management of special education teachers in nonpublic schools. *Dissertation Abstracts International, 48*(10-A), 2600.

Raven, J. C. (1998). *Standard Progressive Matrices.* London: Lewis & Co. Ltd.

Rayner, S., & Riding, R. (1997). Towards a categorization of cognitive styles and learning styles. *Educational Psychology, 17*(1 & 2), 5–27.

Reed, W. M., Oughton, J. M., Ayersman, D. J., Ervin Jr., J. R., & Giessler, S. F. (2000). Computer experience, learning style, and hypermedia navigation. *Computers in Human Behavior, 16,* 609–628.

Reis, S. (1987). We can't change what we don't recognize: Understanding the special needs of gifted females. *Gifted Child Quarterly, 31,* 83–89.

Renninger, K. A., & Snyder, S. S. (1983). Effects of cognitive style on perceived satisfaction and performance among students and teachers. *Journal of Educational Psychology, 75*(5), 668–676.

Renzulli, J. S., & Smith, L. H. (1978). *Learning styles inventory.* Mansfield Center, CT: Creative Learning Press.

Reynolds, C. R., & Torrance, E. P. (1978). Perceived changes in styles of learning and thinking (hemisphericity), through direct and indirect training. *Journal of Creative Behavior, 12,* 247–252.

Reynolds, J. (1991). Learning with style: An introductory workshop. *Journal of College Student Development, 32*(1), 85–86.

Rezler, A. G., & Rezmovic, V. (1974). The learning preference inventory. *Journal of Applied Health, 19*(1), 28–34.

Rezler, A., & Rezmovic, V. (1981). The learning preference inventory. *Journal of Applied Health, 10,* 28–34.

Richardson, A. (1977). Verbaliser–visualiser: A cognitive style dimension. *Journal of Mental Imagery, 1,* 109–126.

Richardson, J. A., & Turner, T. E. (2000). Field dependence revisited I: Intelligence. *Educational Psychology, 20*(3), 255–270.

Richardson, J. T. E. (1990). Reliability and replicability of the Approaches to Studying Questionnaire. *Studies in Higher Education, 15*(2), 155–168.

Richardson, J. T. E. (1995). Mature students in higher education: II. An investigation of approaches to studying and academic performance. *Studies in Higher Education, 20*(1), 5–17.

Riding, R. (1991). *Cognitive style analysis user manual.* Birmingham: Learning and Training Technology.

Riding, R. (1997). On the nature of cognitive style. *Educational Psychology, 17*(1 & 2), 29–49.

Riding, R. J., & Burton, D. (1998). Cognitive style, gender and conduct behavior in secondary school pupils. *Research in Education, 59*, 38–49.

Riding, R. J., Burton, D., Rees, G., & Sharratt, M. (1995). Cognitive style and personality in 12-year-old children. *British Journal of Educational Psychology, 65*, 113–124.

Riding, R. J., & Cheema, I. (1991). Cognitive styles—an overview and integration. *Educational Psychology, 11*(3 & 4), 193–215.

Riding, R. J., & Craig, O. (1998). Cognitive style and problem behavior in boys referred to residential special schools. *Educational Studies, 24*(2), 205–222.

Riding, R. J., & Craig, O. (1999). Cognitive style and types of problem behavior in boys in special schools. *British Journal of Educational Psychology, 69*(3), 307–322.

Riding, R. J., & Dyer, V. (1983). The nature of learning styles and their relationship to cognitive performance in children. *Educational Psychology, 3*, 275–287.

Riding, R. J., & Fairhurst, P. (2001). Cognitive style, home background and conduct behavior in primary school pupils. *Educational Psychology, 21*(1), 115–124.

Riding, R. J., & Rayner, S. (1998). *Cognitive styles and learning strategies: Understanding style differences in learning and behavior.* London: David Fulton.

Riding, R. J., & Taylor, E. M. (1976). Imagery performance and prose comprehension in 7 year old children. *Educational Studies, 2*, 21–27.

Riding, R. J., & Wigley, S. (1997). The relationship between cognitive style and personality in further education students. *Personality and Individual Differences, 23*(3), 379–389.

Riding, R. J., & Wright, M. (1995). Cognitive style, personality characteristics and harmony in student flats. *Educational Psychology, 15*(3), 337–349.

Riding, R., & Pearson, F. (1994). The relationship between cognitive style and intelligence. *Educational Psychology, 14*, 413–425.

Riechmann, S. W., & Grasha, A. F. (1974). A rational approach to developing and assessing the construct validity of a student learning styles scale instrument. *Journal of Psychology, 87*, 213–223.

Robertson, E. D., Fournet, G. P., Zelhart, P. F., & Estes, R. E. (1987). Relationship of field dependence/independence to adaption–innovation in alcoholics. *Perceptual and Motor Skills, 65*(3), 771–776.

Robinson, A. R. (1982). An investigation into the relationship between teaching styles and learning styles. *Dissertation Abstracts International, 43*(2-A), 425.

Rokeach, M. (1960). *The open and closed mind.* New York: Basic.

Rosenthal, R., & Jacobson, L. (1968). *Pygmalion in the classroom. Teacher expectations and pupils' intellectual development.* New York: Holt, Rinehart & Winston.

Ross, J. (1962). Factor analysis and levels of measurement in psychology. In S. Messick & J. Ross (Eds.), *Measurement in personality and cognition* (pp. 69–81). New York: Wiley.

Ross, J. L. (2000). An exploratory analysis of post-secondary student achievement comparing a Web-based and a conventional course learning environment. *Dissertation Abstracts International (Section A): Humanities and Social Sciences, 61*(5A), 1809.

Royce, J. R., & Powell, A. (1983). *Theory of personality and individual differences: Factors, systems, and processes.* Englewood Cliffs, NJ: Prentice-Hall.

Rubovits, P. C., & Maehr, M. L. (1971). Pygmalion analyzed: Toward an explanation of the Rosenthal-Jacobson findings. *Journal of Personality and Social Psychology, 19*, 197–203.

Rudisill, E. M. (1973). *An investigation of the relationships between mathematics teachers' personality characteristics as measured by the Myers-Briggs Type Indicator and their Preferences for Certain Teaching Strategies.* Unpublished doctoral dissertation, University of Florida, Gainesville.

Russell, A. J. (1997). The effect of learner variables cognitive style on learning performance in a vocational training environment. *Educational Psychology, 17*(1 & 2), 195–208.

Sadler-Smith, E. (1996). Approaches to studying: age, gender and academic performance. *Educational Studies, 22*(3), 367–379.

Sadler-Smith, E. (1997). 'Learning style': frameworks and instruments. *Educational Psychology, 17*(1–2), 51–63.

Sadler-Smith, E. (1999). Intuition-analysis style and approaches to studying. *Educational Studies, 25*(2), 159–173.

Sadler-Smith, E. (2001). The relationship between learning style and cognitive style. *Personality and Individual Differences, 30*(4), 609–616.

Sadler-Smith, E., & Tsang, F. (1998). A comparative study of approaches to studying in Hong Kong and the United Kingdom. *British Journal of Educational Psychology, 68*, 81–93.

Saleh, A. I. (1998). The nexus of brain hemisphericity, personality types, temperaments, learning styles, learning strategies, gender, majors, and cultures. *Dissertation Abstracts International Section A: Humanities and Social Sciences, 58*(8-A), 3004.

Salkind, N. J., Kojima, H., & Zelniker, T. (1978). Cognitive tempo in American, Japanese, and Israeli children. *Child Development, 49*, 1024–1027.

Saracho, O. N. (1978). The relationship of the match of teachers' students' cognitive style to teachers' perception of students' competence. *Dissertation Abstracts International, 39*(5-A), 2738.

Saracho, O. N. (1983). Cultural differences in the cognitive style of Mexican American students. *Journal of the Association for the Study of Perception, 18*(1), 3–10.

Saracho, O. N. (1991a). Students' preferences for field dependence-independence teacher characteristics. *Educational Psychology, 11*(3/4), 323–332.

Saracho, O. N. (1991b). Teacher expectations and cognitive style: Implications for students' academic achievement. *Early Child Development and Care, 77*, 97–108.

Saracho, O. N. (1992). The relationship between preschool children's cognitive style and play: Implications for creativity. *The Creativity Research Journal, 5*(1), 35–47.

Saracho, O. N. (1996). Preschool children's cognitive styles and play behaviors. *Child Study Journal, 26*(2), 125–148.

Saracho, O. N. (2001). Cognitive style and kindergarten pupils' preferences for teachers. *Learning and Instruction, 11*, 195–209.

Saracho, O. N., & Dayton, C. M. (1980). Relationship of teachers' cognitive styles to pupils' academic achievement gains. *Journal of Educational Psychology, 72*(4), 544–549.

Saracho, O. N., & Spodek, B. (1994). Matching preschool children's and teachers' cognitive styles. *Perceptual and Motor Skills, 78*(2), 683–689.

Satterly, D. (1976). Cognitive styles, spatial ability, and school achievement. *Journal of Educational Psychology, 68*, 36–42.

Satterly, D. J. (1979). Covariation of cognitive styles, intelligence and achievement. *British Journal of Educational Psychology, 49*(2), 179–181.

Sayles-Folks, S. L., & Harrison, D. K. (1989). Reflection–impulsivity and work adjustment. *Rehabilitation Counseling Bulletin, 33*(2), 110–117.

Scarr, S. (1984). *Mother care, other care.* New York: Basic Books.

Schenker, S. L. (1982). The relationship between matched middle school student/teacher cognitive style and achievement, self-esteem, and attitude toward school subject. *Dissertation Abstracts International, 42*(9-A), 3860.

Schleifer, M., & Douglas, V. I. (1973). Moral judgments, behavior and cognitive style in young children. *Canadian Journal of Behavioral Science, 5*, 133–144.

Schlesinger, H. J. (1954). Cognitive attitudes in relation to susceptibility to interference. *Journal of Personality, 22*, 354–374.

Schmeck, R. R. (1983). Learning style of college students. In R. F. Dillon & R. R. Schmeck (Eds.), *Individual differences in cognition* (Vol. 1, pp. 233–279). New York: Academic Press.

Schmeck, R. R., Ribich, F. D., & Ramaniah, N. (1977). Development of a self-report inventory for assessing individual differences in learning process. *Applied Psychological Measurement, 1,* 413–431.

Schroder, H. M. (1989). Managerial competence and style. In M. J. Kirton (Ed.), *Adaptors and innovators: Styles of creativity and problem solving* (pp. 97–124). London: Routledge.

Seidel, L. E., & England, E. M. (1999). Gregorc's cognitive styles: College students' preferences for teaching methods and testing techniques. *Perceptual and Motor Skills, 88*(3), 859–875.

Serafino, P. A. (1979). Field-dependent and field-independent cognitive style and teacher behavior. *Dissertation Abstracts International, 40*(1-A), 210.

Severiens, S. E., & Ten Dam, G. T. M. (1994). Gender differences in learning styles: A narrative review and quantitative meta-analysis. *Higher Education, 27,* 487–501.

Severiens, S., & Ten Dam, G. (1997). Gender and gender identity differences in learning styles. *Educational Psychology, 17*(1 & 2), 79–94.

Sewall, T. J. (1989). A factor analysis of three learning styles instruments: A test of the Curry model of learning style characteristics. *Dissertation Abstracts International (Section A): Humanities and Social Sciences, 50*(1A), 54.

Shain, L., Farber, S., & Barry, A. (1989). Female identity development and self-reflection in late adolescence. *Adolescence, 24,* 381–392.

Sherman, J. A. (1967). Problem of sex differences in space perception and aspects of intellectual functioning. *Psychological Review, 74,* 290–299.

Shipman, S. L. (1989). Limitations of applying cognitive styles to early childhood education. *Early Childhood Development and Care, 51,* 3–12.

Shipman, S. L. (1990). Limitations of applying cognitive style to early childhood education. In O. N. Saracho (Ed.), *Cognitive style and early education* (pp. 33–42). New York: Gordon & Breach.

Shrauger, J. S., & Osberg, T. M. (1981). The relative accuracy of self-predictions and judgments by others in psychological assessment. *Psychological Bulletin, 90,* 322–351.

Simon, R. S. (1979). *Jungian types and creativity of professional fine artists.* Unpublished doctoral dissertation, United States International University.

Sitko-Lutek, A., Kennington, C., & Rakowska, A. (1998, June). *An investigation into the learning styles of Polish managers.* Paper presented to the Third Annual ELSIN Conference, Sutherland, UK.

Smutz, R. P. (2003). The effect of teaching style-learning style match/mismatch on learning effectiveness in computer-based training. *Dissertation Abstracts International, 63*(8-A), 2845.

Snyder, R. P. (1998). An assessment of the reliability and validity of scores obtained by six popular learning styles instruments. *Dissertation Abstracts International (Section B): The Sciences and Engineering, 58*(11B), 6275.

Spielberger, C. D., Gorsuch, R. L., Lushene, R., Vagg, P. R., & Jacobs, G. A. (1983). *Manual for the state–trait anxiety inventory: STAI (Form Y).* Palo Alto, CA: Consulting Psychologists Press.

Spindell, W. A. (1976). The effects of teacher–student cognitive style similarity on performance evaluation, performance prediction, intelligence estimation and general preference. *Dissertation Abstracts International, 36*(11-A), 7312–7313.

Spotts, J. X. V., & Mackler, B. (1967). Relationship of field-dependent and field-independent cognitive styles to creative tests performance. *Perceptual and Motor Skills, 24,* 239–268.

Stafford, R. E. (1961). Sex differences in spatial visualization as evidence of sex-linked inheritance. *Perceptual and Motor Skills, 13,* 428.

Stahl, S. A., Erickson, L. G., & Rayman, M. C. (1986). Detection of inconsistencies by reflective and impulsive seventh-grade readers. *National Reading Conference Yearbook, 35,* 233–238.

Stansbury, V. K., & Coll, K. M. (1998). Myers-Briggs attitude typology: The influence of birth order with other family variables. *The Family Journal: Counseling and Therapy for Couples and Families, 6*(2), 116–122.

Stensrud, R., & Stensrud, K. (1983). Teaching styles and learning styles of public school teachers. *Perceptual and Motor Skills, 56*(2), 414.

Sternberg, R. J. (1985). *Beyond IQ: A triarchic theory of human intelligence.* New York: Cambridge University Press.

Sternberg, R. J. (1988). Mental self-government: A theory of intellectual styles and their development. *Human Development, 31,* 197–224.

Sternberg, R. J. (1994). Thinking styles: Theory and assessment at the interface between intelligence and personality. In R. J. Sternberg & P. Ruzgis (Eds.), *Intelligence and personality* (pp. 169–187). New York: Cambridge University Press.

Sternberg, R. J. (1996). *Successful intelligence: How practical and creative intelligence determine success in life.* New York: Simon & Schuster.

Sternberg, R. J. (1997). *Thinking styles.* New York: Cambridge University Press.

Sternberg, R. J. (2001a). Preface. In R. J. Sternberg & L. F. Zhang (Eds.), *Perspectives on thinking, learning, and cognitive styles* (pp. vii–x). Mahwah, NJ: Lawrence Erlbaum Associates.

Sternberg, R. J. (2001b). Epilogue: Another mysterious affair at styles. In R. J. Sternberg & L. F. Zhang (Eds.), *Perspectives on thinking, learning, and cognitive styles* (pp. 249–252). Mahwah, NJ: Lawrence Erlbaum Associates.

Sternberg, R. J. (2003a). *Wisdom, intelligence, and creativity, synthesized.* New York: Cambridge University Press.

Sternberg, R. J. (2003b). WICS: A model of leadership in organizations. *Academy of Management Learning and Education, 2,* 386–401.

Sternberg, R. J., & Grigorenko, E. L. (1993). Thinking styles and the gifted. *Roeper Review, 16*(2), 122–130.

Sternberg, R. J., & Grigorenko, E. L. (1995). Styles of thinking in the school. *European Journal for High Ability, 6,* 201–219.

Sternberg, R. J., & Grigorenko, E. L. (1997). Are cognitive styles still in style? *American Psychologist, 52*(7), 700–712.

Sternberg, R. J., & Wagner, R. K. (1992). *Thinking Styles Inventory.* Unpublished test, Yale University.

Sternberg, R. J., Wagner, R. K., & Zhang (2003). *Thinking Styles Inventory–Revised.* Unpublished test, Yale University.

Sternberg, R. J., & Zhang, L. F. (Eds.). (2001). *Perspectives on thinking, learning, and cognitive styles.* Mahwah, NJ: Lawrence Erlbaum Associates.

Sternberg, R. J., & Zhang, L. F. (in press). Developing the leaders of tomorrow: The wrong direction is the wrong way to the right direction. *The Korean Journal of Thinking and Problem Solving.*

Stone, M. K. (1976). The role of cognitive style in teaching and learning. *Journal of Teacher Education, 27,* 332–334.

Stone, M. K. (1982). Teacher adaptation to student cognitive style and its effect on learning. *Dissertation Abstracts International, 42*(7-A), 3083.

Streufert, S., & Nogami, G. Y. (1989). Cognitive style and complexity: Implications for I/O psychology. In C. L. Cooper & I. Robertson (Eds.), *International review of industrial and organizational psychology* (pp. 93–143). New York: Wiley.

Stricker, L. J., & Ross, J. (1962). *A description and evaluation of the Myers-Briggs Type Indicator* (Research Bulletin, 62–6). Princeton, NJ: Educational Testing Service.

Stricker, L. J., & Ross, J. (1963). Intercorrelations and reliability of the Myers-Briggs Type Indicators scales. *Psychological Reports, 12,* 287–293.

Strout, E. M. (1986). Attractiveness of students with convergent and divergent learning styles to teachers with convergent and divergent learning styles. *Dissertation Abstracts International, 47*(2-A), 425.

Stuart, I. R. (1967). Perceptual style and reading ability: Implications for an instructional approach. *Perceptual and Motor Skills, 24,* 135–138.

Stuart, I. R., & Breslow, A. (1965). The question of constitutional influence on perceptual style. *Perceptual and Motor Skills, 20,* 419–420.

Stuber, S. R. (1997). Teaching behavior viewed as a function of learning style and personality type: A comparison of experienced and less experienced instrumental music teachers. *Dissertation Abstracts International (Section A): Humanities and Social Sciences, 58*(6A), 2127.

Suárez-Orozco, M. M., & Qin-Hillard, D. B. (2004). *Globalization: Culture and education in the new millennium.* Berkeley & Los Angeles, CA: University of California Press.

Sun, C. C. (2000). *Thinking styles and academic achievement.* Unpublished manuscript. The University of Hong Kong.

Susabda, E. (1993). The relationship between matched/mismatched students' learning styles to faculty teaching style and academic performance in Christian secondary schools in Southern California. *Dissertation Abstracts International, 53*(11-A), 3854.

Szymanski, M. D. (1977). *The successful teacher in an alternative school: A study of student preference and student and teacher personality type.* Unpublished doctoral dissertation, Georgia State University.

Taft, R. (1971). Creativity: Hot and cold. *Journal of Personality, 39*(3), 345–361.

Tamir, P., & Cohen, S. (1980). Factors that correlate with cognitive preferences of medical school teachers. *Journal of Educational Research, 74*(2), 69–74.

Tan-Willman, C. (1981). Cerebral hemispheric specialization of academically gifted and nongifted male and female adolescents. *The Journal of Creative Behavior, 15*(4), 276–277.

Tavris, C. (1992). *The mismeasure of women.* New York: Simon and Schuster.

Taylor, J. (1994). The stability of school-children's cognitive style: A longitudinal study of the Kirton Adaption–Innovation Inventory. *Psychological Reports, 74*(3), 1008–1010.

Taylor, L. M. (1980). The effects of cognitive styles of professors and undergraduates on the students' course evaluations. *Dissertation Abstracts International, 40*(8-A), 4504.

Tennant, M. (1997). *Psychological and adult learning* (2nd ed.). London: Routledge.

Terenzini, P. T., Pascarella, E. T., & Blimling, G. S. (1996). Students' out-of-class experiences and their influence on learning and cognitive development: A literature review. *Journal of College Student Development, 37*(2), 149–162.

Thomas, C. R. (1983). Field independence and Myers-Briggs thinking individuals. *Perceptual and Motor Skills, 57,* 790.

Thomas, S. A. W. (1971). *The role of cognitive style variables in mediating the influence of aggressive television upon elementary school children.* Unpublished doctoral dissertation, University of California, Los Angeles.

Thompson, R., Finkler, D., & Walker, S. (1979). *Interrelationships among five cognitive style tests, student characteristics, and achievement.* Paper presented at the annual meeting of the American Educational Research Association, San Francisco. ERIC Document Reproduction Service No. ED 174 678

Thomson, D. (1980). Adaptors–innovators: A replication study of managers in Singapore and Malaysia. *Psychological Reports, 47,* 383–387.

Thomson, D. (1985). *A study of Singaporean executives: Their attitudes, disposition, and work values.* Unpublished doctoral dissertation, Henley Management College/Brunel University.

Tiedemann, J. (1989). Measures of cognitive styles: A critical review. *Educational Psychology, 24,* 261–275.

Tierney, P. (1997). The influence of cognitive climate on job satisfaction and creative efficacy. *Journal of Social Behavior & Personality, 12*(4), 831–848.

Tines, E. N. (1974). The effects of comparable learning styles of teachers and students on instructional outcomes. *Dissertation Abstracts International, 34*(9-A, Pt 1), 5809–5810.

Titus, T. G. (1990). Adolescent learning styles. *Journal of Research and Development in Education, 23,* 165–171.

Tobacyk, J., & Cieslicka, A. (2000). Compatibility between psychological type and academic major in Polish university students. *Journal of Psychological Type, 54,* 22–30.

Tokar, D. M. (1995). Evaluation of the correspondence between Holland's vocational personality typology and the five-factor model. *Dissertation Abstracts International (Section B): The Sciences & Engineering, 55*(9B), 4159.

Tokar, D. M., Vaux, A., & Swanson, J. L. (1995). Dimensions relating Holland's vocational personality typology and the five-factor model. *Journal of Career Assessment, 3*(1), 57–74.

Torbit, G. (1981). Counselor learning style: A variable in career choice. *Canadian Counsellor, 15*(4), 193–197.

Torrance, E. P. (1988). *Style of learning and thinking: Administrator's manual.* Bensenville, IL: Scholastic Testing Service.

Torrance, E. P., & Reynolds, R. C. (1978). Images of the future of gifted adolescents: Effects of alienation and specialized cerebral functioning. *Gifted Child Quarterly, 22*, 40–54.

Torrance, E. P., McCarthy, B., & Kolesinski, M. T. (1988). *Style of learning and thinking.* Bensenville, IL: Scholastic Testing Service.

Torrance, E. P., Reigel, T., Reynolds, C. R., & Ball, O. (1976). *Preliminary manual: Your Style of Learning and Thinking.* Athens, GA: Department of Educational Psychology, University of Georgia.

Torrance, E. P., Taggart, B., & Taggart, W. (1984). *Human Information Processing Survey.* Bensenville, IL: Scholastic Testing Service.

Trigwell, K., & Prosser, M. (1996). Congruence between intention and strategy in science teachers' approaches to teaching. *Higher Education, 32*, 77–87.

Trodahl, V., & Powell, F. (1965). A short form dogmatism scale for use in field studies. *Social Forces, 44*, 211–214.

Tse, P. (2003). *The relationship among thinking styles, learning approaches, value attachment, and academic performance of junior secondary school students in Hong Kong.* Unpublished manuscript. The City University of Hong Kong.

Tucker, R. W. (1999). An examination of accounting students' thinking styles. *Dissertation Abstracts International (Section B): The Sciences and Engineering, 60*(6B), 2977.

Tullett, A. D. (1995). The adaptive–innovative (A–I) cognitive styles of male and female project managers: Some implications for the management of change. *Journal of Occupational and Organizational Psychology, 68*, 359–365.

Tullett, A. D. (1997). Cognitive style: Not culture's consequence. *European Psychologist, 2*(3), 258–267.

Tullett, A. D., & Davis, G. B. (1997). Cognitive style and affect: A comparison of the Kirton Adaption–Innovation and Schutz's Fundamental Interpersonal Relations Orientation–Behavior Inventories (KAI and FIRO-B). *Personality and Individual Differences, 19*, 393–396.

Tymms, P., & Gallacher, S. (1995). Primary science: An exploration of differential classroom success. *Research in Science and Technological Education, 13*(2), 155–162.

Van Voorhees, C., Wolf, F. M., Gruppen, L. D., & Stross, J. K. (1988). Learning styles and continuing medical education. *Journal of Continuing Education in the Health Professions, 8*(4), 257–265.

Varma, O. P., & Thakur, M. (1992). Cognitive style and scholastic achievements. *Psycho-Lingua, 22*(2), 81–92.

Vaught, G. M. (1965). The relationship of role identification and ego strength to sex differences in the rod-and-frame test. *Journal of Personality, 33*, 271–283.

Veres, J., Sims, R., & Locklear, T. (1991). Improving the reliability of Kolb's revised learning style inventory. *Educational and Psychological Measurement, 51*, 143–150.

Verma, S. (2001). A study of thinking styles of tertiary students. *Psycho-Lingua, 31*(1), 15–19.

Vermunt, J. D. H. M. (1992). *Leerstijlen en sturen van leerprocessen in het hoger onderwijs* [Learning styles and guidance of learning processes in higher education]. Amsterdam: Swets and Zeitlinger.

Vernon, M. D. (1963). *The psychology of perception.* Harmondsworth, UK: Penguin Books.

Vernon, P. E. (1972). The distinctiveness of field independence. *Journal of Personality, 40*(3), 366–391.

Vernon, P. E. (1973). Multivariate approaches to the study of cognitive styles. In J. R. Royce (Ed.), *Multivariate analysis and psychological theory* (pp. 125–48). London: Academic Press.

Volet, S. E., Renshaw, P. D., & Tietzel, K. (1994). A short-term longitudinal investigation of cross-cultural differences in study approaches using Biggs' SPQ questionnaire. *British Journal of Educational Psychology, 64,* 301–318.

Watkins, D. A., & Dahlin, B. (1997). Assessing study approaches in Sweden. *Psychological Reports, 81,* 131–136.

Watkins, D., & Gutierrez, M. (1990). Causal relationships among self-concept, attributions, and achievement in Filipino students. *The Journal of Social Psychology, 130*(5), 625–631.

Watkins, D., & Hattie, J. (1981). The learning processes of Australian university students: Investigations of contextual and personological factors. *British Journal of Educational Psychology, 51,* 384–393.

Watkins, D., & Hattie, J. (1985). A longitudinal study of the approaches to learning of Australian tertiary students. *Human Learning, 4,* 127–142.

Watkins, D., Biggs, J., & Regmi, M. (1991). Does confidence in the language of instruction influence a student's approach to learning? *Instructional Science, 20,* 331–339.

Wegner, R. C. (1980). The relationship of field independence–dependence cognitive styles with managerial disposition. *Dissertation Abstracts International, 40*(8B), 4012.

Weisz, J. R., O'Neill, P., & O'Neill, P. C. (1975). Field-dependence-independence on the Children's Embedded Figures Test: Cognitive style or cognitive level? *Developmental Psychology, 11,* 539–540.

Wells, L. E., & Sweeney, P. D. (1986). A test of three models of bias in self-assessment. *Social Psychology Quarterly, 49*(1), 1–10.

Widiger, T., Knudson, R., & Porter, R. (1980). Convergent and discriminant validity of measure of cognitive styles and abilities. *Journal of Personality and Social Psychology, 39,* 116–129.

Wieseman, R. A., Portis, S. C., & Simpson, F. M. (1992). An analysis of the relationship between cognitive styles & grades: New perspectives on success or failure of preservice education majors. *College Student Journal, 26*(4), 512–517.

Williams, M. E. (2001). The effects of conceptual model provision and cognitive style on problem-solving performance of learners engaged in an exploratory learning environment. *Dissertation Abstracts International (Section A): Humanities and Social Sciences, 62*(3A), 983.

Willis, J. H. (1995). Stress, cognitive style, and job satisfaction of computer programmers. *Dissertation Abstracts International (Section B): The Sciences and Engineering, 55*(7B), 3002.

Wilson, D. J., Mundy-Castle, A., Sibanda, P. (1990). Field differentiation and LOGO performance among Zimbabwean school girls. *Journal of Social Psychology, 130*(2), 277–279.

Wilson, K. L., Smart, R. M., & Watson, R. J. (1996). Gender differences in approaches to learning in first year psychology students. *British Journal of Educational Psychology, 66,* 59–71.

Wise, T. N., Hall, W. A., & Wong, O. (1978). The relationship of cognitive styles and affective status to post-operative analgesic utilization. *Journal of Psychosomatic Research, 22,* 513–518.

Witkin, H. A. (1954). *Personality through perception: An experimental and clinical study.* New York: Harper.

Witkin, H. A. (1959). The perception of the upright. *Science American, 200,* 50–56.

Witkin, H. A. (1962). *Psychological differentiation: Studies of development.* New York: Wiley.

Witkin, H. A. (1964). Origins of cognitive style. In C. Sheerer (Ed.), *Cognition, theory, research, promise* (pp. 172–205). New York: Harper & Row.

Witkin, H. A. (1965). Psychological differentiation and forms of pathology. *Journal of Abnormal Psychology, 70*(5), 317–336.

Witkin, H. A., & Goodenough, D. R. (1977). Field dependence and interpersonal behavior. *Psychological Bulletin, 84*(4), 661–689.

Witkin, H. A., & Goodenough, D. R. (1981). *Cognitive styles: Essence and origins: Field dependence and field independence.* New York: International Universities Press.

Witkin, H. A., Dyk, R. B., Faterson, H. F., Goodenough, D. R., & Karp, S. A. (1962). *Psychological Differentiation.* New York: Wiley.

Witkin, H. A., Moore, C. A., Goodenough, D. R., & Cox, P. W. (1977). Field dependent and field independent cognitive styles and their educational implications. *Review of Educational Research, 47,* 1–64.

Witkin, H. A., Oltman, P. K., Raskin, E., & Karp, S. A. (1971). *Embedded Figures Test, Children's Embedded Figures Test: Manual.* Palo Alto, CA: Consulting Psychologists Press.

Woodward, J. C., & Kalyan-Masih, V. (1990). Loneliness, coping strategies and cognitive styles of the gifted rural adolescent. *Adolescence, 25*(100), 977–987.

Wu, J. J. (1968). Cognitive style and task performance—A study of student teachers. *Dissertation Abstracts International, Section A: Humanities and Social Sciences, 29*(A), 176.

Wu, X., & Zhang, H. C. (1999). The preliminary application of the Thinking Style Inventory in college students. *Psychological Science China, 22*(4), 293–297.

Wunderley, L. J., Reddy, W. B., & Dember, W. N. (1998). Optimism and pessimism in business leaders. *Journal of Applied Social Psychology, 28*(9), 751–760.

Yando, R. M., & Kagan, J. (1968). The effect of teacher tempo on the child. *Child Development, 39,* 27–34.

Yang, S. C., & Lin, W. C. (2004). The relationship among creative, critical thinking and thinking styles in Taiwan high school students. *Journal of Instructional Psychology, 31*(1), 33–45.

Yellin, D. (1983). Left brain, right brain, super brain: The holistic model. *Reading World*(October), 36–44.

Yiu, L., & Saner, R. (2000). Determining the impact of cognitive styles on the effectiveness of global managers: Propositions for further research. *Human Resource Development Quarterly, 11*(3), 319–324.

Zelazek, J. R. (1986). *Learning styles, gender, and life change cycle stage: Relationships with respect to graduate students.* ERIC Document Reproduction Service No. ED 276 271.

Zelniker, T., & Jeffrey, W. E. (1976). Reflective and impulsive children: Strategies of information processing underlying differences in problem solving. *Monographs of the Society for Research in Child Development, 41*(5), 59.

Zelniker, T., & Oppenheimer, L. (1973). Modification of information processing of impulsive children. *Child Development, 44,* 445–450.

Zhang, D. X. (1985). An exploratory study of creative thinking in adolescents. *Information on Psychological Sciences, 2,* 20–25.

Zhang, L. F. (1997). *The Zhang Cognitive Development Inventory.* Unpublished test. The University of Hong Kong.

Zhang, L. F. (1999a). Further cross-cultural validation of the theory of mental self-government. *The Journal of Psychology, 133*(2), 165–181.

Zhang, L. F. (1999b). Short-version self-directed search (unpublished test), The University of Hong Kong, Hong Kong.

Zhang, L. F. (2000a). University students' learning approaches in three cultures: An investigation of Biggs's 3P model. *The Journal of Psychology, 134*(1), 37–55.

Zhang, L. F. (2000b). Relationship between Thinking Styles Inventory and Study Process Questionnaire. *Personality and Individual Differences, 29,* 841–856.

Zhang, L. F. (2000c). Are thinking styles and personality types related? *Educational Psychology, 20*(3), 271–283.

Zhang, L. F. (2001a). Thinking styles, self-esteem, and extracurricular experiences. *International Journal of Psychology, 36*(2), 100–107.

Zhang, L. F. (2001b). Thinking styles and personality types revisited. *Personality and Individual Differences, 31*(6), 883–894.

Zhang, L. F. (2001c). Do styles of thinking matter among Hong Kong secondary school students? *Personality and Individual Differences, 31*(3), 289–301.

Zhang, L. F. (2001d). Do thinking styles contribute to academic achievement beyond abilities? *The Journal of Psychology, 135*(6), 621–637.

Zhang, L. F. (2001e). Approaches and thinking styles in teaching. *Journal of Psychology, 135*(5), 547–561.

Zhang, L. F. (2002a). Thinking styles and cognitive development. *The Journal of Genetic Psychology, 163*(2), 179–195.

Zhang, L. F. (2002b). Thinking styles and modes of thinking: Implications for education and research. *The Journal of Psychology, 136*(3), 245–261.

Zhang, L. F. (2002c). Thinking styles and the Big Five Personality Traits. *Educational Psychology, 22*(1), 17–31.

Zhang, L. F. (2002d). Thinking styles: Their relationships with modes of thinking and academic performance. *Educational Psychology, 22*(3), 331–348.

Zhang, L. F. (2002e). Measuring thinking styles in addition to measuring personality traits? *Personality and Individual Differences, 33*, 445–458.

Zhang, L. F. (2002f). The role of thinking styles in psychosocial development. *Journal of College Student Development, 43*(5), 696–711.

Zhang, L. F. (2003a). Contributions of thinking styles to critical thinking dispositions. *The Journal of Psychology, 137*(6), 517–544.

Zhang, L. F. (2003b). *The Preferred Thinking Styles in Teaching Inventory.* Unpublished test, The University of Hong Kong.

Zhang, L. F. (2003c). Are parents' and children's thinking styles related? *Psychological Reports, 93*, 617–630.

Zhang, L. F. (2004a). Revisiting the predictive power of thinking styles for academic performance. *The Journal of Psychology, 138*(4), 351–370.

Zhang, L. F. (2004b). Contributions of thinking styles to vocational purpose beyond self-rated abilities. *Psychological Reports, 94*, 697–714.

Zhang, L. F. (2004c). Thinking styles: University students' preferred teaching styles and their conceptions of effective teachers. *The Journal of Psychology, 138*(3), 233–252.

Zhang, L. F. (2004d). Learning approaches and career personality types: Biggs and Holland united. *Personality and Individual Differences, 37*, 65–81.

Zhang, L. F. (2004e). Predicting cognitive development, intellectual styles, and personality traits from self-rated abilities. *Learning and Individual Differences, 15*, 67–88.

Zhang, L. F., & He, Y. F. (2003). Do thinking styles matter in the use of and attitudes toward computing and information technology among Hong Kong university students? *Journal of Educational Computing Research, 29*(4), 471–493.

Zhang, L. F., & Huang, J. F. (2001). Thinking styles and the five-factor model of personality. *European Journal of Personality, 15*, 465–476.

Zhang, L. F., & Postiglione, G. A. (2001). Thinking styles, self-esteem, and socio-economic status. *Personality and Individual Differences, 31*, 1333–1346.

Zhang, L. F., & Postiglione, G. A. (2005). *Thinking styles, culture, and economy: Comparing Tibetan minority students with Han Chinese majority students.* Manuscript submitted for publication.

Zhang, L. F., & Sachs, J. (1997). Assessing thinking styles in the theory of mental self-government: A Hong Kong validity study. *Psychological Reports, 81*, 915–928.

Zhang, L. F., & Sternberg, R. J. (1998). Thinking styles, abilities, and academic achievement among Hong Kong university students. *Educational Research Journal, 13*(1), 41–62.

Zhang, L. F., & Sternberg, R. J. (2000). Are learning approaches and thinking styles related? A study in two Chinese populations. *The Journal of Psychology, 134*(5), 469–489.

Zhang, L. F., & Sternberg, R. J. (2002). Thinking styles and teacher characteristics. *International Journal of Psychology, 37*(1), 3–12.

Zhang, L. F., & Sternberg, R. J. (2005). A threefold model of intellectual styles. *Educational Psychology Review, 17*(1), 1–53.

Zhao, S. H., & Tang, B. W. (1990). Sweet orange turns into trifoliate orange. In T. Si-Tu (Ed.), *Best Chinese idioms* (p. 174). Hong Kong: Hai Feng Publishing Co.

Author Index

Subject Index